# WE CAN'T ALL BE ASTRONAUTS

# WE CAN'T ALL BE ASTRONAUTS

# TIM CLARE

EBURY
PRESS

1 3 5 7 9 10 8 6 4 2

Published in 2009 by Ebury Press, an imprint of Ebury Publishing

A Random House Group Company

The Random House Group Limited Reg. No. 954009

Addresses for companies within the Random House Group can be found at
www.randomhouse.co.uk

A CIP catalogue record for this book
is available from the British Library

The Random House Group Limited supports The Forest
Stewardship Council (FSC), the leading international forest
certification organisation. All our titles that are printed on Greenpeace
approved FSC certified paper carry the FSC logo. Our paper
procurement policy can be found at www.rbooks.co.uk/environment

Mixed Sources

FSC

Printed and bound in Great Britain by Mackays of Chatham, ME5 8TD

ISBN 9780091928599

To buy books by your favourite authors and register for offers visit
www.rbooks.co.uk

*For Maggie*

*'Oh! Ahab,' cried Starbuck, 'not too late
is it, even now, the third day, to desist.
See! Moby Dick seeks thee not.
It is thou, thou, that madly seekest him!'*

*– Herman Melville*, Moby Dick

# PROLOGUE

Not everyone makes it to the end of this book alive.

But I don't know that yet.

I'm under a shop awning in South London, sheltering from the drizzle. My shirt is crumpled, my hair is wet, and I'm shivering. The smell of incense wafts from the shop. It's 10.40 a.m., and normally I would still be in bed, but today, I have a meeting.

I'm meeting someone who has the power to change my life.

See, since childhood I've dreamed of becoming a bestselling author. I've worked and studied and trained for it. It's been something of an obsession. The person I'm meeting could make my dream a reality.

But time is running out. My mate Joe's book launch party is in less than a month. My friends are all going to be there, all of them successful, happy, grown up. Meanwhile, I'm stony broke, single and still living with my parents.

So I've made a deal with myself.

I've got until the launch party to make good on my ambitions. One last push. Either I find success, or it's time to get a real job. I can't waste my life clinging to childish fantasies. Just because my friends have got what they always wanted doesn't mean I will.

So far, I've pulled out all the stops. I've begged for help. I've gone undercover. I've stared into the jaws of death.

And today, in less than twenty minutes, my fate will be decided.

I'm taking a big risk. To get this meeting, I've told some lies. If I get found out, it's all over. But there's a chance I'll finally achieve my dream; a small chance, my last chance – but a chance nonetheless.

As drizzle collects in beads on the roofs of parked cars, I imagine striding into Joe's party and dropping the bombshell.

*Hey guys, how's it going? Oh, by the way, I just found out I've landed a massive book deal. Yep. Bigger than all of yours. I'm minted. So that's nice, isn't it?*

I imagine them slapping me on the back, then calling for a toast. I imagine Joe off in a corner, ignored at his own book launch.

No, that's too much. I picture him warmly congratulating me, basically happy but unable to disguise his jealousy at my talent and good fortune. I repeat the process for Luke, Joel, Gordon, John, Ross, Chris, and all my other successful friends.

*Nice one, you jammy bastard,* they all say. *We always knew you'd come out on top.*

Droplets pat-pat-pat against the awning. Inside the shop, the man behind the counter is listening to the news on a very loud, very tinny AM radio.

God, I want this. I have no idea what will happen. All I know is, nothing will ever be the same.

Well, that and I need a poo.

# ACT ONE

# DRIVE

# 1

It wasn't a bedroom. It was a dream factory.

Hunched in front of a desk, I was alone with my future. The only sound in the room was the whirr of a computer fan, the only smell the aroma of instant coffee and, occasionally, my own eggy flatulence. It was late. I was working on my book. *The* Book.

This was my sixth or seventh redraft. I'd read through it so many times I could barely see the words anymore. I was tired. The monitor was making my eyes ache.

That night, I was supposed to be dealing with a particularly tricky chapter – a lengthy set piece riddled with tortuous logistics and awkward exposition that always seemed to turn out crappy, no matter how many times I rewrote it. Now, armed with the ability to delete whole sections, to add new words, to transform it into anything I liked, I found my will beginning to falter. I didn't know how to make it better. I didn't know if I *could* make it better.

I checked my emails then surfed aimlessly for a bit, telling myself I should just let the problems purl through my mind until a solution presented itself. That was how inspiration worked, wasn't it? After all, I was a writer.

Wasn't I?

'A bit' of online procrastination became an hour, two hours, three. Eventually, I closed the browser, and forced myself to stare at the offending chapter, resolving not to move from my chair until I'd worked out how to fix it.

But no matter how many times I read it through, I couldn't find the convenient tweak that would convert the content from 'crap' to 'not crap'. A little part of me wondered if, perhaps – just perhaps – all the editorial topiary in the world couldn't rescue it. Feeling angry, I stuck my headphones on, selected some appropriately cataclysmic music and slumped back on my bed.

I glared at the ceiling, trying to spot the mistake in the scene, desperate to apply my supposed skills to make it work. I couldn't afford to fudge this. There had to be some answer I didn't see. I had to *solve* it. My frustration hardened into a throb just above my right eye.

After forty-five minutes without progress, I decided to sleep on it. I kept my headphones on and played a hypnosis track that was supposed to aid relaxation and promote positive thinking. Maybe all the frustration was bunging up my creative juices. Maybe I simply needed a warm pair of hands to work the udders of my subconscious. But all I could think of was the damn chapter. In my mind, it had been so brilliant, so action-packed and compelling, but on the page it was limp and clumsy and bad. What was *wrong* with me? Why couldn't I apply all the deadeye editing skills I brought to bear on other people's work? Was I just stupid? Throughout the half hour of supposed 'deep relaxation', my chest tightened, my headache intensified, and I still hadn't fixed the problem.

I kicked off my duvet, and lay there, perspiring, my heart

walloping in my chest. There had to be a way to save this. But what if there wasn't? What if my struggles pointed to a flaw right at the heart of the project? I *needed* this. What the hell could I offer the world if I was too stupid to be an author?

The Book had to go right. I needed the money. I needed the boost to my self-esteem. The Book was supposed to save me. It was supposed to be my redemption, my way out. I wasn't qualified for anything else – I hated work.

What was happening? Why couldn't I tell a decent story?

*I'm an idiot,* I concluded. *I'm a complete moron. I've applied my whole life to learning a single craft and I'm crap at it. I'll never be able to earn a decent wage. I'll never be able to graduate to proper adulthood. I'll have to spend my whole life in poorly paid jobs I hate, knowing that I failed. I've messed up. I had my chance and I blew it and now I'm a failure, twenty-six years old and living with my parents, a pathetic, self-pitying failure. Why did I think I could write? How could I be so arrogant? I'm an idiot. A fucking stupid worthless idiot. Look at me, lying here in the bedroom I grew up in, feeling sorry for myself. I've had all this time to make something of myself and I'm right back where I started. I'm useless. I hate myself.*

It was becoming clear the positive-thinking track had not worked.

Over years, I had gradually chosen to stake everything – my self-esteem, my career prospects, my independence, *everything* – on becoming suddenly and meteorically successful as an author. This might appear self-evidently preposterous, but spend enough time immersed in creative writing and you begin to see your own life as a story, a narrative with twists and turns, and, most importantly, meaning. I'd experienced some shitty breaks, but I'd always kept the faith, and thus, to my mind, the cosmos owed me a spectacular bounce-back.

According to the script, getting published was supposed to save my life. Sure, it was a ludicrous, grandiose fantasy, but it was the only barrier left between me and stark reality – and now, at last, even that flimsy membrane looked ready to collapse.

The reality I was hiding from was this: I was a twenty-six-year-old guy who still lived with his parents. I slept in late and spent most of my time playing video games. I was single. I was jobless. I had no social life. Sometimes just leaving the house made me nervous and dizzy.

It hadn't always been this way.

I'd come so close to getting what I'd always wanted, so *damn* close. I'd studied for years. I'd got an agent. The Book had gone round a series of publishers, and although they'd all turned it down, most had said they thought I was an excellent writer. My friends told me not to worry. My friends said things would come good eventually.

My wonderful, supportive, infuriatingly successful friends.

Luke and Joel, who landed a book deal after meeting their publisher at a party.

Gordon, whose first novel came runner-up in a national televised competition, then got bought for an advance five times the size of the winner's – a book that he wrote in a *week*.

John, who sold his first book on the strength of a single page – a page he'd knocked out the night before the meeting.

And Joe. Joe, who'd scored a book deal bigger than every-one else's put together. A lot bigger. Piss-takingly big.

Once upon a time, we'd just been a gang of uni mates, hanging round in each other's front rooms, pushing beer and cold pizza into our slogan-holes, chatting about our crazy dreams of one day getting a book published. Suddenly, it was five years later and everyone had done it.

Everyone except me.

Eventually, the door opened. My mum entered the room in her nightie to find me clutching a pillow and sobbing.

Even at the best of times, Mum worries about me. If one of my shoelaces is looking a bit frayed, she panics that I'll lose a shoe and get trenchfoot. When I phone home, she answers with: 'Tim? Hello? Is everything all right?' If I actually had the conditions to go with all the lotions, sprays, tablets and assorted remedies she's foisted upon me, I'd be a shambling, haemorrhoidal, rheumy-eyed leper, my tattered skin hanging like grey tickertape from withered, sunburnt arms.

'Tim? What's wrong?'

'Go away.'

To be fair, I'd given her plenty to worry about recently. I was a depressed mess. I spent most of my time trudging round the house looking miserable.

'Come on, love. What's the matter?'

I hugged my pillow tighter. 'I'm an idiot.'

'Oh, Tim. Don't be silly. Come here.' She started advancing for a hug.

'I said go away!'

While my friends grew from students to independent, successful adults, I was stuck at home, getting comforted by my mum. She was only trying to help, but all her cooing and fussing made me feel like a fat, beardy baby.

'Tim… come on, now. What's wrong?'

'I can't do it anymore.'

'What, love?'

'This!' I waved an arm at my bedroom. 'I can't do it! I'm… I'm *tired*!'

Mum folded her arms, looking concerned. 'I don't understand why you're so hard on yourself.'

'Because I messed everything up! And now…' I took a big, shuddering breath. 'Now it's too late.'

I started sobbing again. I could feel my face prickling with heat, and a vein pulsing in my forehead. Rising panic brought with it a sour sort of ecstasy – I was outside myself, watching a hairy, overweight twenty-six-year-old froth and contort in his Scooby Doo boxer shorts. I imagined my friends' pity and disgust if they were to see me like this. I imagined my ex-girlfriend recoiling with confusion and fear. I didn't know what I wanted, except to escape the moment. I realised that, no matter how lofty my aesthetic goals or fearsome my inner demons, no matter how sophisticated or meaningful the psychodramatic terms in which I couched my turmoil, I was essentially a grown man throwing a massive bawling tantrum. Instead of making me back away from the abyss, abashed, this revelation added fuel to the flames. It was the final blow, conclusive proof that I was a pathetic, worthless, cretinous manchild who had completely and irredeemably ballsed-up his life and who might as well die.

'I just… I want to die!'

'Oh, don't be stupid,' said Mum.

How did I get here? How had I managed to sink so low? It was almost impressive.

Almost.

# 2

Idiots are like superheroes. Behind each one, there's a long and tragic origin story.

I grew up a weird kid in a small town. I was always big for my age, inquisitive, articulate and confident – in other words, a gobshite. Short-sightedness meant that, at the age of five, I was lumbered with a gawky pair of thick brown spectacles, which pretty much wrote off any hope of boyish roughhousing and being accepted by my peers.

I think like many weird, creative kids growing up in small towns, I dreamed of one day escaping my small town, of heading off to explore the big wide world outside my small town and of becoming successful at what I loved, which was making up stories. I imagined that one day in the distant future I would return to my small town a conquering hero, buy the biggest house in my small town, and forever after, whenever anyone mentioned the name of my small town, people would immediately think of cool, off-kilter creativity, and me.

Unfortunately, the small town I grew up in was Portishead, and a decade later the name would become permanently associated with a Bristolian trip-hop band who, rather selfishly, chose to appropriate it before shooting to international renown.

But I didn't know that back then. As a child, my precognitive powers were limited to a vague tingling whenever I needed the toilet, and even that wasn't one hundred per cent foolproof. Despite being pretty clever with words and numbers, when it came to predicting real world outcomes, I was (and still am) almost unfeasibly stupid.

As a six-year-old in Mrs Pollock's class, I hunched over a desk laboriously copying out the text of 'The Lion And The Peacock' from children's magazine *Story Teller*. Deciding I wanted to write a story, I'd quickly discovered the difference between *imagining* yourself as a writer, and the taxing spade-work of actually coming up with something to say and then making it appear on a page. Short on inspiration, I turned plagiarist. Though my chosen tale was only two pages including pictures, transcribing its contents seemed to take forever. Still, I pressed on past morning break. Like the pious monks of the Middle Ages who had set down scripture in ornate, curlicued hand, I was concentrating on the long game. I was going to create something brilliant, and for my pains I would receive attention and praise. After adding a series of pencil illustrations, I strode up to the teacher's desk, and proudly handed her my blue jotter.

Alas, Mrs Pollock was a far shrewder scholar than I had given her credit for. I suppose she could have let it go, but even at six and seven, we were well aware of her name's potential for hilarious single entendres, and thus relations were at something of a low ebb.

'This is copied,' she said flatly.

Her powers of deduction left me in baffled silence. The

story was clearly in my handwriting. Where was my acclamation? Where was my reward?

During the long walk back to my chair, I cycled through the many shades of artistic failure – anger, bewilderment, sadness, apathy. It was a new experience for me and, due to lack of practice, I couldn't sustain the feelings for more than a few minutes.

What I didn't realise at the time was that failure is a muscle. You work at it, and work at it, and eventually, you can keep those emotions going for days, weeks, months – even an entire lifetime.

# 3

Back in my bedroom, I was still bawling.

Dad entered in a khaki T-shirt and boxer shorts. He said: 'Come on, Tim, we're going.'

I withdrew, confused. I yelled no. I assumed he was going to try to take me to the hospital. I felt spun-out, terrified. How did I get here? Was I going to get sectioned? Where had my glowing future gone? What was happening to me?

Dad said: 'Being in this room's not doing you any good. Come on – let's go for a drive.'

It was four thirty in the morning. I looked at him as if he had gone mad – which, given the circumstances, was rather ironic.

Dad said: 'Come on, Tim.'

I didn't want to feel the way I did, but I was convinced there was no way out. Still, I wasn't ready for a straightjacket quite yet. The thought sobered me up.

At last, I said: 'Okay.' At least feeling suicidal in a car wasn't likely to be markedly worse than feeling suicidal in my bedroom.

I pulled some jeans on, wiped the beard of snot from my

top lip and chin. He went back to his bedroom, and returned wearing sandals and a pair of shorts.

'Let's go.'

# 4

As a kid, I thought my dad was awesome. He played all sorts of games with me, he spoke foreign languages, he played guitar, and every so often he'd disappear off to a foreign country and return with trinkets and chocolate.

The first stories I remember him reading to me were in German. I would look at the pictures with him and he would translate the accompanying couplets in soft, reassuring tones – rather incongruously, since the book in question, Heinrich Hoffman's 1845 classic *Der Struwwelpeter*, or 'Shockheaded Peter', featured graphic depictions of children burning to death, drowning in rivers, being savaged by dogs and getting their thumbs snipped off by jodhpur-clad strangers wielding shears.

When I was seven, I got bundled off on a family holiday with Mum, Dad, my younger brother, and Mum's parents, who I knew as Nanny and Pop. I associated Nanny and Pop with trips down to their house in Weston-super-Mare, fish fingers and peas and crinkly chips for lunch, and the ducks that swam in the river at the end of their garden. Nanny seemed young (for a grandma, anyway) and was always beaming and enthusing. Pop was a big man with curly grey hair and a loud laugh, who had a repertoire of favourite jokes that he usually told wrong. My little brother, Ben, was almost three years younger than me. I loved having someone to play with and wind up, but I got frustrated when Dad made us play simplified versions of games so Ben didn't feel left out. He lurched from being my best friend to a baby with a minuscule attention span who was always spoiling my fun.

Much as I loved them all, I desperately, viscerally, did not want to go on holiday with them and spent most of the lead-up wishing that some stroke of fate would get us out of it. I was sure the trip would be eye-gougingly dull.

To add insult to injury, on the morning of our departure I discovered that, rather than going in the boys' car with Dad, my brother and Pop, for the entire journey down to Sidmouth I was going to be stuck with Mum and Nan. Ben was too small to appreciate how rubbish the holiday would be, and cheerily hopped into the other car. He was always making me look bad. I considered my limited options, and eventually decided on sulky acquiescence.

I spent most of the long, boring journey south staring out the window, imagining myself riding alongside the car, alternately on a motorbike or some kind of ostrich, crashing through hedgerows, doing insane jumps over ditches. Mum and Nan nattered about programmes they'd watched on TV and getting building work done on the house and how much longer the journey was likely to take and loads of other dull, dull adult stuff. I imagined that, in the other car, they were all playing some brilliant game or telling jokes and laughing and singing. The already tedious drive was made worse when Dad's car had to stop with engine trouble. Mum got out to ask what was wrong and Dad must have surprised her, because I remember her saying: 'Oh God! You nearly gave me a heart attack!'

One of the main reasons I was dreading the holiday was Sidmouth's purported lack of amusement arcades. Video games were one of my biggest loves, despite (or perhaps because of) the fact I didn't have a console or computer of my own. Going to a smoky arcade and watching a skateboarding caveboy olly over snails in Wonderboy was my favourite thing about holidays – more than camping or ice creams or leaping through waves. All of the rudimentary stories I was writing (or, more often, drawing) at that stage were about people getting sucked into games, or baddies breaking out of games, or scenarios nicked directly from games. (I still think there's a gap in the market for a novel about a skateboarding caveboy who ollies over snails.)

In the end, our car got there slightly before Dad's. I followed Mum up some stairs into our holiday flat.

It was every bit as crappy as I had imagined: cramped, soulless, with grey lino and a tiny Formica kitchen. I made an immediate prediction that the holiday would be misery from start to finish. I was correct.

My little brother came dashing in. He was wide-eyed, breathless.

'Pop's gone to heaven!' he said.

The next few hours passed in a confusing welter of sobbing, phone calls, and long, hollow silences. A policeman came. He wrote his name down on a little piece of paper in looping blue biro. Nan spoke in a dazed voice. She kept saying: 'It's just a shell… just a shell…'

While Dad had been parking the car, Pop had suffered a massive heart attack in the passenger seat. He died right there.

I was old enough to know what death was. I felt angry at Ben for not seeming to understand that anything was wrong, angry at the stupid, sudden, naïve way he'd told me. I felt upset and frightened at seeing Mum and Nan cry. Most of all, I felt guilty. After all, this was what I'd wanted, wasn't it? An excuse to go home.

And in the middle of it all, Dad sat down on the floor, and drew a potato.

My brother coloured it in – five different stripes, a red, a brown, an orange, a blue, and a fluorescent highlighter yellow. Dad made a joke about their being odd colours for a potato. He was smiling. I didn't understand. He didn't seem upset at all. He didn't mention the fact that when we set out that morning Pop had been with him, and now Pop was gone and we'd never see him again. Dad just picked up flesh-coloured plastic figures from our Tupperware box of Musclemen, encouraged me to draw them and make up names for them.

And the more I focused on the little man who looked like a balding newsreader or the one who looked like a midget potato, the less real all my messy, unpleasant feelings seemed to be. This, then, was how to deal with the world. You pushed it into a corner and you built yourself a better one.

Before we left to go back to Portishead, I looked up at Dad and said: 'Thank you for helping us through this crisis.' I timed my delivery so all the adults were in earshot. It was the first time I'd used the word 'crisis' – I'd heard it on an advert, and it was the closest thing in my seven-year-old repertoire to gravitas. The words meant nothing to me. I was performing, overcompensating to assuage my guilt. I wanted everybody to think I was unusually sensitive. I remember hugging him, but staring up at the open kitchen cupboard, which contained Sugar Puffs for my brother, Ready Brek for me, and I imagined the two avatars of the cereals, Ready Eddy and the Honey Monster, getting into a big, elaborate fight, and I started trying to work out who I thought would win, and thinking about that was much nicer than being in the cold, tiny kitchen.

Over the following days, weeks and months, nobody talked to me about Pop's death. We went to Nan's house the next day, and I stood in the kitchen watching while Nan showed Mum the cake she had made. It was covered in little marzipan hearts. Pop had died just before Valentine's Day. Once or twice, at home, I caught Mum doubled over, bawling, yelling she wanted her daddy. When I saw these things, I didn't know what I was feeling or what I should do. All I had was the tactic Dad had shown me.

So I threw myself into making stories. Stories made sense. Stories had baddies and goodies and motivation. When death happened it was big and dramatic and meaningful and you could see it. Boom! Ugh! Splat! Stories were somewhere to hide, a sandpit where I could experiment with cause and effect. And at the back of my child's mind, there nestled the vague, unarticulated notion that maybe, just maybe, in amongst the millions and millions of potential stories waiting to be told, there was one that would explain everything.

One that would put things back to how they were.

# 5

Dad and I drove in silence. We passed through the empty streets of Portishead, up out of the Gordano valley and into Bristol. The unpopulated cityscapes didn't look beautiful or picturesque – just indifferent, bland.

As we drove beneath the Clifton Suspension Bridge, Dad said: 'I don't know why, but I'm getting the word "choices". The word "choices" is going round my head at the moment.' He took one hand off the steering wheel to gesture towards his brow. 'I'm not sure where that's come from.' He reminded me of a TV medium angling for information during a cold-read.

'Mmm,' I said. I felt fug-headed, doped-up after my tantrum, and it was hard to speak.

Dad switched on the heater, and we rolled into the mouth of a tunnel.

Dad worked as a languages teacher in a comprehensive school all his life, until one morning he woke up and discovered he couldn't face going in. His doctor signed him off for stress and put him on a course of antidepressants. In the end, Dad never went back. The school offered him and several colleagues early retirement, and he accepted.

Since retirement, he had 'rediscovered his spirituality'. Biblical tracts and books on faith healing had started popping up all over the house. I got a bit squicked out. Then I found out he was going for regular blood tests and would have to be on medication for the rest of his life. He had a 'condition'. Probably caused by stress, the hospital said. The medication ought to control it, but he needed regular check-ups to make sure, because, well, there was a significant chance that – pills or no pills – his 'condition' might kill him.

My dad finally escaped school, only to run smack-bang into his own mortality.

I couldn't look up to Dad as I'd used to. I saw him now as a cautionary tale, someone whose lack of ambition had left him ground down and miserable. I could remember the long hours Dad used to work, the terse arguments between him and Mum that would escalate into yelling. Mum would often tell me how dreadfully stressed Dad was at work, how he was under a huge amount of pressure and how the system was incredibly unfair. When I asked, in equal parts concerned and angry, why he didn't just quit, Mum shot back: 'This is what being an adult is all about. You don't always have choices.'

It jibed with a memory from much earlier. When I was in infant school, I used to come home for lunch. I wasn't a shy kid, exactly, but I felt aware of my own oddness and I liked to spend time alone. After eating my peanut butter sandwiches, cut into squares, I'd go outside into our garden. Our house backed on to the local secondary school. On the other side of our hedge were cricket nets and a playing field. A drainage ditch ran along the border, ending in a large concrete block with a metal drain cover on top. Teenagers would sit on the drain cover and chat and brood and snigger, and I would spy on them through a knothole in the fence. Occasionally, I'd be spotted.

One time, it was two boys in grey blazers. To me, they were impossibly old. The skinnier of the two, his ginger hair cropped short, turned to look at me, grinning and eager.

'Don't come to the big school,' he said, his freckled face twisted in mock-fear. 'They make you do sums.' He produced a horrible red-jacketed eighties paperback maths textbook and opened it at a random double-page spread of endless long-division. 'Run away,' he told me. 'Run into the fields and play.'

When my mum had told me, 'This is what being an adult is all about,' some part of me just slammed the brakes on the maturation process. If that was what growing up entailed, then fuck it – I was off to the fields.


'You can't always choose what happens to you,' Dad continued, reflections of orange streetlights sliding over the windscreen, 'but you can choose your reaction.'

I felt both guilty and stupid because I'd clearly chosen a shit reaction. 'I'm just really rough on myself,' I said, sniffing a little.

'Of course you are,' said Dad. 'Absolutely.'

I closed my eyes, pinched the bridge of my nose. 'If my writing goes badly, I feel like a failure, but as soon as things go well I start rebuilding every stupid big-headed dream that messed me up the first time. I imagine the glossy cover and the books bound and stacked. I imagine giving big readings to packed halls and people applauding at the end. I have this running commentary in my head where I give wonderfully erudite answers to fake interview questions. I keep fantasising about getting a huge amount of money for it, and that money suddenly solving all my problems. I get obsessed. I neglect other parts of my life. I end up talking about it all the time – the Book, the Book, the Book. And… you know, as much as I want to dismiss all these things as delusions of grandeur and stupid bullshit, part of me can't, because I've been *so* close and, well… *I've seen it work*. I've watched it happen.'

That was the stone in the snowball. My friends. My talented, spawny, bastard friends.

# 6

What you have to understand (if you haven't already guessed) is that, at school, I was the gobby, precocious kid that most people hated. I was smart, I knew I was smart, and I made sure everybody else knew I knew I was smart. My friends and I were convinced we were above it all. We thought we were geniuses, our teachers nincompoops and our classmates drooling subhuman grotesques.

In Year 7, me and my mates Will and Cooper spent a whole weekend taping a 'radio show' on the little cassette recorder I'd once used to load my ZX Spectrum games. We called it 'Asylum 7B' and systematically went through every pupil and teacher we didn't like, one of us doing an insulting impersonation while another pretended to interview them. Thus our Design Technology teacher Mr Mickleson confessed that yes, he hated kids and had toxic BO, while Kerry Taylor boasted that everybody fancied her and she'd given three boys blow jobs. The show closed with a series of scatological a capella freestyles where we had a second crack at abusing our most disliked classmates, singing songs about how they had no testicles, their parents hated them and they should just jump off a very tall bridge or building.

We weren't much nicer to our pals. Within the friendship group we were fiercely competitive and mercilessly cruel to one another – a gaggle of snickering blade-sharpeners. Though getting good grades was something to boast about, getting caught making an effort was deeply shameful. Success was supposed to come easily.

Jukesy, for example, earned a scholarship to Bristol Grammar School, spent a year there, then joined us at the local comprehensive in Year 8. He arrived a full year ahead of the rest of us in Maths, he breezed through Science, had excellent spelling and was one of the best artists in the year. We had a minor academic rivalry, but most of the time, the game was to prove how well we could do without really trying. Jukesy and I nearly got thrown out of our Science GCSE exam when, with more than an hour left to go, we sat back, arms folded, to show we'd finished early, and glanced over at each other at exactly the same time, which made us both burst out laughing. One of our smuggest pleasures was showing each other our report cards, where teachers lamented our laziness, while still being forced to give us As.

A couple of years ago, a brilliant article appeared in the *New York Magazine* entitled 'How Not To Talk To Your Kids', summarising about three decades of research into the effects of praise on children. As a fully qualified armchair psychologist, I subjected the data to my own rigorous meta-analysis, and I present my findings here for your perusal.

The basic thrust of recent studies seems to be that children who get praised for being clever rather than for making an effort become less able to deal with failure. Kids labelled as 'bright' are less willing to persist with tasks they find difficult, and tend to prioritise image maintenance over personal development. Psychologist Carol Dweck is quoted in the article as saying: 'Emphasizing effort gives a child a variable that they can control. They come to see themselves as in control of their success. Emphasizing natural intelligence takes it out of the child's control, and it provides no good recipe for responding to a failure.'

Indeed, when a child labelled as 'smart' runs into a problem they cannot immediately and confidently solve, they show more signs of discomfort than peers praised for effort. 'Smart' children are more competitive, quicker to belittle others, and more likely to lie about test scores. They become increasingly risk-averse, meaning that a child labelled a Maths prodigy may lose motivation in English and Art when they realise they might only come second or third in the class. Ultimately, moderate setbacks may convince them that they have been mislabelled, and really, they were stupid all along.

Much as I'd love to descend into a Larkinesque screed, I'll just say that I identified with these findings. I got the highest GCSE results out of any boy in my school. When I told Mum the good news, she raised an eyebrow and said: 'Well, I knew you would. You're very clever.'

Not that competitiveness and image management don't confer limited, short-term advantages.

In Year 10, the format of our Art lessons changed. Instead of eye-wateringly joyless orange-sketching sessions under the glowering supervision of a leather-jowled tosser who clearly loathed kids, we were expected to do our work at home. The classes turned into beauty contests. At the beginning of each lesson, our homework would be spread out over six or seven big adjoining tables, and we, the class, would have to communally decide how to rank the pieces, with A-grade pieces starting on the left, moving downwards to E and F on the far right.

At the time, I regularly drew cartoons for my own amusement, but I saw Art lessons, with their 'serious' subject matter, as an excuse to doss around. There were no exams, and little opportunity to publicly excel.

However, in the first lesson under the new system, everything changed. I watched, aghast, as the class decided that my still-life daffodil only deserved a 'low' C (not unfairly, since I'd dashed it off the night before, not realising anyone but my teacher would see it). Just one guy received an A, and the class heaped admiration upon him. Perhaps crucially, I noticed that the girls in our class seemed particularly impressed. I left seething. The experience triggered a giant burning 'Fuck You' like a Bat Signal in my brain. I would beat everyone. I was clever, after all.

Our next class was in a fortnight's time and I toiled to produce a sterling piece of work. Lo and behold, my pencil sketch of a badminton racquet was held up as an exceptional piece, not just worthy of an A, but on a par with the A-Level students' project work. I got praise and attention and it might have ended there except word of my triumph got around and a rumour came back via Jukesy that there was a new boy in the other class who was 'amazing' at Art and seemed to be getting even more attention from the girls. He'd sketched one of the raptors out of *Jurassic Park* and everything. Mentally I cracked my knuckles, and the desire to assert myself as number one powered me through the next two years.

Using my parents' camcorder, me and my mate Will made an animation showreel. We drew on our experience collaborating on the live action movies *Fucking Solid Kung Fu Bastards* – which we'd shot with friends up in the woods behind my house, attacking each other in long, unchoreographed fight scenes with hunting knives, metal nunchucks, French bangers and lighters sprayed with aerosol to make flamethrowers – and *Who Gives A Nam*, a hard-hitting polemic against the Vietnam War, in which the Viet Cong were identified by the Gordano School jumpers tied round their heads. Our first animated feature was a Japanese historical thriller called *The Ninjas*, which centred round a war between three rival ninja clans, the Yellows, the Reds and the Blacks. In a key scene, one of the Yellow ninjas steals a giant gold coin (we used a chocolate doubloon left over from Christmas) from the Black ninjas' hideout (which looks suspiciously like the top of a walnut chest of drawers) then sneaks over to plant it in the Red ninjas' compound.

'Ah ha,' he says, voiced by Will, 'I'll just put this gold in the Reds'… in the Reds' base.'

Which he promptly does, before teleporting out. We chose ninjas primarily for their famed teleportation abilities, which made entrances and exits much quicker to animate. Also because Ben, my little brother, had a large Tupperware tub of plastic ninja figurines.

After at least half a day's work, the film was complete. I sent it to Aardman Animations, the makers of Wallace and Gromit, taking full credit in my covering letter. I used their politely encouraging but noncommittal response as leverage to win a grant for animation equipment. I set up a studio in the garage, even had a fat photographer from the local paper come round to take a picture of me and my plasticine models.

'Just remember us when you get that Oscar,' my teacher told me when I received the (modest) grant, only half-joking.

I told Dad I needed a lightbox and he dutifully complied, constructing one from wood and Perspex, then I used it to create and film 2D pencil animations. I read books on lighting and focus and set construction and the history of animation. I wrote out storyboards. I pondered the physics of the laces on a falling man's hoodie.

At no stage did any adult say to me: 'Kudos for working your backside off, Tim.' Lots, however, made remarks to the effect of: 'My goodness, you are talented,' or 'One day, you're going to be a big star.' Any achievement was either in the past (I'd apparently popped out of the womb with a prodigious aptitude for stop-motion animation) or in the future (this was merely preparation for some nebulous project twenty years hence) – it certainly wasn't going on now.

Eventually, I applied to an actual animation studio to go for a week's work experience. When Will found out they'd said yes, he wrote to them too, and ended up coming the same week. As our first day approached, we grew rabid with excitement. We bandied about ideas for films and wondered what brilliant projects they'd set us to work on.

We spent the first day sweeping and tidying the workshop, and getting grumbled at by a scotch-breathed boss with a nose like a giant red bollock, between phone calls where he negotiated with pernickety clients over the exact shade of blue for the man's jumper in their thirty-second indigestion tablet commercial. The 'animators' working there were a bunch of miserable stoners who spent most of their time doing paperwork, planning or balancing budgets. Nobody smiled. On the second day, we found out the boss was in London attending meetings for the rest of the week. The mood amongst the staff shifted. Instead of doing paperwork, everyone smoked roll-ups and played *Mortal Kombat 2* on the PlayStation. When we asked what we should do, they looked stumped for a while, then had us spend the next three days sculpting tiny fried eggs, rashers of bacon, sausages and burgers, for possible use in a Teflon commercial. My burgers were eventually rejected and thrown away, on the grounds that they were 'too grey'. One afternoon, on my way to the loo, I noticed a biro cartoon on their pinboard, depicting Gromit crucifying Wallace with a hammer and nails. To cap it all, every bit of art in the building was clearly shitloads better than anything we'd ever produced.

The whole set-up looked difficult, and unlikely to win me much personal acclaim. At best, animation was a team sport.

At the end of the week, as I watched Will shake hands with the boss, the staffroom mini-basketball and net hidden behind his back, I decided I didn't want to be an artist.

At school, I quit Art. At home, I gave up drawing – permanently, as it turned out. I told myself I'd proved my point – I could've done it if I'd wanted to.

Besides, after some jockeying for position between disciplines, creative writing had lurched into first place as the medium most likely to satisfy my massive, sucking need for recognition. At fourteen I entered my first creative writing competition, the Weston-super-Mare ghost story competition, sponsored by politician Jeffrey Archer, and came joint first in my age group. The story was about an old man who gets possessed by the ghost of an ancient warrior, battles a demon, and ultimately explodes into a soupy mess. At fifteen, my English teacher, Mr Walton, gave me a leaflet for the Bridport Young Writers Competition, a national short story competition.

I entered, fully expecting to win – I even wrote a note to 'future Tim' in my jotter: 'What's that? I won first, second and third? Oh, goodo!' I needled my dad, asking him whether he thought my story would place. He gave me a weary grin and tried to brush off the question as politely as possible, but I kept at him until eventually he put on a sarcastic newsreader voice and announced: 'Due to a fire at the Bridport post office, Tim Clare has been declared the winner of this year's short story competition.'

I felt indignant at his lack of faith, and said that if he was so sure I wasn't going to win, would he agree to match the prize money in the event of my winning so I could buy an electric guitar? He agreed.

Needless to say, I had the last laugh.

My win set a dangerous precedent. I had a hundred per cent hit rate with writing competitions. I had acted like an arrogant cock and the world had rewarded me. Worse, I was convinced that my success had arisen out of some hardwired genius node rather than all the hours and days and weeks I'd spent reading and writing and honing my craft. With my hubris at critical mass, I decided it was time to start writing a novel.

And sure, my egotism was unfortunate, but it existed against the backdrop of my being a gauche, insecure teenager who had no idea how to talk to girls and who was being viciously bullied. My competition-winning short story was about a guy who gets rejected by a girl and then turns out to be a suicide bomber who blows up the café across the street. Ooh... twist!

Yet the real fantasy of the story wasn't the overblown 'now you'll wish you'd been nicer to me' suicide, but the idea that someone would be gutsy enough to tell a girl he liked them. I'd never come close, because I was sure what the reaction would be. And though I got the attention of my peers through mucking about in class, I was fast discovering that attention wasn't the same as respect.

Writing appeared to be the one thing that made me worthwhile. I was lonely and miserable, I got pushed around at school, and so I constructed a puffed-up, destiny-laden version of myself as a kind of life raft. Of course, I didn't have the self-awareness to realise that it was precisely this aloof defensiveness that made me come across as a right bell-end, prime target for a dressing down.

More importantly, I didn't realise that you don't know your destiny until it happens. Back in the present, my dreams of being a big author were circling the plughole while Will was running his own film company.

Of course he fucking was.

# 7

Dad nodded, easing the car through a bank of red traffic lights. 'I totally understand why you feel that way. You're in such a competitive friendship group. I mean, it's like you've all grown up training to be footballers, and now Joey D's been picked to play for the Chelsea first eleven, Luke and Joel have been picked for, uh...' He circled his hand '...Aston Villa, say, and you... you've been turned down by Bury.'

My knowledge of the beautiful game is scant, but I recognised the odium Bury connoted. I waited for the silver lining, but it appeared Dad had finished.

'Yes,' I said, at last.

I had met Joe on a creative writing holiday in the Herefordshire countryside. I was in my second year of university, and he was in the year below me. I'd like to think we clicked pretty quickly – Joe was a good poet, but more than that, he had drive. He wanted to be brilliant. He enthused about authors he thought were great – he enthused about *sentences* he thought were great.

Throughout university we met up to do writing exercises together, sometimes with other people, sometimes just the two of us. We had what usually gets called a 'healthy rivalry' – if one of us wrote something good, the other would confess admiration through gritted teeth, then set about trying to top it.

But there was no topping this. Dad was right: Joe's first book had been snapped up by editors around the globe, whereas mine had been universally rejected. Same dream, same route – but only one of us hit paydirt.

Joe's novel was due to be published in a few, short months. I was bracing myself for the big launch party the way you might prepare for your best friend's wedding – if said friend was marrying your childhood sweetheart and you were fat and divorced. It wasn't just about his book – the whole gang would be there, Luke, Joel, Gordon, John, Chris, Ross and loads more people besides, friends who were making successes of themselves as writers, poets, stand-ups, musicians, film makers, all celebrating the crowning moment when we finally made the leap from a bunch of struggling student artists to a grown-up clique of *creative professionals*. Then they'd all raise their glasses and toast each other in turn, until they came to me... oh dear. The runt. The disappointment. Every time I thought about it, I felt sick.

'You think of all the Premiership soccer academies,' he said, 'taking kids out of schools. They've only just been forced to provide these children with lessons alongside their train-ing. It's ridiculous, really. Out of all the kids they take on, only a tiny percentage end up making a living playing Premiership football. All the rest find themselves on the scrapheap at eighteen, no education, no real prospects. And yet they're bound to know someone like Wayne Rooney who's gone on to make literally millions and millions of pounds. Some of them might find jobs teaching kids football, I suppose, or as referees or something, but they've been promised so much... it must feel terrible.'

I found myself nodding heavily. 'I expect it does.'


I had never been a huge Phil Collins fan, but a year earlier, as I sat in my rented bedroom with the phone to my ear, I reflected that I had, indeed, been waiting for this moment all my life.

'Basically,' the woman on the other end explained, 'we're looking for a young, unpublished author to feature in a series of programmes on Channel 4. They'll be meeting up with agents, publishers and famous authors, trying to get noticed and get their "big break".'

Oh Lord.

Part of me was surprised but another, far more prominent part was thinking, *Well, naturally.* I cast a wry smile heaven-ward. *So this is how You propel me to international literary stardom. Nice twist, big guy.*

'What we'd want you to do is...'

While the woman continued talking, a million jewel-encrusted futures pirouetted through my mind. This, surely, was a key moment in my life's journey and, by extension, a future pivotal scene in art history. I started to take a mental inventory of my surroundings, hitherto ordinary objects now backlit with the eerie glow of posterity. The running sock draped over my disused weights bench, its heel brown with grime, instantly acquired a drab melancholia. In years to come the world would attribute such verve, such rare insight to this

Big Author, and yet, back then, when it all began, he was struggling to keep the minutiae of his life in some semblance of order. It was so goddamn poignant I almost welled up.

'Hello?'

I realised I was still on the phone. 'Yes?'

'So do you, then?'

'I'm sorry?'

'Do you have a book?'

A pause.

'Yes.' I had three chapters. 'Well, I mean I've got a bit of *redrafting* to do...'

'That's fine. It's just we want whoever we choose to actually be going around promoting their novel, you know, trying to get the right people to read it, trying to beat the system. You don't have an agent already, do you?'

'No,' I lied, then added the peculiar intensifier, 'not at all.'

The Book started out as a bit of fun. I thought about the people and places I'd always wanted to see in a novel, and I wrote about them. I created a teenage boy named Joshu, and placed him under the stewardship of a fierce military regime in a country torn apart by civil war. When the story began, insurgent forces were closing in on the town, and Joshu, a weak, introverted kid, was the only one who could stop them. I kept writing because I wanted to find out what happened next. In my youthful enthusiasm, the only critical scrutiny I subjected my writing to was whether or not I thought it was 'cool'.

But a funny thing happened to me on the way to 'The End'. I started sharing what I'd written with others, just short extracts at first, then longer sections, then bona fide chunks. I read bits out, transported Joshu's predicament off of the page and into the heads of real people.

And real people said they liked it. That felt good. Some real people said: 'I love it, Tim. It's amazing. I want to hear more.' That felt very good. They loved what I'd written and they weren't even my mum.

*I love it, Tim.* It felt so good they might have just as well been saying: *I love you.*

In the fullness of time, this conflation would prove disastrous.

The way I wrote started to change. This was no longer a diversion, something to tinker with as an escape from work. This was a project. This was a Book.

My governing criterion duly shifted.

*Cool?* I castigated myself. *What do you mean, cool? Do you really think Dickens sat down at his escritoire and asked himself,* Now, what can I write about that's cool? *What about* À La Recherché Du Temps Perdu? *Is that cool? I suppose you imagine that William Faulkner won the 1949 Nobel Prize for Literature because the judges thought his bittersweet vignettes on the absurdity of the human condition were 'cool'.*

All at once my erstwhile delight seemed a backward, shameful thing. Eager to atone I set myself deadlines, ambitious quotas, told people 'I'll have it finished in a month', then, like some overzealous Party cadre, found myself guiltily hiding productivity shortfalls behind a welter of grin-faced propaganda. I pushed through page after page, usually with no idea where the story was going or what my characters were thinking, but reassured by the steady trickle of words. Working in this manner I produced scenes four and five thousand words long where people stood in rooms and talked at length about epistemology, told meandering, ambiguous parables, and explained the rules to made-up board games in intricate detail, often unprompted. Though I still drew warmth from those early embers of praise, the creative process became increasingly grim. I began to have doubts.

In an effort to rekindle the old fire, I reread the initial sections that had met with such praise. To my dismay, I found I no longer enjoyed them; clunky sentences seemed to have sprung up everywhere, like grimy skulls unearthed by a plough. Each one was an indictment, every instance proof that I was a fraud, a mere scribbler, a deluded imbecile. Whole chapters were scrapped. Conscious of my slackening resolve, I cracked the whip still harder.

Writing soon lost the glow of the delicious skive and began to feel like entering a gladiatorial arena. In my infinite wisdom, I took this as a fine augury and congratulated myself on being such a mature, conscientious artist. Other fair-weather fabulists might only write when they enjoyed it, but not me – I was going to be a Big Author, and Big Authors aren't afraid to do their time in the trenches. Comforting syllogisms plugged the gap between expectation and reality like packing foam: Writing a masterpiece is difficult. Writing the Book is fucking difficult. Therefore, I am writing a fucking masterpiece. 'No Pain – No Gain' became my mantra. A masochistic sense of destiny ensconced itself deep in my system like a bad case of tapeworm.

This teetering scaffold of rationalisations was most obvious when I was interacting with other writers. Given that I had devoted four years of university to studying literature and creative writing, writers accounted for roughly ninety per cent of my social circle, including my flatmates and my girlfriend.

At a reading in an East London pub, I got chatting to a fellow creative type who said he thought writing should be enjoyable, and that if you were having about as much fun as bringing the shopping in from the car, it was a sign you ought to take a break. I coldly informed him that authors who believed that would 'amount to nothing' – particularly harsh considering he'd just bought me a pint.

When, at a seminar on publishing, the author Geoff Dyer explained *quite unapologetically* that he wrote at his own pace, and that new ideas and solutions often arose while he procrastinated, it was all I could do to stop myself gathering up my torch and pitchfork and demanding he be burnt as a heretic. Did he not *realise*, I interjected, my voice growing shrill, the danger of espousing such views? Writers were by nature an indolent bunch – the last thing they needed was another excuse for sloppy standards and loose living.

I smiled as I said it but my heart was crashing in my chest. I genuinely believed aspiring authors were sheep in need of a Strong Shepherd. Without realising it, I had turned into a Writing Nazi.

But there was far worse to come.

In a characteristically inspired piece of scripting by the Inscrutable Immutable, my screen test with the TV company fell on the same day as my interview for a full-time position at Norwich Union. I was desperately strapped for cash – the obligatory 'rags' phase, I told myself – and as an Arts graduate living in Norwich, I was in no position to be choosy.

That morning I found myself in the main function room of the Maids Head Hotel, located in Norwich's delightfully named Tombland district. Its sign was afflicted with some form of electrical malfunction that prevented the red bulbs in the 'M' from working, meaning that, at night, the hotel bore the unfortunate moniker: AIDS HEAD.

Two guys in pastel-blue shirts sat with their backs to a huge mullioned window. They had brought a desk with them; a slightly wilted daffodil was propped in a vase next to their notes. The light from the window picked out the fizz over their glasses of sparkling mineral water. Dust motes hung in grand static constellations, making the room feel like the world's biggest aquarium. Biggest and most rubbish.

Rob, who wore a blue pinstripe shirt and had hair like the fur of a clockwork monkey, perused the CV the job agency had faxed them. 'Looking at your education history it seems that you've got a bit of an interest in writing.' He rolled the last word out with a mixture of amusement and patrician disdain, as if I had spent four years studying a Foundation in Spelunking. 'Is that, uh, something you think you might want to be pursuing in the future?'

The people at the job agency had briefed me very specifically for this moment. Norwich Union, they explained, had the power to offer me a starting salary anywhere within a three grand range. Notwithstanding the fact that much of their local operations were being packed up like a carnival sideshow and outsourced to India, they liked to reward people who they thought they could train up, people they could turn into 'long-term assets' for the company. If I impressed them with my eagerness to scramble up the corporate ladder, I might get offered as much as eleven grand p.a. And there was a gym discount, too.

'Ah, no, no,' I said, shaking my head. 'No, it's just a hobby. I mean, I suppose if I got lucky... But it's not really...' I looked down at my polished black toecaps. 'It's not really a viable career.'

'I want to be a writer more than anything,' I told the camera. 'Ever since I can remember I've wanted to tell stories. I love it.'

Zara was sitting cross-legged to the left of the camera, a clipboard balanced on her knee. She wore liquid black shoes, her dark hair was sculpted into sleek, bold curves and though she was relatively young, her face bore just a hint of wizened conker.

We were sequestered in a tiny office on the second floor of the University of East Anglia's English and American Studies department, recording my screen test. For nearly half a decade, my academic life had centred around this building.

'So your ambition is to be a professional writer?'

I nodded vigorously. 'God, definitely. It's what I've spent my whole life working towards. I mean, I'm not even sure if I have a choice anymore. I'm not qualified for anything else.'

It was true. Aside from successfully passing my Diving Theory test (yes, I really mean Diving Theory; up until university I was a keen member of the Strode Road Sub Aqua Club) and my certificate in Basic Food Hygiene, all my qualifications, experience and achievements were related to creative writing. I couldn't even drive.

Zara cocked her head. Over lunch she had confided that John Peel was 'a grumpy arsehole' with 'a very dark side'.

'How would you feel if you couldn't fulfil your ambition?' she said.

'Well, I… uh… I guess I'm always going to keep trying. If this book fails I'll just try again with another one.' I shrugged and looked away. 'Of course I'll be disappointed, but I don't write for fame or money or attention. I write because I love it.'

But the words had a terrible, counterfeit weight to them. They rang as hollow as the spiel I'd come out with at the Norwich Union interview that morning.

I soldiered on. 'Getting published is the big dream. So many people these days are working on a book. Everyone thinks they've got a novel inside them. There are loads of civil servants and bankers and doctors who secretly want to become successful authors – but how many successful authors fantasise about becoming civil servants? Ever since I was little, I knew it was the best job in the world. I've always written stories, ever since I learned how to make words. I just…' I glanced at Zara, who smiled approvingly. I went for the *coup de grâce*. 'This isn't a side project. Writing is my life.'

That much, at least, was true.

I got a phone call that week telling me my interview had been successful.

Unfortunately, the call was from Norwich Union.

On my first day, Dennis gave me a tour of the office, showing me various departments that were undergoing 'a transitional period'. Dennis wore a blue pinstripe shirt and looked like a gull. He'd say things like: 'Okay, this team deals with policy retentions. We're not quite sure what the status of these guys is going to be over the next few months. Some of them are over in India training staff at the moment so this may be one of the areas where we, uh, have to juggle things around a bit.' Then he led me over to a cluster of eight or nine desks.

'Here's where you'll be working,' he said. 'Deaths.'

There were two bars on the left side of the screen: one represented your expected output, the other showed how much work you'd actually done. The 'expected output' bar was constantly ticking upwards.

I sat on the black swivel chair and Dennis put his hand on my shoulder. 'I'll leave you to get on with it,' he said. 'If you need any help, everyone round here knows what they're doing. Just ask someone like Janice.' He nodded towards the middle-aged lady with the pixie cut and powder-pink blouse. She did not look up from her typing. Cyan stats shone in the twin pools of her dilated pupils. Every office has a Janice. Dennis walked away.

I was delirious from lack of sleep. The previous evening, I had gone to bed, shut my eyes, and stayed awake the entire night. I hadn't been conscious of being wracked with anxiety or sadness – I'd just felt heavy and inert, like meat on a slab. I'd lain there, not sleeping, knowing I would have to get up in the morning, put on a shirt, walk through the chill, greyscale streets and enter an office.

'Are you okay?'

I blinked, looked up.

Janice was squinting at me. 'Are you okay?'

'Uh... yes. I'm fine.' I realised I must have zoned out for a couple of seconds.

'You know, um...' She pursed her lips. 'You know we're not really allowed to sleep at our desks.'

Okay. More than a couple of seconds.

Janice looked genuinely concerned. 'Do you need to go home?'

I glanced down at my hands, then at the glowing productivity bars, then back to Janice. 'I don't know.'

Dennis came over. 'Is everything all right?'

'I just... I haven't been sleeping very well,' I said.

'Perhaps you should go home,' said Dennis, letting three of his fingertips rest gently on my shoulder.

'Okay,' I said.

I got out of my chair, walked out the building, went to Boots and bought two packs of sleeping tablets. I'd never needed sleeping tablets before. I ate four, went to bed, and slept.

I stayed in bed the whole next day. The following morning, I phoned in and quit.

The world of work had always been an odious place where I traded my limited competence for meagre wages, wasting the best years of my life performing menial, meaningless errands. But now, the whiff of opportunity had thrown the whole farce into sharp relief. It had reminded me there was more to life than productivity charts and customer retention procedures – that some people actually got paid to do stuff they *liked*.

For two whole days I lay in bed with the curtains drawn, a dark little cloud swirling in my chest. If I was such a soft prima donna that I couldn't stomach working in an office while I tried to catch my big break, I was screwed. I had no income, and apparently no tolerance for the realities of modern living.

Then my phone rang. I'd passed the interview.

Yes, the other one.

Shooting the TV series took place over a week at the Hay-on-Wye Literary Festival, a nauseatingly self-congratulatory ultra middle-class clusterfuck populated by bellicose, cauldron-paunched academics and have-your-cake-and-eat-it mums sporting half a dozen papoosed babies while supping Sauvignon Blanc and liaising with the office on their mobiles – people more successful than me, basically. The premise of the show was that I, an aspiring author, was there to try to blag an audience with the big-name authors, editors and agents, in the belief that doing so might open the door on a glittering literary career. Of course, I knew that in real life, this would be a bad move – the equivalent of gatecrashing a prospective employer's private dinner party instead of sending a CV – but my director told me we had to exaggerate things a little to create drama. Besides, they had already phoned ahead to secure interviews with industry names. All I had to do was pretend I'd tracked these bigwigs down through tenacity, chutzpah and a series of crazy gambles, and that the three-person film crew following me at all times had nothing to do with it.

Thus my role was reduced to hammy pantomime as I pretended to beg and cajole and sneak about like a cat burglar in the service of my ambition.

On the second day, as we stood amongst deckchairs in the middle of the festival site, my director handed me a sheaf of canary-yellow A5 paper.

'What's this?' I said.

'They're for your book,' she said.

I looked down. The paper was blank. 'I don't understand.'

'Well, in this scene, you're going around the festival, handing out fliers, trying to promote your book.'

'Right, but—'

'You're trying to get a lead that'll take you to a big cheese.' She grinned and swung her fist in a kind of 'go get 'em!' gesture.

I hefted the 'fliers'. There were about a hundred and fifty of them. All about us middle-class festival goers clumped from tent to tent via a network of astroturfed walkways.

'So I should just—'

'Yeah. Just... you know, hand them out. And say to people: "Hi, I'm Tim Clare. I'm a writer. I don't suppose you know where I need to go to find a big name in publishing?"'

'But how would they—'

'Oh, they won't. We just need footage of you on the hunt. We've got to see you having some failures to make it more exciting. Can't have your victory coming too easily!' And she gave me a wink. 'We'll probably record a voiceover for this bit, with you talking about how your mission wasn't going very well. Anyway. Off you go.'

And so I spent the next half an hour shambling awkwardly about the festival site, handing blank scraps of paper to strangers and telling them my name was Tim Clare, that I was a writer, and did they... no, sorry, of course. What? Oh, yes, it's just a piece of paper. Sorry. We're filming.

The interviews themselves didn't go much better. None of the production staff knew the title of my novel, much less what it was about, so I ended up having to pitch my whizz-bang teen Fantasy to dour, melt-faced editors from serious literary lists, who, for their part, resisted the urge to slit their palsied wrists as I rattled on about dog-faced boys and totally sweet underground mech battles.

One chat with a literary agent bucked the trend, and seemed to be going well. We talked over coffee, sat at a table beneath a big red and white sun umbrella. I'd quickly learned not to admit my novel was Fantasy – instead, I claimed it was 'sort of a William Golding-inspired type of thing'.

'Well,' said the agent, stroking his beard, 'that does sound interesting. I'd like to read it.'

I heard a hiss from behind the camera, saw my director mouthing something at me. I frowned.

'Give him a flier!' she repeated.

'Uh...' I reached into my pocket, took out one of the yellow pieces of paper. 'I, uh... I've been handing out fliers about my book.'

I held out the crumpled page. He accepted it with obvious reluctance, turned it over in his palm.

'I don't understand.'

'It's...' I tugged at my hair, caught between maintaining the fiction my director had insisted on and not appearing mentally ill. 'I'm trying to promote my book.'

There was a long pause, then the agent placed the blank flier on the table, next to his empty coffee cup.

'I think this,' he said, 'is the kind of thing that would put me off.'

He never read my book.

I was surprised at how draining filming was. We'd start at eight and end at midnight every day. On camera, I was about as natural as an animatronic haddock, stammering and flinching my way through hours of scripted 'antics' while feeling increasingly fraudulent. My director responded by encouraging me to be loose and spontaneous.

'Let's see what happens,' she'd say. 'You know – be crazy.'

Some of my friends were down for the festival too, and while we filmed I'd see them about the town, lolling in deckchairs, drinking cider, chatting about the bagfuls of second-hand books they'd bought. As far as I could tell, they were having the time of their lives. Joe, who, at this stage, was still Joe Schmoe, a wannabe, like me, had been whooping it up with his bogus press accreditation, going to hundreds of pounds' worth of events for free, getting boozed at multiple parties, pining for a girl with hair in strawberry-blonde ringlets, and cringing when he and his parents sat at the next table along from Zadie Smith and his dad kept pointing and saying her name to embarrass him.

I really missed my friends. I'd thought filming would be a whirlwind of socialising, but most of the time we had to find quiet areas with no one around, so I could do pieces to camera. Perhaps this was the price of fame Britney Spears had sung about so poignantly in 'Lucky'.

The festival site itself is quite small, so authors and celebrities can often be found mingling amongst regular festival goers. My director urged me to collar recognisable 'names' for a chat, without explaining what she wanted me to chat to them about.

We'd just finished shooting a bit to camera near the performers' hospitality tent when author, presenter and celebrity wit Stephen Fry strolled past.

'Go on, Tim!' my director whispered, stepping out from behind camera to give me a dig in the ribs.

I turned to look at him. 'Oh, hello,' I said.

He stopped, saw the camera, then turned to face me. 'Hello,' he said.

I considered my next move. What was I supposed to be stopping him for? Was I pretending he was one of the people I wanted to read my novel? Did I think he might be able to get me an 'in' with an important editor? What the hell was I doing?

My mouth had gone dry. My brief hesitation widened into a long, uncomfortable silence, while Stephen Fry waited for me to say something. But I couldn't think of anything.

Eventually, looking mildly confused, he walked away, leaving me wearing an apologetic grin – the entire miserable transaction captured on film for posterity. Minutes later, almost exactly the same thing happened with Julian Clary, neither of us seeming to know who I was supposed to be or what I wanted.

By the end of shooting, I felt exhausted, self-conscious and very small. The 'climax' to the series was a segment where I 'blagged' entry to an exclusive Channel 4 party – a twist I felt insulted the audience's intelligence more than strictly necessary, given that the show was commissioned by and shown on Channel 4 – then schmoozed with the supposed great and good of the UK publishing industry. After shooting a clutch of moments where beaming editors slapped me on the back and assured me they'd love to read my manuscript, it was time for the film crew to head home. I asked if they minded my staying a bit longer – I'd met so many friendly, connected people, it seemed silly not to hang around and chew the fat with my new literary pals.

I watched the tail lights of the crew's car disappear up the long, stony drive, then headed back to the party. Music blared from three interconnected tents festooned with garish lights. All across the field, guests yammered in tight clutches, quaffing free champagne. I couldn't see any of the people who'd been so nice to me. Perhaps they were inside, getting some food.

I plunged into the busy tents, smiling and trying to look like I belonged. After joining a queue, I found myself waiting for the knife at a lavish cheeseboard. A man was cutting himself a thick tranche of something blue and veiny. Then I realised it was Channel 4 News presenter Jon Snow.

'Hello,' I said, before I could stop myself.

He frowned. 'Hello.'

Oh God. Not this again. I tried to smile politely, realised I had nothing to say, then stared down at the brie and waited for him to go.

Walking back through the tent, I felt increasingly conspicuous. I cast around for a familiar face. Just beneath the far awning, I spotted a chap who'd spoken to me earlier – an editor with trendy rectangular spectacles and a dun-coloured jacket. He'd been really enthusiastic, telling me he thought my book sounded 'great' and 'he'd love to chat' about it further. He didn't appear to be speaking to anyone, so I shuffled and apologised my way towards him as discreetly as possible.

As I came close, I pretended that I'd just spotted him. 'Oh, hello,' I said, this time meaning it.

He gave me a strained smile, nodded. 'Hi.'

I stopped. 'How's it going?'

'Actually–' He began sidestepping around somebody '–I was just going to get a drink. See you later!' He trilled his fingers in a patronising little arpeggio, then began walking away.

'Uh, okay.' I gave him a kind of lacklustre half wave, but he already had his back to me.

I turned, and almost crashed into one of the agents I'd spoken to the previous day.

'Oh, hi!' I said, brightening.

'Hi,' she said, slim but pearlescent with sweat. She glanced over my shoulder, mouthed something to someone behind me.

'How's it going?' I said.

'Fine,' she said, picking at her watchstrap. 'And you?'

I shrugged. 'Yeah, okay. I, uh... I don't really know anyone here.'

'Right.' Her gaze drifted back over my shoulder.

'Would you, um—'

'Sorry – I'm being summoned.' She gave someone the thumbs up, nodded vigorously, then turned back to me. 'Have a nice time, anyway. Uh... Tim, was it?'

'Yeah.'

'Have a good time.' She patted my shoulder, then pushed a little, encouraging me to step aside so she could get past.

And so it continued. I wandered the party, returning to the faces who had been so welcoming, but with the camera gone, each erstwhile chummy publisher or agent gave me an apologetic smile, made their excuses, and backed away. I ended up sitting on a sofa, alone, nursing a glass of wine, feeling like a classic chump. I cut such a pathetic figure that eventually one of the burlesque dancers came over to check I was all right.

'Are you okay?' she said. It took me a few seconds to register that she wasn't in character – for most of the evening hired girls had been flouncing about in pseudo-twenties flapper garb, hooting salutations in exaggerated posh accents.

'Uh... yeah, I guess so.' I tugged at my forelock, a nervous habit that irritates the bejesus out of my friends. 'I just feel a bit out of place. I don't really, uh... These aren't my people.' It was an odd turn of phrase, but the moment the words left my lips, I knew they were true. Sure, I'd spent my entire academic career studying to be an author, sure, I loved books and read with a hungry fervour, sure, I could appreciate a well-stocked cheeseboard, but unless I had a bona fide published book under my belt, to these folk I would always be an outsider.

The dancer nodded. 'God, I know how you feel. Don't worry. No one wants to speak to me, either.' I must have looked surprised, because her face went serious, then she added, 'I'm from Surrey.'

'Oh, that explains it then,' I said, then laughed at my brilliant and apposite zinger.

She grinned. 'Yeah. Takes a few weeks away before you lose the stink.' She stood, patted me on the shoulder. 'Anyway... enjoy the party.' With that, she stood and drifted off into the crowd.

The encounter left me feeling funny all the next day. Not undignified-tingle-in-the-trouser-region funny, just funny odd, thank you. The only partygoer who had been honest and nice had been the one person who wasn't a member of the publishing industry. Somewhere deep inside me, a grit speck of doubt began rankling – why was I working so hard to impress these people?

As I rounded the corner on the way to one of Hay-on-Wye's many pubs, I passed a trio of teenage girls, who started giggling. Not entirely unused to being an object of derision for this demographic, I tried to look indifferent and kept walking. I heard one of them say, 'Excuse me,' and bravely pretended I hadn't heard, rather than taking the bait and getting my gait/dress sense/haircut mocked.

'Excuse me,' the girl called out again, 'are you Tim Clare?'

I stopped. I frowned. I turned around. 'Uh... yeah.'

The girl was wide-eyed. Also, I now noticed, very attractive. As were her friends.

She smiled from behind a fringe of full red hair. 'Are you the one that's been doing that programme?'

I was so taken aback I had to think for a moment. 'Uh... yeah.'

'Umm...' The girl giggled again. To my growing amazement, I realised that she wasn't sniggering at me. She was *shy*. 'I, umm... I do some writing. Would you mind if I asked your advice?'

'Uh... sure.'

Ten minutes later, I was in the snug of a local pub, meeting up with Joe. We got ourselves a couple of ales and found a table in the back. Joe was tall and slim, with a head of long blond hair. I thought it made him look a little like Vega, the gorgeous but narcissistic masked Catalonian cage-fighter from *Streetfighter II*. He was staying with our other friends at a campsite a few miles out of town. We talked about some of the famous authors he'd already seen. Neither of us had been to the Hay Festival before. We'd never encountered so many role models in one place. Throw a stone in any direction, and you'd more than likely hit someone who was making a living doing what we'd always longed to do.

As we sat supping our pints and admiring the horse brasses, Joe smiled and said: 'You know, it's weird – for the first time this week, I feel like it might actually be possible. We might actually be able to do this.'

By 'it' and 'this', he meant, of course, 'being a writer'.

I smiled. I was thinking about the fit girl who'd asked me for writing tips.

'Yeah,' I said. 'I think so too.'

I took a long, luxuriant gulp of ale. It was great having a mate like Joe to share the week with – someone who understood the slow-ripening pleasures of aspiration and hard graft. I decided then and there that his loyalty would not go unrewarded. As soon as I had signed my big book deal, I would use my newfound celebrity within the industry to make sure his novel got published too. After all, what are friends for?

I raised my glass.

'Cheers,' I said.

'Cheers.'

# 8

'Oh, I don't know.' I made a show of taking a long, surly tug on my bottle of Corona. I was wretchedly drunk. 'It feels weird, I guess. I've heard so many stories about the Edinburgh Fringe but I've never been. I don't think I've ever been to Scotland, even. And now I'm here, I feel a bit out of it.' I took another gulp of beer, gazing at happy people queuing for comedy shows. 'I mean… I always wanted to come one day, but not like this. It's just things are so bad at home right now, I thought it was best I got away, give me and my girlfriend time to clear our heads, like. I had to travel all the way from Norwich by train. The journey was horrible – eight and a half hours or something fucking ridiculous. And now I'm here… it's almost surreal. There's so much going on, I keep forgetting that my whole future's up in the air. I'll be smiling, having a good time, then I remember there's a massive shitstorm waiting for me when I get home. I feel like I'm in hardcore denial… Fuck that… I don't know *what* I feel.' I necked the dregs, set the bottle down on the table with a sigh. 'So. What about you? Are *you* having a nice festival?'

The skinny, bespectacled flierer shuffled awkwardly. The only interaction he wanted was the handing over of a glossy card advertising a topical satire show and perhaps my agreement to attend. My troubles were my own.

It was late summer 2005, three months after the TV series at Hay. I was drinking in the Pleasance Courtyard, Edinburgh, while all around me enthusiastic up-and-coming writers, actors, comedians, poets, musicians, entertainers and other assorted artists plied their trade and competed for a slice of the Fringe Festival audience.

A month earlier, I had moved into a new house in Norwich with my long-term girlfriend. I was doing freelance writing work to cover the bills, and waiting on my agent to read my redrafted novel. I had been offered a position working from home as Features Editor for a national magazine group. I even had my own study. Career, commitment, no more playing PlayStation till four in the morning with drunken flatmates. This, then, was growing up.

Two days before my arrival in Edinburgh, my girlfriend came home late, rather worse for wear. She sat down heavily in a green club chair that belonged to our elderly landlord, a spry, plummy ex-Major. When he had showed us around, he had used phrases like 'as sure as God made little apples' and 'but then you're robbing Peter to pay Paul, d'you see?' while showing me how to do things like open a window or turn on a heater.

'You all right?' I had said, hovering at the edge of the room. Like me, she was an aspiring writer. We'd done the same course at uni and we'd met through the Creative Writing Society. We'd been going out for two and a half years, living together for most of them, although not like this – just the two of us.

My girlfriend sighed. 'I think we should break up.'

The room lurched.

'You're just tired. You don't mean that.'

She sighed again. 'I think I probably do.'

'Ah.'

It's at times like this you turn to your closest friends for support, but unfortunately most of mine were up in Scotland doing a month-long run of their Fringe show – a mix of stand-up and performance poetry, under the collective name of Aisle16. I felt this qualified as an emergency, so I got on a train and headed north in search of sympathy, wisdom and a dash of perspective.

The problem with perspective is it doesn't always work in your favour. Sometimes you take a step back and realise that not only is the picture frame wonky but the nail you drove in has a crack rising from it that goes all the way up the wall, widening at the ceiling to a dark fissure that in all probability compromises the structural integrity of the house. A few days at the Fringe convinced me that not only was my relationship about to go gurgling down the shitter but, compared to the hardworking artists there, I was a washed-up faker.

Over their sixty-year histories, relations between the original Festival and the Fringe have oscillated between convivial and frosty. Since the Edinburgh International Festival launched in August 1947, performance at the main Festival was strictly by invitation from its Artistic Director. Previous Directors include Sir Ian Bruce Hope Hunter, Sir John Richard Gray Drummond, the seventh Earl of Harewood George Henry Hubert Lascelles, and the superbly monikered

Robert Noel Ponsonby. While they may well have been competent, responsible custodians impressively conversant in contemporary performing arts, one can't help feeling there's something about those names that's a little, I don't know... establishment?

In the first year, a handful of theatre companies not invited to take part in the Festival decided to turn up anyway, hoping to attract some of the culture-loving crowds to their own, less traditional shows. The initial dynamic may have been parasitic, but sometimes parasites are useful – like those little birds that hop about inside hippos' mouths, pecking at scraps of food lodged between teeth, food that would otherwise rot and spread decay. Soon, the Fringe was drawing its own, distinct audiences, some of whom fed into the main Festival.

More than half a century later, the Fringe I was attending had over two thousand shows a year, sold over 1.6 million tickets and boasted a three-quarters share of Edinburgh's annual Festival audiences. Walking down the Royal Mile in Edinburgh's Old Town upon my arrival, I felt simultaneously like Marie Antoinette addressing peasants at the gates of Versailles, and a honey-snouted bear beset by angry bees as hundreds of grinning, pushy performers in oh-so-wacky costumes vied for my attention, my approval, and, ultimately, my money. It was as if rumours of easy food had attracted more and more little birds to the hippo's mouth, until its maw was crammed with thousands of tiny, struggling bodies, its smooth back plastered with shit and a constant, asinine twittering in its big grey ears.

I knew that the Fringe had a reputation for consisting of needy twats doing ever needier, twattier things in the name of artistic freedom and experimentation, but the fact remained that even the most incompetent, vapid attention-whores were doing better than me, because their work was reaching an audience. While my best efforts languished, unread, on my hard drive, some perpetually bescarved nihilistic rich kid playwright's bid to shock his laissez-faire parents into noticing him was being watched, night after night, by people who had paid to attend. Sure, the first comedian I saw there delivered her conspicuously laugh-free set with the kind of rapid, dry-throated desperation one associates with someone begging an encircling gang not to mug them, but the smattering of polite, relieved applause she received at the end was a few dozen handclaps more than I'd ever got. The worse the show, the more painful I found its artists' relative success.

To cap it all, Luke, Joel, Chris and Ross – the friends to whom I had come running for comfort – were having a brilliant time, working like dogs but performing their irritatingly well-written show to large, appreciative audiences.

Luke and Joel I'd met at uni, through the whirlwind of nerdy delights that was the Creative Writing Society. Where Luke was engaging, extroverted and baby-faced, Joel was wry, measured, and bore the cruel, beardy countenance of a depressive Icelandic coastguard.

I'd first encountered Ross at poetry gigs. An upbringing split between Scotland and Essex had rendered his accent a hybrid drawl, while chronic asthma chopped his sentences into halting Goldblumian rhythms. Combined with an uncommon aptitude for wordsmithery, these happy accidents conspired to make him one of the most compelling performance poets I had ever seen, glowering under black locks as he chanted elaborately crafted bollocks.

With his close-cropped hair and dead eyes, Chris was the member of the group I knew the least well. He had taken a somewhat eccentric route into live poetry, via an initial desire to join the armed forces then a switch to training as a lawyer. I'd already deduced that his unusual career path had conferred upon him some very particular skill sets:

i.   he could fieldstrip a casual statement in a matter of seconds, parsing it down to its core assertions, then rebuild it as a kind of improvised siege engine to send crashing back into its originator

ii.  he had the emotional vocabulary and empathy skills of a pork scratching

iii. he was much more popular than me with girls

As a quartet, they were doing great. The critical reception to their show had been excellent, an Arts Council grant meant that their spell in Edinburgh was free of the usual financial hardships associated with a Fringe run, and the shared challenges created a bonding experience that the four of them would treasure for the rest of their abundant, joy-filled lives. Plus, having donned the comportment and snazzy white suits of an ironic performance poetry boyband, the single males of the group were doubtless sowing their wild oats with the aggressive efficiency of a global agribusiness conglomerate.

Surrounded by ambition and success, I could feel my self-image shrivelling like a burger. My nine minutes of fame on television counted for nothing – the tiny amount of interest my appearance had inspired had fizzled away already. I had to repress the impulse to cry out to people, *Hey, hey, I'm an artist too!* Partly because shouting stuff like that is weird, but also because I was starting to wonder. If I really cared, wouldn't I be up here plying my trade? Might I be a fraud?

Back at the flat after the show, people showered, fixed themselves food, cracked open beers. One of Ross's half-finished poems was taped to the white kitchen door, Swiss-cheesed with blanks like a Mad-Lib. He said he'd put it there to keep it in his mind while he tried to fill the gaps. There were so many gaps, in fact, that it was impossible to tell what the poem was supposed to be about, and its enigmatic final line, 'Chocolate doubloons – and it's not even Christmas!' left me none the wiser.

As well as my four mates in the show, there was a vague constellation of satellite characters and hangers-on; friends, helpers, and people they'd met at the festival. Even amongst my mates, I felt like an outsider – after a fortnight of gigging daily, they chatted in a tangled argot of catchphrases and allusions.

Me and Chris sat in the front room, chugging beers and playing Xbox. Chris had rigged up the digital projector from their show so that we could play *Star Wars: Battlefront* on a screen roughly the size of a professional snooker table. I was temporarily content. I mean, it's not like boozing and having frenetic computerised lightsaber battles on a massive screen made me forget that my life was in a flat spin – they just dulled the emotions that might have prompted me to do something.

'Really sucks about your girlfriend, mate,' he said.

'Mmm,' I said, attempting to make Darth Vader pull off a Force Choke. I had never seen any of the *Star Wars* movies, but acquaintances had assured me that this sort of quasi-magical sadism was very much in character. 'Well. I'm kind of hoping that we can sort it out.' Darth Vader slashed at the dust with his lightsaber like a frustrated golfer searching for his ball in the rough.

'Yeah.' Chris nodded sagely. 'It was tough when I broke up with my girlfriend. But you can get good things out of it. Ross had a big creative burst after his break-up. Joel suddenly started writing poems and performing again when he split with his girlfriend. I wrote the best poems I'd ever done when it happened to me. I bet you end up writing the best stuff of your life.'

If there was one thing I desperately needed at that moment, it was for a respected peer to come along and substantially raise the bar.

'Right,' I said. 'Great.'

Luke Skywalker charged forward, controlled by Chris, and my cack-handed Darth Vader fell to a welter of flashing blade strokes.

Later that evening, on our way to get blotto, we called in to our friend Yanny's flat. Yanny – otherwise known as Ian – was part of the Fringe too, doing street performance in his then super-zeitgeisty 'chav poet' character, who, truth be known, was pretty much Yanny plus a couple of sovereign rings and a Burberry cap. When he'd approached the Arts Council for funding, he'd been told he was a shoo-in, on account of his chronic arthritis meaning he was registered disabled. This provided my rampant envy with yet another target. Why oh why wasn't poor time management recognised as a legitimate disability?

Yanny was staying in a flat above a university psychology department, at the top of a long, dank flight of concrete steps. We traipsed up as a gang – me, the Aisle16 boys, a couple of friends who were crashing at their flat, and two of the attractive young girls who, by day, went around handing out fliers for the show. It was a tough climb, and when Yanny answered the door, still dressed in his white tracksuit and medallion, most of us were wheezing like fag-knackered geriatrics.

'Come in, lads, come in,' he said, beckoning in his best approximation of an Essex barrowboy, his voice so coarse and bass-heavy that at times it resembled an idling tractor engine. 'Make yourselves at home. Anybody want a beer?'

We shuffled into a spacious flat that managed to be at once baroque and skeevy, all green baize club chairs and leather tomes, creaking floorboards and huge wilted pot plants. In the lounge, a huge, ghastly portrait of some anonymous old lady glowered down from above a gaping fireplace. As people chatted and found perches, I wandered into the bedroom. Dog-eared paperbacks were heaped in stacks ten or twelve deep around a tatty chest of drawers and a double bed. The whole flat had a weird vibe to it that I couldn't place. Rooms go for such a premium during the Festival that owners often rent them out to performers for an exorbitant profit then bugger off for the month. The flat Yanny was renting was still overflowing with the private minutiae of a stranger's life. It was as if the owner, instead of leaving, had faded into the wallpaper and remained there, watching us like a ghostly pervert. The hair on the back of my neck prickled. I took a breath. A hand clamped down on my shoulder.

I jerked round.

It was Yanny.

'Here Tim, you seen the dildoes yet?'

'Uhh...' I racked my brains, as if this were the sort of experience that might have slipped my mind. 'No, I don't *think* so.'

'Oh, mate.' Yanny rubbed his palms together and beamed. 'You've got to see the dildoes!' He squeezed deftly past me, round stacks of books, and pulled open the top drawer of the chest of drawers. It was full of boxer shorts and – oh! I gave a little start – a neat collection of three dildoes. I'm not sure why I reacted with surprise. I mean, if a trusted friend says they're going to show you some dildoes, and then they show you some dildoes, reality has tallied precisely with expectation.

Yanny took out the biggest, a flesh-coloured affair perhaps three feet long with some sort of gusseted middle and two 'heads' (I believe the technical term is a 'double-dong'), gripped either end with a fist and proceeded to flex it like a strongman bending an iron bar. 'All I did was open the drawer, you know, having a bit of a sniff around, and it was full of pants and dildoes!' he reported cheerily.

'Not... your dildoes?' I queried, uncertainly.

'Nah, they belong to the geezer whose flat this is. All of

this shit is his.' He gestured – using the prosthetic appendage – about the room. Creepy or not, the place reeked of wealth and success. It was like an anti-prophecy, a glimpse of everything I would never achieve for myself.

My gaze kept returning to the gigantic phallus. In the end, I had to cast around for something else to focus on. I reached down and picked the first paperback off the top of the nearest pile. The cover was roadmapped with downy white creases. In big, blue capital letters, it read: *Toxic Parents: Overcoming Their Hurtful Legacy And Reclaiming Your Life.* Several pages had been folded over at the corners and it fell open naturally at these. I saw at once that whole passages had been underlined in blue biro using thick, heavy strokes that stood out like staples when you turned the page. There was a questionnaire, all filled in, again with violent slashes of ballpoint pen.

Now, at this point, I should have stopped reading. Most of us have experienced that tingling push-pull feeling where you realise you have the opportunity to invade a stranger's privacy without their knowing – the email inbox left open on an internet café computer, the intimate letter somehow discarded in the street, the gust of wind that lifts a skirt just high enough to reveal a bum cheek decorated with a tiny circle of heart tattoos. Over the years, I've found I'm much more likely to take advantage of one of these 'accidents' to peek into the life of a stranger than into the life of someone I know, where such knowledge might confer some personal advantage. I suppose my rationalisation is always, well, I'm never going to meet this guy, I can't connect the information to a face – where's the harm in snooping?

I glanced up, and saw that Yanny was absently slapping one end of the double-dong against his palm like a cosh. Any chance of my attention straying from the book evaporated.

It seemed like an exploded version of Larkin's 'This Be The Verse', its chapters apparently split into categories. Whoever had read it had circled the subsections entitled: 'The Inadequate Parents' and 'The Controllers' ('Why Can't They Let Me Lead My Own Life?'). Long passages about parental incompetence and emotional frailty saddling the child with an inevitable legacy of suffering and low self-esteem had been circled then annotated with marginal notes, mostly 'Yes!' or just '!!!'. The reader seemed to have picked out the sections that condemned bad parents, while the advice on taking responsibility for one's life and moving on had been left blank. In the questionnaire, one of the questions went something like: 'Have you ever fantasised about murdering your parents?' The reader had marked the 'Yes' box with a big blue tick, fat and deep from where the pen had rolled back and forth, back and forth, etching it into the page.

I slapped the book shut.

'What you reading?' said Yanny, cocking his head.

'Oh, nothing. Just some… book.' When I went to put it down, I saw that the paperback beneath it was also a self-help book, something about 'healing psychic wounds', and by tilting my head to read the spine of the next one down I saw that it too was a self-help book, as was one the beneath that, and the one beneath that. Looking round, I realised that practically every book in the room was pop-psych. A few had generic, *You Can Do It!*-style 'personal improvement' titles, but most were so specific (you know, *So You've Got Herpes*, or *Beat Your Emetophobia Today!*, that sort of thing) it bordered on ludicrous to believe that one person could require them all. I began to suspect someone was pulling our leg. It was as if they had set up the entire flat as a piece of guerrilla installation art, planting bizarre clues about the owner that built up into this ridiculous, impossible conglomeration of quirks, fetishes, and peccadilloes. Doubtless, in the lounge, the other chaps had just discovered the scorched remains of a gorilla suit in the fireplace, while a green-tinted monocle crunched beneath one of the girls' heels.

But as I thought some more, I realised that owning books relating to various psychological problems was not that absurd a proposition for someone either working or studying in a university's psychology department. Nor, really, was it strange or shameful for an adult to own what amounted to a very modest collection of sex toys. Presented with a smattering of value-neutral objects, my knee-jerk reaction had been to construct a figure of puerile derision, one I didn't have to compare myself to or feel jealous of.

I put the book down on the pile and followed Ian through to the lounge, where everybody was drinking and smoking and trying to out-quip each other. Banter shuttlecocked between the loudest males, but I loitered in a corner, lost in thought.

What would a stranger make of my room, back in Norwich? A brand new bed, a brand new chest of drawers, both of which my parents had bought for me, most of my possessions still crammed into cardboard boxes stacked three levels high – one was full of self-help books. No posters or pictures on the walls. Clutter all over the floor; socks trampled flat, half-read books left face down to keep the page, a pair of dumbbells, their embossed lettering crusted with rust. A small plastic radio and tape player, the cassette inside it a pirate copy of a hypnosis CD – Side A for relaxation and general positive affirmations, Side B for successful slimming. On the bedside table, the bottle of 'Rescue Remedy' my mum had bought for me, supposedly able to deliver 'support at times of emotional demand' in the form of a pump-action spray. Next to it, a 'One-a-Day' pull-off calendar of Chinese propaganda posters, several weeks out of date.

Some time very soon after I and my girlfriend had moved into our new house, remembering to tear off the previous day's calendar page had become a source of huge anxiety to me. Every morning I'd wake up, and the calendar would be wrong, and I'd have to remember to rip off the old date or it would go on being wrong, sitting there like an indictment, proof that I couldn't handle the most meagre of adult responsibilities. It was like a timer I had to keep on resetting, or else something terrible would happen. Soon, just looking at the calendar made me feel stressed, just *thinking* about that endless ripping of days and days and days tied my stomach in knots, so I tried to push it to the back of my mind, which of course meant that I would often forget to tear the date off at all, and then it would go two days late, or three, which made me feel even more useless, and so my feelings spiralled.

Eventually, I had given up. A mere calendar had defeated me. Time stopped.

Unfortunately, my anxieties found new things to latch on to. Despite a lack of anything worth stealing, I became convinced that burglars would, at some stage, attempt to break into our house. I nervously tapped the single-glazed windows with an index finger, scrutinised the locks, peered down into the back garden imagining approach routes, checking for spots where a criminal might lurk unseen. At night, I would lie in bed, sleepless, staring up at the ceiling while mentally augmenting the house with layer upon layer of security measures – first double-glazed windows, then replacement five-bolt mortis deadlocks for the doors, then additional sliding bolts for the same, then a security chain, then movement-activated security lights for the back garden, then a spyhole in the front door, an alarm, gravel to replace the back lawn, remote control metal blinds for the windows, a mail cage, closed-circuit television both inside and outside the property, metal plates to reinforce the doors, at which point my imagination would start garlanding the fortress with razor wire, conning towers, packs of slavering guard dogs.

But these make-believe safety measures only fed my fear. In my paranoid fantasy, each additional layer of security made our house more conspicuous, implying there was something inside worth protecting, attracting ever-more enterprising burglars and thus necessitating a higher level of protection, the cycle continuing until, in my mind, under cover of darkness hundreds of black-clad thieves swarmed towards an armoured citadel, imbued with the wiliness of ninjas and the tenacity of fresh-risen zombies.

My heart racing, I would start at the slightest noise. The

thought that an intruder might be in the house would harden into a conviction. I would tense up, tell myself not to be so stupid, then worry that I was ignoring my instincts. Surely I'd heard that noise? That one, just then. What on earth could've caused that, if not a burglar? More than once, I got out of bed, stepped out on to the landing, crept to the top of the stairs, then tiptoed my way down into the darkness, until I stood between the kitchen and front room, my hand poised on the light switch, listening furiously, knowing that to turn the lights on would allay my fears once and for all, and yet terrified of what I might see. What would I do if the 60 watt bulb revealed a gloved stranger, frozen in the act of stuffing my non-stick wok into a gunnysack marked 'SWAG'?

So I'd stand there, waiting, afraid. Eventually, after minutes in awkward solitary tableau, I'd muster the courage to flick the switch.

*Click.*

There was the front room, with its armchair and little TV, and a green plastic box full of printed-out drafts of my novel chapters.

*Click.*

There was the dining room, books stacked on the table, and past it, the kitchen. Taking deep, relieved breaths, I would usually flick the lights back off, then turn, and go back upstairs to bed.

One night, however, maybe five days before travelling to Edinburgh, I had switched the lights off, but instead of leaving, I had walked through the dining room into the kitchen, and had stood there, letting my eyes adjust to the dark, listening to the hum of the fridge. Back when we'd been shown round the house, one of my first thoughts was: *God, this reminds me of the flat we were in when Pop died.* I didn't tell my girlfriend, because we were desperate to find somewhere, and it seemed stupid.

In the cool, empty kitchen, I silently admitted to myself that I was miserable. Growing up sucked. Everything felt wrong. From here on in, life was only going to get worse. More burdens, less freedom, my inadequacy and incompetence thrown into ever sharper relief.

Taking a tea towel from its peg, I wedged myself into the generous gap between the refrigerator and the wall. The painted wall was cold against my back, the fridge's hum so loud that I could feel it vibrating against my chest. I wadded up the tea towel, stuffed it into my mouth, and began to scream.

Back in Edinburgh, after we left Yanny's flat, we went out and got smashed. It was Fringe Sunday, traditionally the busiest day of the entire festival, and Monday would be Ross, Joel, Chris and Luke's only day off that month, so they each planned to spend it in the nauseous, agonised doldrums of a monster hangover. Surrounded by revellers we staggered from bar to bar, knocking back pints, becoming more obnoxious and stupid but less aware of it, tongues loosening and inner philosophers rising up to seize the podium.

Eventually, some time approaching six in the morning, we were blundering out of a bar when Luke said, 'Hey, shall we climb the mountain?'

Arthur's Seat is not really a mountain. It's a mild hill that rises just over a quarter of a kilometre above the city. An Iron Age fort once stood on the east side and the panoramic views at its summit make it a magnet for pissed-up Fringe goers every August. Although the ascent ought to be a casual jaunt, there's nothing like drinking solidly for nine hours to turn a casual jaunt into an epic, punishing quest.

Though the hill is visible throughout the city, it took us some time to wend our way through the streets and work out how to reach it. In the process, we weeded out our less tena-cious members as, one by one, companions decided they were too drunk to go hiking. Putting one foot in front of the other began to demand such intense concentration that we separated out into a long, straggly column. Conversation shut down as all our mental resources got rechannelled into gross motor control. I watched the damp grass roll past beneath my shoes and wondered what the hell I was doing.

Over the course of the evening I had talked to a lot of people – my friends, random performers, flierers and other noble foot soldiers of the Fringe – and as I did so, I started to realise I'd been a bit hasty in my assessment of my friends as 'jammy bastards'. It became clear that performing at the Fringe was tough – crushingly tough, in fact. Handing out fliers and constantly acting as a shill for your show was no more fun than selling double-glazing. In fact, for most people, it was worse, because they weren't even getting paid. Every day, these performers were met with a barrage of resentment, hostility, and indifference. Some were new to the Fringe, others were middle-aged veterans who still hadn't managed to finesse their love of the Arts into a career and who struggled to make a living. I listened with mounting dread to stories of performing to empty rooms, of rowdy, abusive audience members, of returning from the Fringe thousands of pounds in debt.

As for my friends, each told me privately that he was knackered, worn down by the constant gigging and the unpredictable audience numbers and varied temperaments of his fellow performers. Tensions were flaring. Cabin fever was setting in. Each member was quietly wondering what the point of it all was. On top of this, I discovered that Yanny's funding had been pulled at the last minute. But with accommodation and a slot on the Royal Mile already booked, he'd had little choice but to come up and foot the bill himself.

And what of the Aisle16 flierers? Lost in self-pity, I'd dismissed them as stipended grunts with no ambition or discernible personalities, but I found out that one of them, Kate, played guitar and wrote songs. It made me realise that they were artists too, up in Edinburgh for a month, selflessly breaking their backs to help promote someone else's show, looking on as other people lived out their dreams.

But climbing Arthur's Seat, suddenly we were all equals. Groggy, lumbering, we made our way up the hillside. My fingers closed round nubs of rock still slick with last night's rain. Tendons in my shoulders tightened as I pulled myself up another couple of feet. Bit by bit, motion by motion, I was climbing the hill. I glanced up, and saw Chris some way ahead, strangely animated, nimble as a mountain goat. He was bolting from rocky outcrop to rocky outcrop, beckoning like Gollum, showing us the way, extending a hand to help pull people onwards. Even farther up the hill, Luke was climbing on his hands and knees, finding new routes, beating new paths, sometimes having to backtrack and try again. And when I looked behind me, I saw Kate, the flierer, facing the same challenges we'd faced, overcoming the same obstacles, doing her best to keep up, but enjoying herself all the while. Then some way beneath us all was Ross, whose asthma makes climbing difficult.

It wasn't until two days later, on the train back to Norwich, that the revelation hit me.

I remembered how we'd worked to get up that hill, the personal battles we'd each fought, and I thought, yeah man, we're all at different stages but we're climbing the same mountain. There's no sense in envying people just because they're a little farther up – you ought to rejoice, because the very fact they've made it proves that there's a safe path for you to follow. And for every person who's ahead of you, there's another, like Kate, down behind you, and you need to be conscious enough to turn round to them and say, 'Hey, I've made it this far, you can too,' and extend your hand to help them, because, you know, the view at the top's nice and everything but it's the sides of the mountain that sustain life, not the summit. You need to learn to take pleasure in the *process* of climbing, not in the promise of a final reward, because once you've reached the top, there's nothing to do but come back down again. Too many of us huff and puff, resenting the work it takes to get to the top, when the true achievement is just letting go, being totally in the moment, and appreciating the cool, wet rock beneath our fingertips.

After all, if it didn't need climbing, it wouldn't be a mountain. It'd just be some ground.

Meadows flickered past outside the carriage window. Evening sun hit a row of pines, exploding into dozens of bronze lances. My phone buzzed. It was a text from Chris. He said: 'Hey mate. Nice to see you. Good luck with everything. I've put you in my phone as Tim16.'

As small gestures of friendship go, it was one of the sweetest and best-judged I've ever received. Right when I needed it most, here was a message that said: *whatever happens, your mates are here for you.*

And if my friends had so much faith in me, why didn't I? I was a good person. A talented person. A strong person. Sure, I had some mountains in my path, but my trip to Scotland had taught me that a mountain's not a burden, it's an opportunity. I could do this. I was in a new home, starting a new life. I had a girlfriend I really cared about, a brand new job and a novel that was almost finished. Commitment and maturity can be frightening, and when people are frightened, they lash out. My girlfriend didn't want to leave me. She was just feeling the same doubts I'd experienced, and looking to me for reassurance.

Was I a little boy, or was I a man?

A warm serenity began to spread through my body. For the first time in months, I relaxed. As the buffet cart went by, I ordered a G&T. I listened to the tonic fizzing as I poured it over the ice, kicked back in my chair and took a contented sip. I thought to myself, *I can do this*, and just like that, I knew everything was going to be all right.

When I got home, my girlfriend told me she was seeing someone else. Within twenty-four hours I was back living with my parents in my teenage bedroom, where I had a nervous breakdown and ended up on tranquillisers and antidepressants. I lost my job with the magazine group and my agent sent the latest draft of my novel back saying it was deeply flawed and perhaps I should take a break from it. Oh, and Kate, the flierer? Her first album got to Number 1 in the UK charts and she went on to win the Brit Award for Best Female Artist.

Of course she fucking did.

# 9

The day I got home, immediately after splitting up with my girlfriend, something broke. I remember being on my knees in my parents' converted loft room, and I was howling and screaming like those bereaved mothers you see on the news after a bombing or a natural disaster, and I was dizzy, and I couldn't breathe, and I got a nosebleed. When people talk about rough break-ups or grief, they tend to resort to lots of metaphors related to physical pain – it really hurt, it was like getting kicked in the guts, it felt like my heart had been ripped out, etc, etc. For me, it was the opposite. I felt like I had been shot full of anaesthetic. My whole chest cavity felt icy and numb, as if the contents had been carefully, surgically removed. My primary emotion was terror.

It's a mark of what an incredibly fortunate and privileged life I've led that this was the worst thing I'd ever gone through, but at the time that was scant consolation. I only knew I'd be okay when, later, Dad managed to take me to the doctor.

Unfamiliar phrases like 'severe depressive symptoms' and 'persistent suicidal ideation' got tapped into my medical records. Being 'suicidal' didn't feel how I'd expected. I didn't want to off myself in the melodramatic, *Brief*

*Encounter* sense – on the contrary, imagining my own death calmed me down. Suicidal thoughts were soothing, pleasant even – they made me feel peaceful, like there was a way of regaining control.

When the doctor suggested tranquillisers and antidepressants, I baulked. I didn't want to be on pills, I mumbled. The doctor looked at me over her reading spectacles, and said that I had one of the most severe cases of depression she'd seen in her professional career.

Deep inside the bleak cavern of my psyche, a tiny fist clenched.

*All right!* I thought to myself. *My first shot at genuine depression, and it turns out I'm freaking awesome at it!*

And at that moment, I knew there was a way back out of this.

The problem was, another, larger part of me was thinking: *You've really got to knuckle down now. No more excuses. Writing's all you've got left. Don't screw that up as well. It's time to prove yourself. You can show everyone you're not a fuck-up. You can fix this. If you get a book deal, you can fix this.*

Back in the car, Dad said: 'You know your friends all think the world of you.'

'I doubt it.' His football pep talk had failed to lift my spirits, and I was sulking.

'No, seriously. They do.'

I rolled my eyes. 'How do you know?'

'Because I've spoken to them. They've told me.'

'When?'

'I phoned Luke,' Dad said. 'When you were really bad. I spoke to him.'

I rose in my seat. 'Did you?'

Dad nodded.

'Really? Why?'

'Mum and I were just so worried about you. I didn't know what to do.'

'I'm sorry,' I said. I was mortified.

Dad shook his head. 'You've got nothing to be sorry about. And all your friends are really rooting for you.'

'Oh come on, Dad. It wasn't like you were going to phone him up and tell him your son was suicidal and he was going to say, "Well, actually, John, privately we all think Tim's a right dickhead."'

'Don't be ridiculous.'

'I'm not!'

'You are. Why would they waste time on you if they didn't like you?'

'I don't know.' I let out a sigh, slumped in my seat. 'I really don't know.'

A year after we'd sat in that Hay-on-Wye pub, toasting our futures, I was there when Joe got the phonecall from his agent.

A few of us were lounging about in his rented East London flat, drinking cups of tea and listening to music. Joe's pad was a little too metropolitan for a shrinking violet like me. Noise from the bar downstairs often bled through the floor-boards until two in the morning, and the pneumatic drills on the building site next door started at eight. Rats scurried about the floor at night, gnawing at overflowing bin liners. One morning, Joe and his flatmates woke to discover someone had broken in during the night, taken a prodigious dump in the middle of the floor, then wiped his or her backside on several towels.

When Joe's mobile rang, nobody paid much notice at first.

'Yep... okay... yep...' Joe was nodding, smiling. As the call went on, he seemed to grow taller. 'Right... So what's the next stage? Okay.' We started to sense something was up. Our conversation tailed off. We turned to look at him. 'Yeah... okay... right then. That's great! Thanks very much. Bye.' He hung up, looked at us. His face broke into a massive grin. 'I'm going to be published!'

He jumped in the air, began hugging everyone in grabbing distance. His flatmates, none of whom were writers, showered him with praise.

'Congratulations! Oooh, I'm so excited!'

'Thanks.'

'Well done, Joe! This is fantastic. Are we invited to your book launch?'

'Of course!'

Soon it was my turn. I rose a little reluctantly from the sofa, patted him on the back when he embraced me.

'What did they offer you?' I said, not really wanting to know the answer.

When he told me, I felt myself flinch. The offer was a big one. More money than either of us had ever got for anything.

'I'm going to call my parents!' Joe said. Seconds later, he was excitedly relaying the news to his mum and dad.

Joe had told me his agent was sending his book out to publishers, and I'd read it and knew it was really good, so it wasn't a massive surprise that an editor was interested – but the speed and the size of the offer caught us all off-guard. It was happening. It was *really* happening. Just not to me.

I smiled, because everyone else was, and quietly, selfishly, hoped things would stop there.

A week later, I was back in my bedroom in Portishead, and my heart was racing.

'Yeah, I think the initial offer was big because it was supposed to be pre-emptive,' I told Luke over the phone. In the week since Joe had received his news, I'd started presenting my expert opinions on the cut-and-thrust world of UK publishing to anyone who'd listen. Sometimes, I almost believed them myself. 'They wanted to offer over the odds to frighten off any potential competitors.'

'Well, it hasn't worked,' said Luke.

I inhaled sharply. 'What do you mean?'

'Haven't you heard? The offer's already been beaten.'

'Oh shit.'

Over the next few weeks, I came to dread Joe's calls. He'd ring to give me progress reports and solicit advice. Each time we spoke, the money involved had gone up. He'd tell me the latest figure and I'd feel as if I'd been slapped, but at the same time, I wanted to know more, because he was my friend, and his life had just taken a hugely exciting twist.

His book was caught in a fierce bidding war. A debut

novelist's market value is notional – he or she has no sales record, no string of hits or history of muted disappointments. Editors often try to couch this process in robust-sounding cod-economic jargon, but essentially it's about a combination of gut instinct and balls – which, of course, is why so many editors love it, despite themselves.

In a book auction, the higher the advance rises, the greater the number of copies a publisher must sell in order to recoup their investment. Every time somebody significantly ups the top bid, the level of expectation rises a notch. Since, at this stage, almost nobody but the bidders have read the book, it creates an echo chamber where editors inadvertently stoke one another's excitement. A publisher starts off bidding for a promising young author – two rounds later, and the asking price is so high that anyone who pays it is going to have to shift a huge number of copies to turn a profit. Suddenly, they're battling it out for what will *have* to be the biggest literary debut of the year.

And that's not to say, of course, that it won't be. Just that it's a huge gamble.

'You should go with whoever offers you the most money,' I said, pacing back and forth on my bedroom's furry grey carpet with my mobile pressed to my hot, clammy ear. On the one hand, hearing about his escalating fortune while I didn't have two brass farthings to rub together made me feel physically sick, but on the other, I was afraid that if I didn't get involved I'd be forgotten about. By casting myself as his consultant I got to kid myself that I was part of this world too, and that we were somehow still equals.

He was being feted by the various auction participants – going to presentations, receiving heaps of free books. He told me that two imprints of the same publishing house were bidding against each other for his novel – that he'd gone up in the same glass elevator twice in a week and that he had to pretend to be as impressed the second time as he was the first. He'd started dropping terms like 'lead title' and 'Booker submission' into our conversations, while, for my part, I'd tried to sound blasé, when really I was delirious with jealousy and awe.

'It's not just about the money,' he said. 'I need to think about who's going to publish it best, what sort of authors I'm going to be appearing alongside.'

'What's that got to do with…'

My bedroom door opened. It was my mum, carrying a pair of burgundy loafers.

'Tim?' she said. 'I got these on the way home at Asda. I can take them back if you don't like them but I just thought if you tr—'

'Not now!' I mouthed, swatting her away with my free hand.

'Sorry!' Mum whispered, retreating. I waited until the door clicked shut.

'Joe,' I said, pulling myself up to my full height, 'listen, mate. The most reliable indicator of how well you're going to be published is how much money they offer you.' I knew he wanted kudos, that he wanted a chance to get into the McSweeney's set, with young, zeitgeisty authors like Dave Eggers and Zadie Smith. 'Taking less because you're desperate to chase down trendy stable mates is stupid.'

'Fuck you.'

Joe's meteoric ascension left me feeling the pressure like never before. Where was my breakthrough moment? Where were the editors beating a path to my door? As the bidding continued, I repeatedly tried to get in touch with my agent. She'd had the final draft of my book for over two months, and still hadn't read it. I'd spent ages rewriting it and I was desperate to get things moving. How could I become a bestselling author when my masterpiece was stuck in her desk drawer?

When I wrote to ask what was going on, she sent me an angry reply saying that she was very busy after the London Book Fair, that she'd been very patient with me and all my inadequate redrafts, and that if I wasn't happy with the speed she was going then I could go and try my luck finding another agent, but otherwise, I'd have to wait.

I rang Joel in need of counsel.

His diagnosis: 'It sounds like you've got a shit agent.'

I'll admit, it was tempting to compare Joe's treatment by his agent – regular calls, close editorial feedback, plenty of encouragement – to my own, but then I wondered how many of her other clients she was having to sideline in order to devote her time to him. Our old creative writing tutor was also one of her authors, and I'd heard he was complaining to his students that he couldn't get through to her by phone or email. Maybe, I reasoned, this was how it worked. Maybe it wasn't that I had a shit agent, but that my agent had a shit author.

Joe wasn't the only one doing well. Over a matter of months, all my best friends found success at the one thing I'd always wanted to do. Their achievements made my failure feel all the more odious. They'd made getting published look easy. I'd given it my best shot, and I'd failed. I couldn't blame circumstances, because Joe had proved that even my fantasy of a wild cash bonanza was possible – the auction finally petered out at the 'insano' level, with the rights to his novel sold all round the world. My dream *had* been achievable. After all those years, it had come true – only for someone else.

I remembered nights at Yarmouth dog track, waving fivers at the bookies with the chalkboards, yelling over the rail as six greyhounds took the near bend in a spray of damp sand. There'd usually be at least a dozen of us, and, in a group that large, there was almost always someone who came away with a profit. One guy I know won over six hundred quid when he correctly picked first, second and third place, and spent the whole night buying everyone beers. Of course, just because one person in a gang of twelve wins money down the track, it doesn't follow that betting on dogs is the path to riches.

But just try telling that to the bloke with his pockets full of twenties.

# 10

Back in the car with my dad, I began to sob.

'What's the point?' I said. 'I can't cope with the most basic problems in life. I'm afraid of everything. I can't do what I want to. I'm a stupid fucking idiot. There's no point living. I just want to die.'

'Tim, would you stop saying that,' said Dad, growing angry.

'But it's true! What's the point in lying? I can't fucking pretend anymore! I'm *tired* of putting a brave face on it for other people's benefit! I'm tired of struggling to get somewhere and always getting knocked back! I haven't got any fight in me!' My voice grew parakeet-shrill. 'How many times have we had this conversation? And I'm still not better! I'm still a mess! I don't say I want to kill myself just to piss you off! I say it because I hate myself! I say it because I want to die!'

'Right!' Dad slammed his fist against the dashboard. 'If you want to die let's fucking die together! I'll drive the car into the fucking central reservation!'

My dad cannot swear convincingly. It always sounds awkward, like he's trying to rap. Thus my reaction was not fear, but acute embarrassment.

'Dad...don't,' I said, referring to the profanity rather than the death-threat.

But my father was lost in his own private *Thelma and Louise* moment. His sleep-deprived eyes were like ping-pong ball halves. His heel hit the accelerator.

Okay, okay, I hear you. You're wondering, how is it that someone so extraordinarily fortunate, with a loving family, his health, his youth and kind, supportive friends, can still be so gut-mashingly depressed that he'd slit his wrists if only he wasn't such a coward? How could I be so *ungrateful*?

And yes, on one level I accept that I was being a total dick – an ugly combo of Art Student ennui and 'I'm so Goth I shit bats' pseudo-teenage wangst. Maybe, in the midst of all my self-pitying sobs and moans of 'I'm such a fucking idiot', what I really needed to hear was, 'Yes, Tim, you are – now what are you going to do about it?'

Half the world would *love* to have my problems:

'Oh, I'm really depressed because no one will buy my dog-boy adventures, I'll have to spend the next six months eating Haribo and playing Super Nintendo!'

O foul harlot fate! What vile transgressions did I commit to warrant such cruel and wretched punishment?

But right there in the middle of it, it wasn't funny at all. I felt like all my beliefs about myself and the world were coming unglued. I felt as if I was dying.

Like a lot of people, I spent a significant portion of my adolescence unhappy. I didn't feel confident or attractive. I walked around school with my head down, scared of making eye contact with the wrong person and getting a barrage of insults flung at me. At home, I would regularly throw huge temper tantrums, scream blue murder at my parents and break stuff, because they were the only people in the world I could safely direct my anger towards.

One day I overheard my mum telling someone about a millionaire businessman she'd heard talking on the radio who attributed his success to sitting down as a teenager and reading literally hundreds of books on self-improvement from cover to cover. Two thoughts hit my brain simultaneously: first, I could read. Second, I'd like to be a millionaire. Thus began my voracious pop-psych habit. Without much of a religious faith to speak of, I gravitated towards self-help books as a way to power me through the cruddy slough of teenagerdom, hoping that I could suck up all their positivity and competence through some sort of intellectual osmosis, and transform myself into a bulletproof shoo-in.

The problem is that, for all their professed humanity, most pop-psych books focus on plucking totally non-representative statistical freaks from the masses and holding them up as appropriate models for your own behaviour. These people, CEOs, top athletes, world leaders, prominent scientists, military commanders and religious spokespersons, supposedly embody behavioural patterns and lifestyle choices that everybody could and should emulate.

Of course, it should be obvious to any reader that you can't build a world economy on these jobs alone, and most pop-psych books are careful never to claim that you can. There'll always be slack-jawed muppets out there who'll sleepwalk through their lives of prolish drudgery, but you – oh *you*, you cheeky beggar, you have a chance to be actually worthwhile. There's rarely any mention about the relationships that allow these grand roles to exist – we're assured that these vaunted winners' achievements were a direct, inevitable function of their inner qualities.

So a 'great pacifist' isn't discussed in terms of how wonderful and receptive the crowds were who flocked to hear her or him, who recognised value in the message and worked to show their support and act on it. A 'great author' is seldom talked of in terms of the hundreds of thousands of intelligent, adventurous readers who worked to actively interpret and appraise the novel, who were switched on enough to create value and meaning from printed word and then acted beyond that to propagate the work and encourage discourse around it.

The pop-psych books I read were all about the transcendent glory of being the astronaut clumping through moon dust – they had nothing to say about the millions upon millions of people back on Earth who made it possible simply by giving a shit.

The books I read stoked my desire to achieve, assuring me that success in my chosen field would airlift me out of all my woes. On top of that, they encouraged me to view my life as a story, where problems were superficial and temporary, existing only as plot twists. My gawkiness and lack of social status became like watching *Teenage Mutant Ninja Turtles* – when you see a whole bunch of purple-hooded Foot Soldiers surround the Turtles, you don't feel a sick, hollow feeling in your gut and think, 'Oh no. The Turtles are all going to die,' you think, 'Awesome! We're about to see them tear through like thirty robot ninjas!' because the Turtles are heroes and they always win.

So, although I didn't believe in God anymore, I grew from teenager to adult with this strong, internalised narrative about how my life was supposed to play out. And if you have a robust faith in a personal story, and your own destiny, when it becomes obvious that things aren't going to happen that way, the kickback's a killer.

You've screwed up. Your heart feels like the black space behind the Game Over screen. If you really believe that you were given the requisite tools and opportunities to achieve your ambitions, that you were *meant* to be a golden success, then this failure is utterly your fault. It's a double-whammy – you don't get to live your dreams, *and* you're fucking useless.

There's a shadow side to believing the universe is a benign and equitable place. It's comforting to think we'll reap what we sow, but if life is fair, it follows that everyone deserves the misfortune they receive too.

To an extent, we're all prone to this kind of distorted thinking. Studies have shown that drivers who are demonstrably at fault in a fatal collision (because they were drunk, for example, or they fell asleep at the wheel) recover faster and are less likely to suffer from Post Traumatic Stress Disorder than drivers who couldn't have done anything to avoid the crash. The 'at fault' drivers know they exhibited an obvious 'wrong' behaviour, which in future they can take measures to avoid. However, the 'not at fault' drivers didn't make a mistake, so there's no action they can take to eliminate the risk of a repeat. Getting back behind the wheel, they're acutely aware that a fatal accident could happen any time, anywhere, no matter how fastidious their road safety. Indeed, the only way to be absolutely sure of avoiding a collision is to stop driving altogether, which many people do. It's why those who've suffered sudden, traumatic incidents often become severely agoraphobic – the outside world feels like a sprawl of uncontrollable variables and potential disasters. Casting around for threats gets very tiring very quickly – far better to sit in a locked room, with your back to the wall, in a sequestered environment with minimal surprises.

In some ways, agoraphobics have hold of a truth most of us are wilfully blind to. We have considerably less control than we care to admit.

When you start writing your magnum opus you become like the crazy guy building an ark in his back garden. Sure, people will laugh – that's the whole point, goddammit – but one day, oh the Flood, oh the soggy vindication. Of course, actually caulking the hull or sanding splines is a pretty odious task, so you may not have got around to it yet, but that's okay – the ark is your statement of intent, and whenever your boss gives you a dressing down at work or you look at your bank statements and feel sick, you can always head out back and hammer a few nails into the stern. Whenever your microwave dinner and solitary evening in front of the television leaves you feeling hollow and bereft, you can always put on your captain's hat and watch yourself making salty seadog faces in the bedroom mirror. Whenever you're kept awake listening to your neighbours making noisy love to speed garage after midnight, you can imagine their bloated, mollusc-crusted corpses drifting with the current, bumping gently against the prow of your fine, broad boat.

But keeping the fantasy alive means never testing it against reality. That was my mistake. I finished my ark, stood back, and waited for the rain.

And waited.

And waited.

# 11

We were approaching the entrance ramp for the motorway. Beyond the concrete crash barrier, dawn was haemorrhaging through thick clouds, staining their undersides fuchsia, indigo, lemon and peach.

'Dad... don't be an arsehole.'

He did not respond.

'Dad...' I was nervous now. 'Dad?' I was almost completely sure that he did not intend to kill us, but my faith in his driving abilities was less robust.

I first discovered my father was fallible when I was a teenager, and he took me to a dry bobsleigh run in Germany. I agreed to go down it with him. The track was a kind of concrete half-pipe and the bobsleighs ran on casters. Your only control was a single lever at the front that operated the brakes.

At the top of the hill, we climbed on to the bobsleigh together, me sitting between his legs. Dad immediately released the brakes, and in a couple of seconds we were hurtling round tight corners.

I said: 'Dad, we're going too fast!'

Dad let out a gleeful, gobliny laugh.

I yelled: 'Dad! Slow down!'

He kept the brake lever completely floored. He was enjoying frightening me.

Up until that moment, I had been having a rotten holiday. I was edgy and withdrawn – back at school, I was being bullied, but I'd been too embarrassed to admit it to my parents.

Sitting on the bobsleigh, staring danger right in the gob, I realised life was too short to be scared all the time. This was a chance to let go. I said to myself: *Come on, stop being such a baby. He knows what he's doing. Chill out and enjoy the ride.*

For the first time in weeks, I relaxed.

On the next corner, our bobsleigh exited the track. My head slammed against the concrete and I slid approximately six metres, taking a layer of skin off my back. Dad did much the same. An attendant would later assure us that we were 'very lucky – all the real injuries happen when you get hit by the next person coming down'. To make up for it, Dad took me to a swimming pool the next day. I got whiplash injuries coming out of the slide and spent the rest of our holiday in a neck brace.

'Dad – slow down!'

Dad did not slow down. 'I thought you said you wanted to die?'

I was both scared and acutely embarrassed. I felt like I was trapped in some awful drama improv class. Dad's latest spiritual tome was *The Tibetan Book Of Living And Dying*. His friend Nigel had bought it him for Christmas. Now he was desperately trying to engineer some kind of ersatz breakthrough moment where, confronted with my own impending demise, I was supposed to cry out, 'Stop! Please! I want to live! I want to live!', and the realisation would slam through me like a blast of turbulence, mutating into waves of hot joy. 'I want to live!' I'd proclaim. 'I want to live!' Doubtless the sequence would finish with the camera switching to a long shot, watching our car disappear down the motorway, the sun an amber disc rising in the east.

What actually happened was I looked at him with an expression of anguished humiliation and said: 'Dad – *please*. Don't be a twat. You might hurt somebody.'

He inhaled through his nostrils. He slowed down. My bowels remained mercifully unevacuated.

We drove back along the motorway towards Portishead. Sunlight caught the windscreens of hundreds of cars lined up in lots by the Avonmouth docks.

After a few minutes of awkward silence, Dad said: 'I'm sorry about that thing I did back there. You know, speeding up and everything. I'm sorry if I frightened you.'

I didn't respond, because, loath though I was to admit it, his excruciating am-dram stab at shock psychology had actually had an effect. Don't get me wrong – as a life-affirming object-lesson, it had utterly failed. But as a satire on the suicidal impulse, it was sublime. The basis of satire is disingenuously accepting your opponent's position then pushing it to its logical conclusion, thus exposing the underlying absurdity. On top of that, there's nothing like seeing your dad have a go at an activity to make it seem suddenly uncool, and, as it turns out, offing oneself is no exception.

As we headed home, I realised that, from that point on, whenever the dark clouds gathered, they would bring with them an image of my bleary-eyed dad in his khaki shorts and sandals, driving slightly over the speed limit, saying, 'Let's fucking die together!', and I would withdraw from beneath the Reaper's scythe blade, mortified, cringing.

# 12

A couple of weeks after the car debacle, I got an email.

It was from a production assistant, telling me about a new television show. I wasn't sure where he'd got my email address from – perhaps from the university, or from the film crew I'd made the series with before, or from one of the creative writing websites I'd put work on. The programme was going to be called *Million Pound Giveaway*, he said, and, as the name suggested, they would be giving away actual pounds sterling. I just needed to think up some brilliant reason for wanting the cash, he said, something fascinating or poignant or funny – which I took to mean 'the pathetic end of self-consciously wacky'.

Maybe this was my chance, I thought. To get back in the game. To rekindle interest in my book. Perhaps some important publishing exec would see my performance and try to snap me up immediately. Perhaps *two* important publishing execs would see me, and start a bidding war against each other, like with Joe's novel. Surely it was worth a shot?

But I knew the production company wouldn't let me on TV just for wanting to be published. I had to find some way of converting all that internal drama into something unusual, something immediate, something *visual* – a metaphor for all that I had been through.

Before I had time to talk myself out of it, I emailed back my idea. The assistant got back to me the next day. He liked it. He invited me to come for a screen test in London. A couple of days after the screen test, I got the call. I was going to be on telly again.

I waited in the green room, reading through a lengthy contract that seemed to boil down to: 'I hereby grant the TV company the rights to do whatever they like with footage of me, including using bits out of context, making stuff up, etc.' There were bits with dates and sums of money on I didn't understand. I signed it anyway. Two other participants on plastic chairs sat across the room from me.

The silence was making me fidgety and anxious.

'So,' I said, 'what are you two asking for?'

'Well,' said the first, a smartly dressed man in his mid-thirties with a reedy, public school accent, 'I want money to travel to Kenya, to meet my biological father for the first time.'

I looked to the second, a tall, attractive girl in a white vest top, her mousy hair scraped back into a ponytail.

'Boob job,' she said. 'I want to be a glamour model.'

The man threaded his fingers, rested his chin on his knuckles. 'How about you? What are you asking for?'

'Ah,' I said. 'Ah.'

'Four years, three therapists, two failed relationships and one breakdown – ladies and gentlemen, my name is Tim Clare… and I am a writer.'

I stood before a panel of five slouching, ire-filled plutocrats, clasping and unclasping my hands, shifting my weight from foot to foot as I rattled through a spiel co-written by me and the production assistant. I licked my lips and went for the final push: 'In the book I've been working on for the last four years, the main character is part-dog. So... I'd like to hire a dog costume to promote the book myself. I'll wear it for an entire month while handing out fliers, touring and, I suppose, eating my tea and sleeping, as part of an expertly orchestrated PR stunt. I am asking for one thousand pounds. Thank you very much.'

There was a long pause. The panel members and I regarded each other with – what felt to me like – shared confusion. *How did we all get here? What are we doing?* their bemused expressions seemed to say.

First to speak was gruff, boggle-eyed Scot Duncan Bannatyne, a self-made multi-millionaire with a background in ice cream, nursing homes and health clubs.

'Ah no, Tim,' he said. 'This is a joke, isn't it? This is a joke.'

'Uh, no, it's not.'

'Yes it is, Tim.' He put down his notepad. 'This is a joke.'

'It's not,' I said, and I was shocked to realise that I believed what I was saying. 'I really care about it.'

'No you don't,' he said. 'You've come here today to have a joke with us. I'm not interested. I'm out.'

Next was Simon Jordan, burly chairman of Crystal Palace Football Club. He wore a sharp suit, a chunky watch and polished shoes which, combined with his shoulder-length blond hair, made him look like a surfer dude dressed up for a court appearance.

'Have you got over that breakdown?' he muttered, looking utterly bored. Sniggers came from the crew.

'Well, I...' I could feel my cheeks prickling with heat. The honest truth was, I didn't know.

Anne Summers founder Jacqueline Gold and MOBO awards founder Kanya King were both equally dismissive. The format of the show required me to try to convince a majority of the five-strong panel to support my request. Unfortunately, none of the production staff had told me this. So with four wealthy patrons having declined to finance my scheme, I found myself desperately courting disgraced peer and best-selling author Jeffrey Archer, unaware that it was a lost cause in every sense. I tried to rally my courage for a last hurrah.

'Ten years ago,' I fawned, leering through the glare of studio lights, 'almost to the day, I won twenty pounds of your money when I came joint-first in my age group in the Weston-super-Mare ghost story competition. It was the first money I ever got for writing. It was the first time I got confirmation from the outside world that I was good. It inspired me to keep going. It made me believe that one day, I could be a published author.'

Some of the production staff laughed and clapped. Mr Archer looked uncomfortable, then, realising a response was required, rose to his feet.

He held out a greasy palm. 'I want my twenty pounds back.'

Not only had I failed to convince the panel to give me money – my performance had been so poor that they were asking me to recompense them.

I was ushered into a second room where national television host and latter-day king of middlebrow reading habits Richard Madeley was waiting to interview me. Now, I'm rather fond of Richard Madeley. Not for his charming dearth of tact, nor for his tendency to advance his own pet theories on any topic from quantum physics to cerebral palsy when interviewing a guest who has devoted their life to studying said subject. No, I like Richard Madeley because when my mum tripped over a sheepdog in a pub in Cirencester, he helped her up. She had hurt herself quite badly (she needed stitches) and he happened to be on hand – apparently he was really nice. It's difficult to be cutting about someone after they've been nice to your mum.

Richard's role on the programme was presenter and confidante. I think the idea was that, after the contestant, i.e. me, had taken a drubbing from the smug, corpulent millionaires, he was on hand to soften the blow and represent the sympathetic audience at home.

I sat down and was greeted with: 'Tim, that was a dreadful idea.'

It was, of course – the entire show fell into that yawningly wide category – but I'd assumed that, as the presenter, he'd have adopted a more neutral stance.

'It was a bad idea,' he repeated. 'You were planning to dress up in a dog costume as a publicity stunt, right?'

I nodded.

'No one would have come – the press wouldn't be interested,' he said, then added, 'Trust me, mate,' which was a bit presumptuous.

'Uh… okay.' L'esprit d'escalier was strong that day, and later I realised that what I should have said was: *Yes, of course it was a shite idea. That's the point, isn't it? This is a programme about funding shite ideas. If they wanted to invest a million quid wisely, they'd give the lot to cancer research, or fighting child poverty. This is a TV show about crass, self-obsessed myopic swine wallowing in pools of filthy lucre and dragging out even the most meagre display of charity into a lengthy and demeaning public spectacle. And yes, I'm a party to this nonsense; yes, I'm partly to blame for turning up here and meekly suckling at opportunity's gristly teat, but that's only because I desperately want to get published and be a Big Author.*

And that's when it hit me.

Ah, the Book – the one true constant in my tumultuous life. The Book had survived all the downs and ups, contrived somehow to be never quite finished, to always need one last redraft, as if it knew that, without its steadfast companionship, my life would dissolve into a morass of contentment and financial security. For every problem it created – isolation, self-doubt, a sallow, semi-necrotic complexion – the Book promised a solution: legions of fans, critical affirmation, and a three-month sabbatical in the south of France on the royalties. The Book was God.

Rattling home from London on the train, suddenly I recognised the poison that ran right through my life, like an expletive through a stick of rock.

The Publishing Dream. The myth of the Big Author.

These false idols had driven me to ruin. They had tormented me, causing untold sleepless nights. They had soured all my relationships: towards successful writers, I felt a gnawing envy; towards unsuccessful writers, a practised scorn; towards non-writers, mere indifference. They had blinded me to everyday pleasures and filled my heart with greed. Worst of all, they had turned me into Jeffrey Archer's willing bitch.

Scraping and grovelling at the feet of that smarmy, arse-countenanced hack was the last straw. I had given everything to writing, and my reward was suffering and humiliation. There had to be more dignified ways of making a living. Scat porn, for example.

All my life, I had believed that I was unhappy because I had not fulfilled my dream. Now I was starting to wonder whether the dream itself was the source of my unhappiness.

The Buddha discoursed eloquently on the spiritual bene-fits of letting go. Yet as Confucius wisely remarked: 'He who sits on fence gets it up the backside.' The idea of merely leav-ing my ambitions to wither on the vine while I descended into a slough of boozy middle-aged cynicism seemed a less than attractive prospect. There was no room for half-measures – after all, I didn't want to wind up as some insufferably preten-tious *artiste manqué* who still calls himself a writer after decades of inactivity and insists he'd write a book 'if only I had the time'.

It was make or break time.

Whatever my faults, I was an intelligent, adult human being. My intellect, my ability to self-identify as having made mistakes, my awareness that I'd actively constructed an unwholesome and inefficacious worldview – all of those things ought to count for something, ought to give me at least a fighting chance at tearing the whole lot down and replacing it with something more healthy.

I needed to make a choice.

Did I really want to give my life over to writing? Was becoming a Big Author really my destiny, or just the fantasy that a younger, insecure me had created as an escape hatch? Wasn't the last step towards contentment accepting myself for who I was, imperfections and lack of status included? Or was that just cowardice? How did I know that ten, twenty years down the line, I wouldn't curse my meekness at backing down just when I was *so* close to getting what I'd always wanted? I'd come so far. I'd *suffered*.

I owed it to myself to at least investigate the matter. I knew I'd never truly give up unless I proved to myself once and for all that big ambitions, and, in particular, my dream of becoming a famous writer, were all mired in the same massive crock of shit. I needed to do what they'd made me pretend to do on Channel 4. Rather than fantasising and speculating, I needed to meet people who'd actually experienced the highs and the lows, proper role models, professionals, and genuine failures. Either I'd return from my odyssey buzzing with hope and inspiration, well in with all the biggest wigs in the industry, or I'd be so appalled by what I saw that I'd be able to stride away from the shower of superficial bastards with my head held high. I was a bright chap. If I acted now, I still had time to retrain in a safely pensionable career.

Joe's book launch party was just a few months away. There, I'd have to stand with gritted teeth while all my chipper, talented mates raised a glass and toasted his glorious victory. Not only would I be surrounded by success stories, but people I hadn't seen for ages would be approaching me, asking what I was up to: 'Hey Tim! How's it going? Still working on your novel? What was it called again? Isn't this party great? Have you read Joe's book? Brilliant, isn't it?'

Just imagining it made my stomach churn. I couldn't go on in this wretched limbo, struggling but never getting anywhere. I couldn't stand the humiliation of feeling like a hanger-on. I had to do something.

So I gave myself an ultimatum.

I would have one last shot at making it. I'd ask myself the big questions, go to any lengths necessary. If I still hadn't sealed the deal by the time Joe's launch party came around, I'd get out of the game for ever. And maybe that would be for the best. Perhaps I needed to search elsewhere for fulfilment.

It was a win-win plan. At least, I hoped it was.

I knew one thing for certain – I couldn't face another year of happy pills and comfort eating in my teenage bedroom while Dad shuffled round the house like Marley's Ghost. I had dire visions of myself a decade down the line, still living with my parents, the three of us bonded by an ugly web of mutual resentment and shame, I, an overweight recluse with a full deck of social disorders, first on the suspect list when neighbours' dogs began turning up headless and rogered.

# ACT TWO
# MAKE OR BREAK

# 1

'Are you, I wonder, one of those people who finds the physical part of writing a bore and a chore?' read the article. 'Already there are in use in the United States – and they have been demonstrated here – machines designed to ease the lot of the editor and sub-editor. Sections of the typewritten original are displayed on a species of television screen, before which is a keyboard. By pushing the appropriate keys, the operator can delete or alter words and passages and perform all the other sub-editorial operations.'

*Ha ha*, I chortled to myself, *people in the seventies were such backward twats.*

I was browsing the November 1971 edition of *The Writer*, twenty-five pence worth of A5 magazine printed in black-and-white with a British racing-green cover. I owned several other issues from the same year, given to me in my teens by my mum's mum, my nan.

The June poetry competition called for poems 'commemorating the year 2000 A.D.' Most of the resultant entries, lamented the competition editor in a later issue, were 'dreadfully gloomy'. A.H. Tudor foresaw 'a divine punishment', while Ethel M. Wildgust plumped for 'a frightening nullity'. Though Mrs Olive J. Derbyshire bucked the trend with her arresting couplet, 'Out of the ashes of internecine strife – / The Phoenix of sacred Utopian life!', the first prize went to one Hugh Tomlinson of Marple Bridge, Stockport, for his visionary work: 'Musings of a Drowsing Dionysian Into a Video-Recorder A.D. 2000'. 'Again,' wrote the competition editor, 'I grieve that the market for poetry is so restricted; many of these entries deserve wider readership.' Mr Tomlinson trousered a princely two pounds and a well-deserved place in literary history.

For all their quaint archaisms, the magazines offered compelling evidence that, in over thirty-five years, very little had changed. There were features on self-publishing and coping with rejection, readers writing in to condemn inconsiderate editors or crow over modest triumphs, plus the ubiquitous slew of adverts touting everything from 'essential market knowledge', to 'detective training with ex-Inspector, Metropolitan Police'. One advert in particular caught my eye:

**SEND NOW FOR**
**FREE KNOW-HOW GUIDE TO WRITING SUCCESS**
**How To Write and Sell Articles**
**How To Become a Successful Story Writer**
**YOUR SUCCESS IS CERTAIN... ONCE YOU KNOW-HOW**

It had been marked in blue ballpoint pen with a large asterisk. When I checked the pile of magazines Nan had given me years before, I discovered a slim introductory manual and several 'blueprints' from 'The British American School of Successful Writing'. The booklets were no more than twelve pages in length, and so small that I hadn't spotted them amongst copies of *The Writer.*

'An end to the fumbling of the self-taught beginner bewildered by continual rejections,' the manual teased. 'An end to time wasted in trial-and-error attempts which are doomed from the start. Instead, you learn how to supply the demands of editors, publishers and producers. You learn exactly what buyers of fiction and non-fiction want from a writer.'

A strange, nauseous compulsion made me read on:

*The 5-point test for a selling title... the 25-point Fiction Market Analyser... the 6 major emotions which will excite a reader's attention... how you must characterize to sell... Tolstoy's hint... what Proust did... Description guide to hair, eyes, complexion, lips, ears, teeth, etc... The sort of husband a heroine should get...*

It went on and on. It was tacky, horrible, writing as just another service industry... and yet, wasn't this exactly what I had been searching for? Wasn't I hunting for truths so hideous that they would permanently sour my authorial lust?

Though the marketing bumf left me feeling sceptical, if an author really could use these techniques to build a successful novel identikit-style, then the whole myth of a 'creative gift' suddenly looked very shaky indeed. According to the Know-How Technique, art was just a matter of slavish adherence to fixed principles – one could train a monkey to do it given time and sufficient bananas.

However, as far as I was aware, my grandmother had never enjoyed a career as a bestselling author. What had gone wrong? Had the blueprints failed her? She was coming down in a couple of days 'to look at some wallpaper'. I decided to use her visit to discover the truth.

We sat at a table in the back garden of my parents' house. It was a bright spring afternoon, the kind that somehow transformed the drab Gordano Valley where I'd grown up into something lush and abundant. One morning the previous year I'd woken to see a deer foal standing in the middle of the lawn, nuzzling shyly at the wet grass. Its incongruity had seemed to radiate outwards until everything, the garden's sparse woodchip borders, the ivy on the corrugated roof of our garage, the tattered cricket nets in the adjoining field and even the plump, broccoli-headed trees on the hillside looked new and alive and miraculous.

We were sitting in the shade of the garage; the instructions that came with Nan's medication said she had to keep out of direct sunlight. I popped open the capsule from a Kinder Egg with my teeth and started assembling the toy – a canary-yellow anthropomorphised hatchback – while we spoke.

'I think I was, in a way, wasted.' Nan's voice became quieter as she went on. 'If opportunities had come my way… If I'd been praised a bit more and had a bit of encouragement… I think I could've done quite well.' The emphasis fell on 'well' rather than 'quite'. I got the impression that Nan felt she could have done not just quite but *very* well.

'Back at school I got a lot of praise for my English. My grade teacher always told me that I was going to get a cap and gown. She was very sure that I would go on to university.' But Nan dropped out of school just before the fourth year. 'You either had to do Sciences or Art, and I wanted to do Art. I *so* wanted to do Art. Back then, pupils didn't get to choose. Your teachers placed you based on wherever they thought your natural aptitude lay. The person who really tipped the scales was my Domestic Science mistress. She wanted me in her class. Why, I don't know. I wasn't a particularly good cook, my sewing wasn't very clever either...perhaps it was just a case of numbers.' She tried to appeal the decision, going to see the vice-headmistress, but to no avail. Sure that she could never get the requisite five passes in Science that would get her into university, Nan quit. 'You didn't have choices in those days.'

It was hard for me to feel too much enmity towards Nan's Domestic Science teacher. Whether she had seen in my grandma a potential county-standard cross-stitcher or simply plucked a random girl out of the crowd to balance quotas, without her intervention it was very possible that I would not exist.

I brought up the copies of *The Writer*, and the Know-How manuals. 'Yes...' Nan looked almost wistful for a moment. 'Well, people had been saying to me I ought to take up writing. I used to transcribe the minutes for the PTA, you see, and I'd add a little flourish here and there and people had told me how brilliant they thought it was. So, you know... I pursued that for a while, and then...'

I clicked the hatchback's front wheels into place and glanced up. 'And then what?'

'Well...' Nan sighed with her whole body. 'I was going through... a *difficult* patch in my marriage at the time. I wasn't very happy.' I didn't press her for details because I'd heard from my mum just how 'unhappy' Nan had been. 'Unhappy' didn't really cover it. 'Yes. So... I gave up.'

'Do you regret giving up?' I said, and as the words came out of my mouth I realised what a stupid question it was.

She shrugged. 'I think things might have been very different. But, like I say... if I'd had somebody who believed in me...' She turned to look at me. 'When I see your talent, Tim, it makes me so hopeful. I think it's wonderful that you're going out there and you're trying and you're working at fulfilling your dream, and I know... I feel *sure* that sooner or later things are going to go very well for you indeed.'

She was doing the grandma thing. I pulled a face.

'That's very sweet, Nan, but with all due respect, you've been saying that for years. You also think I'm a brilliant guitarist, a superb cartoonist, and a concert-standard vocalist. At some point a bloke's got to take a long honest look at himself and give up all his unrealistic fantasies. I've tried to be a big writer, and I haven't got anywhere. I'm not suggesting that makes me a bad person – I just think it might be best for me if I quit while I've still got time to retrain as something else and live a life.'

Nan rolled her eyes, then aimed a reprimanding fore finger at my head. 'Now, you listen, I've been having a word with the Man Upstairs–' She meant God (she lived in a bungalow) '–and whatever you think, He's up there and He's watching over you – you just have to be patient. I remember that short story you did, the one about the old man that you entered for that competition.' She was talking about the story that won the Weston-super-Mare ghost story competition back when I was fourteen, the one that earned me twenty quid of Jeffrey Archer's ill-gotten pelf. 'When I first read that, I thought, "My goodness, this is wonderful." The language was so fantastic, so vivid. I could really *see* all the characters and hear how they talked.'

I shook my head. 'That's very sweet, Nan.'

'I've got so much faith in you.'

'Brilliant. I'll use that as a jacket-quote: "I've got so much faith in him", Tim's nan.'

She tutted. 'Don't be so cheeky! Anyway, if you want to talk to someone in the family who's had proper literary aspirations, you ought to talk to Pa. He's done a lot more than I did.'

Pa was my father's father. In my childhood, I had looked up to him as a kind of impossibly sagacious gentleman scholar. As far as I was aware, he didn't do anything except compose music for the piano and muse on worldly affairs. His vocabulary was rangy and he could discourse at length on any given topic with little or no prompting. I gave him short stories to read and he produced elaborate mini-critiques in the ponderous high-flown language of a broadsheet theatre review. In one story I gave him, the 'twist ending' revealed that the protagonist's fantastic adventure had, in fact, all been a dream. Pa lauded the tale's 'multitudinous ancillary cast' and noted that 'the presence of the single feather on the hero's pillow helps lend the narrative a credence it might otherwise have lacked'. I didn't always understand what his comments meant but I accepted them with what I felt was an appropriate reverence.

They often say creativity skips a generation. Certainly, neither my mum nor my dad were especially arty – Dad played the guitar and my parents both enjoyed music, but they were consumers rather than producers.

Looking back at my parents' parents, I remembered how both Nan, on my mother's side, and Pa, on my father's side, had taken a particular interest in my work, reading poems and short stories, offering feedback and insight.

'Perhaps you're right,' I said to Nan. I went to visit Pa the very next day.

Pa slid Omi's rocking chair to one side and crouched in front of the bookshelf, searching amongst the antique tomes and doughty encyclopaedias for three volumes he had written himself. We were in the lounge of my grandparents' detached house in Weston-super-Mare, just minutes' walk from spectacular panoramic views of the Somerset Levels. After a short while, he crossed the room, books in hand, and held them out for me to take. I gazed down at his life's work. All three were bound in leather – one red, one green, and one blue – his name embossed in gold capitals on each cover: L.H. CLARE.

They were my grandmother and grandfather but I knew them as Omi and Pa. They had met just after the Second World War. The war had ended just as Pa became old enough to serve in the army. He found himself stationed in Germany and, as I understood the story, had broken the ice with Omi by asking to borrow a ping-pong ball. Not long afterwards, he had brought her back to England and married her. More than once, Mum had said that marrying Omi was Pa's one big romantic gesture, and it had frightened him so much he had spent the rest of his life playing it safe. She was only half-joking.

It was a glorious spring afternoon, the sky a cloudless cyan, and the sun was streaming through the bay windows behind his armchair. As we talked, golden rectangles of light slowly moved from the fireplace, across the cream hearth rug to the tips of my toes.

Pa was wearing the clothes that – in my mind, at least – he always wore: beige trousers and a cocoa-brown jumper over shirt and vest. Every so often, he would adjust his spectacles or run a fingertip across the bristles of his moustache. Above the fireplace, a rosewood mantel clock tick-tick-ticked between four dark green wine glasses, marking his long pauses.

Recently, there had been concern that Pa's once-brilliant mind was beginning to fade. Omi – an ex-member of the Hitler Youth who once belted an amorous American soldier with one of her crutches – was complaining that, increasingly, Pa did not answer when she demanded he fetch something. Over the course of our conversation, it became clear that Pa remained an extremely erudite and articulate man. My grandmother was the type of woman euphemistically referred to as 'formidable'.

'I began to write because people kept telling me I ought to. Lots of people, in fact. They said: "Anyone who's managed to survive what you've been through ought to write a book about it!"'

'I suppose it would have been pretty tricky to write one if you'd died,' I quipped, then felt a belated nip of guilt.

Pa smiled. 'Yes.'

In 1969 my grandfather was diagnosed with throat cancer. 'It came at a very inconvenient time,' he explained, speaking slowly and deliberately in the voice he spent months constructing from scratch – a hodgepodge of croaks and belches that allowed him to fully aspirate each of his words. He took a rasping breath through a hole in his trachea, part-hidden behind a turkey wattle flap of skin. 'I'd just made the move from teaching in the school system to university, and I was trying to write a thesis. In those days, there weren't the same treatments for cancer. Mostly, if you got cancer, you were dead.'

Pa survived, obviously, but only after two years of invasive surgery, and at the expense of his voice. 'I visited a speech therapist who helped me build the muscles in my throat by giving me a straw and getting me to pick pieces of paper up off the table by sucking.' He pursed his lips to illustrate. 'But I was a child again. I had no words. The speech therapist said she had to go away for a couple of weeks, and gave me some books that she said I ought to read. There was one by an American doctor who had had the same operation as I had – a tracheotomy. It had some exercises for strengthening the throat. I practised them and, when my speech therapist came back, I could talk again.'

I asked Pa what regaining one's voice entailed.

'There are two main methods. One involves swallowing air and speaking from the stomach, but I didn't like that because it was a bit unpleasant for other people – you're just burping, really. The other one, the one I use, involves sort of trapping a bubble in your throat, and then you speak against the bubble. It takes a lot of patience, but over the years, I got better at it.' He sighed. 'The tricky thing is, it's very quiet. If you try to push harder to make your voice louder, the bubble bursts.'

Not being able to talk at much more than a whisper put paid to Pa's aspirations of lecturing. With a lot of extra time on his hands, he turned to writing.

I looked at the three books on the couch next to me. He'd had them bound at the university. The blue one was his first, his thesis. The second, the green one, was a memoir of his experiences with cancer: *No Island All My Own*. The third, the red one, was his attempt to break into the popular philosophy genre – a collection of short essays entitled *Thought Starters*.

'That was the one I really hoped would get somewhere,' he said as I ran my thumb across the cover's embossed lettering. 'I got a few complimentary letters back from some of the publishers I sent it out to, but... nobody really wanted it, I suppose. I was disappointed.' Pa's way of speaking meant that his sentences lacked tone and inflection. My understanding was that he was never a hugely demonstrative man to begin with, but stripped of familiar tonal cues almost everything he said came out sounding matter-of-fact.

'It was more important to you than your memoirs?'

'Yes. I mean, I thought writing about my illness might help some other people who had suffered the same thing, and I included some of the exercises I'd used, but *Thought Starters*... it's not terribly sophisticated as philosophy goes but I suppose I thought the little essays might prove interesting to people. I thought they might be useful in an educational context.'

I couldn't help making the obvious connection between Pa losing his physical voice and his taking up the pen. I put it to him that he had turned to dreams of becoming an author as a form of compensation, an alternative means to get his voice heard.

'I just think I had rather more time on my hands,' he said.

But didn't he feel a sense of failure? Hadn't he put his self-esteem on the line when he sent out those manuscripts?

'Not really. There was no financial imperative. I didn't have any of those pressures. I just wrote because I felt I ought to. Once it was finished, and on paper, I had done all I had to. That was enough for me.'

I felt baffled and frustrated by Pa's sanguine attitude. I had hoped, nay *expected*, that he would break under interrogation and confess that his life had been a hollow, tragic sham, and that, secretly, he had always dreamed of finding ultimate validation in being published. For the purposes of my quest, I had hoped that Pa would reveal himself to be someone I could simultaneously blame for my ambitions while holding up as evidence of said ambitions' ugly consequences. On the contrary, he seemed pretty chilled out. As far as I could tell, not getting published had made no more impact on his life than a somewhat disappointing holiday.

Our conversation was interrupted by Omi's yells for assistance from two rooms away. With a resigned shake of his head, he rose from his armchair. While he was out of the room, I flipped *Thought Starters* open at a random page. The first fresh paragraph began:

Although ideals may temporarily inspire, they can also mislead and ultimately depress. They are shadows, unreal, unattainable, which can dissipate energies better employed on attainable goals. Take, for instance, the matter of romantic love. A young man, in his natural desire to find a partner, may carry in his mind a vision of the perfect woman – beautiful, intelligent, athletic, pure, faithful – or whatever his particular ideal virtues may be. In reality such a woman does not exist and sooner or later the young man is likely to be disappointed. More serious consequences could follow, such as the onset of acute depression, disillusionment, and the contracting of an unhappy marriage.

As I turned the page, I heard Omi shout, '*Lawson!* What on earth do you think you're doing?', followed by an indistinct crash.

The young man would relate more successfully to the opposite sex if he started out by realising not just that it was biologically different but that it was equally fallible. Little benefit can result from self-deception. The individual whose visions are greater than the ability to realise them can present a very pathetic spectacle, as can a nation which inherits the pretensions but not the power of a previous age.

On reading these last two sentences, I experienced a horrible vertiginous twinge. Was this the secret to Pa's nonchalant attitude? Had he recognised his modest literary competence early on and tailored his vision accordingly? Was I some crumbling Soviet satellite state, issuing angry edicts to the superpowers and parading two dozen troops through the square in full military regalia while my single, obsolete tank squadron rusted in a warehouse?

Pondering this, I closed the book, but as I did so, an A5 piece of paper fell from between the pages. I bent down to pick it up. Written in blue ballpoint pen, it was a series of numbered bullet points – a plan. Underlined at the top of the page were the words: *No Island All My Own*. This was the outline for my grandfather's memoirs.

Each numbered bullet point had a subtitle next to it, often with possible topics spidering out from it:

> 1 *The 1960s – change – national*
> > *- ethnic*
> > *- religious*
> > *- ethical*
> > *- educational (comp. school)*
> 2 *The Onset – Age 40*
> 3 *Moment of Truth – Cancer*
> > *Cobalt – 99.9% chance*
> 4 *Spiritual Forces*
> 5 *Hospital – Operation – spiritual experience*
> 6 ...

The list went on, but I heard Pa coming back along the hall and quickly replaced the piece of paper inside the book. I wasn't sure why I didn't want him to catch me reading it. I suppose that, compared to the finished manuscripts in their professionally bound grandeur, a yellow, somewhat creased bit of paper seemed a bit personal.

Pa had told me the story of his 'spiritual experience' several times before, but when he sat back down I asked him to repeat it.

'I'd been for five operations altogether,' he said. 'This was my sixth. The other five I'd been fine for but the doctors had decided that the treatments I'd been getting hadn't worked, so I had to have the full operation.' He gestured towards the hole just above his breastbone. 'I was very, very nervous. I thought I was going to die.

'As they were wheeling me down to the operating theatre, I heard a voice. It said: "Whither thou goest, I will go." It was so clear I looked around to see who had said it. It was a human voice. I think it was the most human voice I've ever heard in my life. Suddenly I felt this incredible calm descend over me. I knew I would be all right. I felt at peace – buoyant, even.

'The mood lasted for days afterwards. An Anglican priest came round the ward offering patients communion and I accepted. I hadn't been particularly spiritual up until that point. I realise there could be all sorts of explanations for what I heard, but, for me, it marked a change in my whole way of thinking.'

Pa had no need for the god of literary posterity – he had a genuine faith. A tentative one, perhaps – he believed in biblical ethics while accepting the possibility that Christ might have been a bastard, that the resurrection might not have happened and that God might not even exist – but a faith nonetheless. Did my lust for fame and success represent my own pathetic striving after a kind of eternal life? And if so, did I really have it in me to seek permanent excommunication?

During the journey home, I was uncharacteristically quiet. Before I had put back the slip of paper, one subtitle in particular had caught my eye:

*Self-importance*, it read. *Learning to take a backseat; being humbled.*

# 2

The clock was ticking. I'd set a deadline, committed myself to drastic action. The problem was, I had no idea what that drastic action should be. Under the gun, with my entire future at stake, I fell back on the strategy that had got me through my first two and a half decades. I procrastinated.

My environment didn't help. The longer I spent at home with my parents, the more I could feel myself regressing, melting down into a huge blundering morass of sloth and neediness. Trudging round the house feeling blue about my social life, career prospects and physical appearance, it was all too easy to leave boxer shorts on my bedroom carpet for Mum to pick up, to mope glum-jowled about the kitchen until Dad offered to make me a sandwich. These were exceptional circumstances, I told myself, dispatching thugs with headshots on my Xbox 360 while out in the garden Mum pegged my washing to the line.

To give them and me a break, every week or so I'd stuff some clothes into a rucksack and head up to London to crash on friends' floors, kidding myself I was a cool, free-living bohemian rather than a depressed, slightly smelly moocher. With my scruffy hair and sad, trudging gait, I wandered from house to house like Columbo without a case.

One evening, I met up with Joe and Luke in a bar in Angel. When I arrived, they had both been drinking for some time. Luke insisted on buying a round, and came back to our table with three bottled beers and three double gin and tonics.

'There you go, lads,' he said, and took a swig of beer. He'd spent the day getting wined and dined with his editor while they discussed his new book. 'Everything's going great. I feel really positive.'

'That's awesome,' said Joe. His book had just been sold to several more countries, including America and Israel. 'Sounds like it's all coming together.' He held out his beer bottle for us to clink. 'Cheers.'

'Cheers!' said Luke, enthusiastically knocking his bottle against Joe's.

'Cheers,' I muttered, tilting the mouth of my bottle in their general direction. 'I'm delighted for you both.'

'How's it going with you, Tim, anyway?' said Joe, patting me on the back.

'Oh. You know. Normal.' Their cheery avuncular concern was getting right up my jacksie. They both seemed so bloody content. I felt like I was glimpsing my rotten future. Joe's launch party would be like this, times ten. Maybe times eleven.

I hadn't told either of them about my plan, yet. I'd decided I was better off keeping it secret, in case, like everything else in my shabby life, it all blew up in my face.

'No joy with the book yet?'

'No.' My shoulders slumped. 'I guess all my Fantasy stuff was too odd for the publishers.'

'Why don't you write something normal?' said Luke.

'Yeah,' said Joe, 'why don't you write something more commercial? You know, just to make some money?'

'Exactly,' said Luke, nodding. 'Then maybe, once you've got a couple of books under your belt, they'd be more likely to look at *Yoshi Speaks Back*.'

'My book's called *Joshu Replied*.'

'Even better.'

Luke and Joe looked at me with expectant grins, chuffed at having solved all my problems.

'Right,' I said. 'I'll just dash off a couple of bestsellers then. Piece of piss.'

'That's not what I said,' said Joe. 'Just... you're a good enough writer. Why don't you try doing something less obscure?'

'Is that what you think I've been doing?' I took an angry tug on my beer. 'Writing deliberately wanky nonsense so I can't get published?'

'No, I ju—'

'What's the point in writing what *other* people want to read?' By now, I was practically yelling. 'Does the world really need another novel about dysfunctional middle-class relationships? I want to *care* about what I write – otherwise, what's the difference between me being a writer and selling double-glazing?'

Luke shrugged. 'You might make some money selling double-glazing.'

'Piss off.'

Something in our conversation went on rankling long after my hangover had faded. Luke and Joe had been on to something

– was it really so surprising that my tale of canine fascists and a giant spider in a fuchsia housedress hadn't instantly screamed mass-market appeal to the editors who'd read it? Was I too peculiar to follow in my friends' footsteps? As I pondered these questions, a name kept springing to mind – the name of the one person who might be able to give me some answers.

People say you should never examine your idols too closely – it can only result in disillusionment. But disillusionment was exactly what I was hankering after. My novel had been turned down by publisher after publisher, but their kind, slightly patronising comments had invariably suggested that I was a good writer who ought to have another crack – who ought, indeed, to keep on cracking until such time as I got my just deserts. Again and again, friends and relatives had said: 'You have a gift. Don't give up and you'll be rewarded.' This simply would not do. My fanatical belief in the publishing industry as a pure meritocracy had already led me to dark places.

I suspected the myth of the Big Author didn't accord with reality, but I needed proof, so I asked myself: who's my role model in all of this? If I could find a disparity there, surely the whole house of cards would come toppling down. If, on the other hand, I found a success story, then that was the template I needed to follow to finally make good.

During my third year at university, I did a week's work experience at a new books magazine called *Ink*. I'd never done any real journalism before. Around the office, stacks of novels formed a paperback metropolis. When the editor let me loose doing a couple of reviews, I was rabid with naïve glee – finally, I was going to see my words in print!

I still remember the day the issue I'd worked on was due out. As I headed out to pick up a copy from the newsagent, my whole body rattled with excitement. This was it! I envisioned these first few articles snowballing into a rich, impressive portfolio that would see me taking centre stage in the world of arts journalism, my incisive commentary and caustic reviews demonstrating that my literary success was no fluke, but the inevitable fruit of a shrewd and unflinching critical eye.

On the way to WH Smiths, I stopped at Norwich library to check my email. There was a message from my publishing tutor: 'Tim – have you seen this? Such a shame.' At the bottom of the email was a link. I clicked on it, and discovered that *Ink* had folded two days previously.

Bugger. Just one more innocuous scratch in the death by a thousand cuts.

Though my fantasies of a lucrative side-career as a critical behemoth perished during delivery, I gained something far more valuable during that wageless week – a new favourite author.

On my second day in the *Ink* office, I slit open a padded A4 envelope and a bunch of glossy postcards fell out. When I picked them off the floor I realised that some of them weren't postcards at all – more like top trumps. There were pictures of weird, fluorescent daemons, treble-chinned misanthropes and staring dolts, all with stats underneath – odd, unquantifiable stuff, like 'bastard rating'. I was perplexed.

I stuck my hand into the envelope and discovered it was stuffed with books (something I ought to have anticipated, given the fact I was sitting in the office of the largest book review magazine in Great Britain). I fished one out. It was called *Dummyland*, by a guy I'd never heard of, Steve Aylett. Here's what I read:

> In the doll forge a dozen steaming mimiques stood rigid in a row. Behind them the express fiend machine was coughing sparks to the floor, its piston knuckles shuffling like a coinwalk trick. Lacquered eyes witnessed the head of rituals, the Grand Dollimo, entering via the gifts of a scaffold. He consulted a mechanical grimoire, a hinged mandala on its cover, and looked impassively down on the slurry-floored assembly area. He muttered, perusing the checklist. 'Brass springs under cardboard skin, eyes the same colour as the facial flesh, unguessable inner life. Good.' He called out. 'Accident faucets on.'

It took me weeks to unpack this first paragraph and work out what was actually going on. By the time I'd got it sussed, I was hooked.

Since then I'd devoured everything of his I could get my hands on – no easy task, given that high-street bookshops seemed perpetually bereft of his stuff and nobody seemed to have heard of him. This apparent disconnect made me nervous. Affecting an easy indifference towards literature, or just doffing your chapeau to the classics, is a safe, safe game. By comparison, liking something fringe, or unpopular, or just liking something a *lot*, can be a lonely business. Often, it invites the accusation that you're being deliberately perverse.

I never found anyone who enthralled me in quite the same

way, whose prose could slug me hard in the guts and leave me wheezily asking for more. Perhaps it was his unorthodox plot-lines: in *Atom*, meatheaded hoodlums engage in an extended bun-fight after someone filches Franz Kafka's preserved grey matter from the City Brain Facility; in *Resenter*, a chap decides to store his pent-up rage externally – it ends up burgeoning into a writhing conglomeration of flesh and sticky dendrites, and as it tears the city asunder he feels impassive as a doped toad; *Shamanspace* deals with the ethics and logistics of killing God; in *Ears, Goodbye*, the narrator is threatened with having every bone in his body broken, but points out that, due to 'the hundreds of tiny cartilaginous ones in my ears' any such attempt would prove impossible, since by the time all the bones in one ear had been broken, those in the other would have healed; as for *The Inflatable Volunteer*, I still don't under-stand what it's supposed to be about, but it blew my head clean off my shoulders.

His work has some common recurring themes – an antipa-thy towards mimes features strongly. In one interview, he justi-fied the prejudice thus: 'Well, they're obviously calling attention to themselves, and simultaneously being spooky and obscure, while clearly expecting some reaction from onlookers. The combination of all these things leads me to conclude that they want to be destroyed.' It's the kind of observation that might have been made about Steve Aylett himself – or me, for that matter. Chefs are also frequent targets of derision, as are lawyers, the police, the government and the general public.

Reviewers – including such luminaries as Alan Moore and Michael Moorcock – regularly went apeshit over his work, but for all the praise Aylett had made little commercial impact, and no one I knew seemed to have heard of him. As far as I could tell from his sporadic online interviews, his finances were in a parlous state at best. On receiving the somewhat tongue-in-cheek Jack Trevor Story Memorial Award, he said: 'Other than humour and imagination, I think the Prize is index-linked to authors who, no matter how many books they have published or in print, manage to have no money or exist in massive debt. I just put money on a table and it becomes gauzy and disappears.' Less amusingly, he'd often talked of unhappiness, of lacking certain key coping skills, and of how he felt human existence was a kind of hell.

Was this really the life I wanted to emulate?

If it was soul-crushing pessimism I wanted, Steve Aylett seemed to be the go-to man. After all, if a guy as talented and original as him couldn't find fame and fulfilment as an author, what chance did I have?

So I wrote to him, asking about his writing, his life, and how he managed to combine the two.

For a long time, I didn't hear anything. Then, about a month and a half after my initial email, Steve sent his reply – a massive, discursive treatise on writing, publishing, and life in general, included both in the body of the email and as three separate attachments in different text formats. He also included an appendix with selected quotations from his own work and suggestions for further reading.

I think it's fair to say that Steve Aylett is fastidious about language. On his website, a note beneath the 'Interviews' section reads: *IN THE CASE OF MISQUOTES ETC,*

*VERSIONS REPRINTED ON THIS SITE RESTORE WHAT WAS ACTUALLY SAID.* A week after the first email, he sent me a message, requesting I insert a single, four-word sentence into one of the paragraphs.

What follows is not the full, unexpurgated text. It's not 'what was actually said'. I hope my favourite living author can forgive me.

Steve was my age, twenty-six, when his first novel, *The Crime Studio*, was accepted by a small press and published. 'I'd been writing stories while properly thinking about being a writer since I was ten or earlier. I didn't have a clear idea of how a writer lived, but I knew there were people who actually got paid for doing this thing I was doing anyway, and wouldn't it be good if that was a job?'

By the time of our correspondence, he had released fourteen or fifteen books, none of which had made much of a commercial impact, despite being rapturously received in cult circles. 'People go on about *Slaughtermatic* a lot for some reason, and *LINT*.'

*LINT* is a literary biography of a bizarre, freewheeling pulp writer called Jeff Lint, a writer whose career seemed to echo Steve's own in many important ways, a writer who simply wrote what pleased him then realised too late that he also wanted some commercial success, a writer who happens not to exist.

*Slaughtermatic*, on the other hand, is a zingy hyper-violent SF crime novel, and probably as first-glance coherent as Aylett gets – crime artist Dante Cubit accidentally duplicates himself in a bungled time-travel heist and the two get up to all sorts of giddy mischief culminating in a frenetic gun battle and a tank covered in melted glass. Central to the plot is an enigmatic – and ostensibly dead – cult author called Eddie Gamete. Cubit filches one of Gamete's multifaceted satirical works, *The Impossible Plot Of Biff Barnabel*, and eventually meets the author, safely ensconced in secret high-tech luxury, right in the middle of the city. Gamete claims he sticks around 'because there is no more infernal amusement than the spectating of civilisation's bind'. I'd always thought of Eddie as Steve's personalised flavour of the Big Author myth – a happy trickster, aloof from the masses, appreciated by the discerning few, relatively powerless but free to say or do whatsoever he chooses.

'I'm very into originality, which is not a valued commodity at large. Many people will say they crave originality, but the moment they're faced with it in reality, it becomes clear they really, really don't. I think some make the claim because they never expect to be called on it. Others don't realise how they really feel about it until that moment. When people decree that there's nothing new under the sun and you then present them with something new, they retreat to a default position which tells a lot about the person. For many it's a fuzzy blankness. The funniest is a withering superiority.

'It makes sense, though, because creativity is the bringing into being of something that wasn't there before – originality, in other words. Not the duplication of something that's been seen before. Genuine creativity is originality. But, because it hasn't existed before, people don't have a slot of the right shape to fit it into, in their minds. There are no receptors.' This, incidentally, was the four-word sentence Steve had wanted me to add. 'So it feels uncomfortable in an obscure way, it's like anti-matter or something. Like a new colour you can't see directly until you get used to it.

'I've wondered why people aren't just honest about wanting the same old Martin Amis, Jeffrey Archer, Tom Clancy, Don DeLillo, Zadie Smith and other literary flat-earthers – I mean, it's not a crime. But I've realised they're sort of lying to themselves about it too, so they claim they want originality. I'd prefer honesty about this, it would avoid confusion and wasted time. It's taken years for me to accept that most people really do prefer more of the same – because it just seems so insulting to them – but I've finally had to believe it.'

I knew Steve felt very strongly on this subject. In one interview I'd read, he'd castigated serial killers – not for murder, but on the grounds that they were 'boring', adding: 'Why do the same thing repeatedly?' At the same time, his lumping together of Zadie Smith and Jeffrey Archer suggested that he hadn't read very much of either.

'For a lot of writers the industry works a bit like aversion therapy,' he went on, 'so that creativity becomes associated with pain and lack. So the writer's no longer fiending after it – why would he? You can maybe get back into it by disengaging completely from the publishing world for a long time, but I don't know.

'I'm now in a cycle of going "So long, you suckers!", quitting the day job, being only a writer for a while, then slouching back again… It can get wearing, working but still having no money for basics, seeing piss-poor empty books being hailed, people defaulting to the bland every time. Ebay and Amazon's "Buy Used" button have eliminated author royalties.'

Sometimes, Steve wished he had chosen a different career entirely: 'Some sort of ichthyologist would be interesting. Marine biologist. Swimming, dolphins, women, blowfish – everything a man could want.'

But for all that, it was clear that there were still parts of the creative process that he absolutely loved. Steve has synaesthesia – a neurological condition in which two or more senses are paired. 'Books fall on me whole, as coloured shapes that contain all the information sort of fractally. I can best describe the visual as a giant chiming glob of varicoloured vibrational bubble gum, with other structures pushed through it, slowly rotating in glittering space. And the idea is to make a book that contains the feeling and ideas that this thing is. And you know what belongs in the book and what doesn't. At the end of it you have a book that will create that buzz for the reader. It's not exactly transcription, it has more dimensions than that, and it's a beautiful thing. Clicking these space-sculpture shapes together, making ideas that haven't existed before – you know those ones because they really fizz, they're mischievous. Maybe they know they're not going to be welcome and they love that in a trickster sort of way. *LINT* has some beautiful shapes in it. Some of the ideas have whole little nervous systems pulsing away in there. Same with a lot of *And Your Point Is?* And it's a beautiful thing when that stuff comes together from directions that can't be pointed to, it's like the best moments in life when things let go and something surprises you, and there seem to be possibilities and a sort of vibrating richness.

'The problem is – though I'm not blocked and I still have these whole books cropping up, I'm not sitting down and making them at the moment, not much. So I have about twelve books stacked up like planes ordered into a holding pattern, and I'm not letting them land. I'm not sure why I should. I know exactly what they are, and they make up most of the second and more interesting half of my career, and I'm just not sure at this point why I should. When I whine about this crap to friends they say "Oh you'll keep on doing it because you're a writer, you can't help it, it's a compulsion," or whatever, but I wonder. I wonder. Are you beaten if you walk away, or if you keep showing up for a beating? Who has power in which of those situations?'

It was the first time I had heard my predicament summed up in such bleak terms. Friends and family had always told me, 'You can't give up. You must go on,' without really stopping to consider what such a path entailed.

'Actually those friends of mine are probably right about me. I will keep on writing, so I'm really fucked.'

His words left me dizzy with dread. Here was a guy who knew exactly how crappy a life pursuing the Publishing Dream could be, a guy who felt it was all an unrewarding, irredeemable hoax, a guy beaten down and impoverished by his efforts – and yet *it still wasn't enough to stop him trying.* There was nothing noble in his struggle – it was like the final battle in *Way of the Dragon*, <SPOILER ALERT> where Chuck Norris refuses to give up, even though he's all bloody and pathetic and his leg's broken, and he keeps trying to fight until eventually Bruce Lee grabs him round the throat and snaps his neck.<END OF SPOILER>

At the end of my letter, I'd told Steve about my predicament and asked his advice on my make or break dilemma. Given everything he'd been through, I assumed he'd wholeheartedly endorse my giving up writing for ever. I was right to be turning my back on this filthy, punishing business, wasn't I?

'It depends whether you got into it for approval. I've had to come to terms with the fact that to a great extent I didn't. So I can only justifiably be pissed off in regard to work not being reflected by pay. And in regard to changing the world, the ineffectiveness of satire was one thing I knew from the start – it's obvious even to a child – but I still do it because I have these obscure unappliable notions of justice and so on which I can't seem to get rid of.

'The fantasy that's lost is that the two things – writing good books and being financially rewarded for writing – can coexist. And that useless "justice" thing that's stuck in the corner of my mind sort of chafes at that.'

After digesting Steve's response, I felt frustration mixed with a lingering sadness. Though he'd given me very real proof that talent can go unrewarded, that writing can be a desperate grind, and that all my cooing relatives' assurances that 'One day you'll be a big success, Tim, I know it' were probably utter bollocks, he hadn't actually shown me how to kick the habit. He'd experienced all these depressing things first-hand, claimed to have at least suspected them for most of his life, and yet he couldn't bring himself to walk away from the fight.

And I knew why. I knew because I'd felt it too. It was the tug of brain chemistry distorted by a lifetime of intermittent reinforcement, the same impulse that sends a gambler back to the bookies day after day, delirious with debt. If you win, it's easy enough to back off – it's the losses that lock you in. The gambling addict on a losing streak thinks: *If I walk away now, this has all been a waste. One more flutter. One last hurrah. This time I can make it right. This time I can win it all back. This time, this time, this time… Just one big win and I can redeem myself.* And the gambler fantasises about the freedom, and the sweet ecstasy of release, and maybe treating pals to nice things and repairing past transgressions and receiving adulation in return. And it all seems so poetic. *Of course I feel like walking away. That's how the story goes. Temptation in the desert – then godhood.*

Clearly, seeing how bad things could get in the trenches wasn't going to suffice. If I wanted to prove Steve wrong, or else rid myself of those 'obscure unappliable notions of justice' that he had talked about, I needed to find out once and for all whether the publishing industry gave two hoots about my beautiful, gleaming destiny. It wasn't enough to just canvass individual authors for their opinions – the plural of anecdote isn't data. Chastened as I was by Steve's grim perspective, I couldn't help but think of Joe's tales of being courted by rival publishers, listening to presentations by different marketing departments as actual experienced professionals explained how brilliant they thought his book was and how they'd make it a bestseller. He'd written exactly what he'd wanted to write and the industry had lapped it up.

Which story was the truth? I knew which one I *wanted* to believe. Even with Steve's baleful warnings ringing in my ears, the siren song of big bucks and stardom blared louder. A single dissenting voice was easy to dismiss.

I needed a wider perspective. I had to climb into the machine, smell its grimy cogs and either seize the controls or break the last vestiges of my delusion amongst its clanking guts.

If Steve was right, no team of benevolent pixies lay poised in a London office, waiting to weave a sparkling future around me and my supposed masterpieces; no matter how good I might be, the book world did not owe me a career.

If he was right, my choice was stark: either I found a way to smother my dreams, or I would face a future like my hero's – struggle, weariness, despair, and a smoked-glass opacity in my eyes as again and again I headed back for another beating.

# 3

One morning I opened my inbox to discover an email with the heading: *FW: From Amanda Ross, the most powerful woman in publishing!*

Crikey, I thought, and adjusted my spectacles. A quick glance at the 'To:' list revealed I was one of approximately fifty recipients. The forwarded email had originated somewhere deep within the manky guts of the publishing industry. It was prefaced with the words: 'If you thought your boss had issues, think again... (this from the boss of the company that makes *Richard & Judy*)'

My chum Richard Madeley and his wife Judy Finnegan were frequently referred to as the king and queen of the UK publishing industry. Following in the yeti-sized footprints of the rampantly successful Oprah Winfrey Book Club, in 2004 their late afternoon programme began showcasing a select few books every year, catapulting featured authors to megasales and stardom. But it seemed this wholesome couple were just a front – the email's subject heading implied that Amanda Ross was the master puppeteer, her hands looming over the publishing world, spidery digits tugging at strings, flimsy marionettes dancing in her vast shadow.

The email read as follows:

I did not get to **see** or sign Maryam's card.

Can I remind you **all** that the Cactus Birthday tradition is mine, and I effectively pay for it, so if you can't make it happen that I get to sign the card then I will stop it.

To stop this happening in future, you are **not** to circulate **any** cards to **anyone** before I have signed them. What happened today? Did Maryam get a card with a space in the middle? No? Then who didn't do their job?

This sounds draconian but you have forced me to be that way, as you cannot make the simple system work. I am upset about this as I implemented the Birthday tradition to show staff Simon and I care about them. I am upset I didn't sign Maryam's card.

Amanda Ross

Managing Director


Lots of people who had forwarded the email had added comments about how 'hilarious! LOL' and 'mental' they thought it was, but I was interested in only one thing – how could I get to speak to this person? Serendipitously, Amanda's details were included at the bottom of the email, so it was a simple matter to copy and paste them into the 'To:' box before formulating my letter of introduction. But how to grab her attention?

The more I thought about it, the more I realised she must get dozens of emails from needy arselickers every day, all angling for a piece of the action. Straight flattery was unlikely to make much of a dent, and it wasn't like I was important enough to show up on her radar. The odds seemed stacked against me.

But then, I'd spent most of my life training as an attention-seeker. I knew the drill. I didn't need her approval – I just needed her to notice me. My email read:

To: Amanda Ross
Subject: The Publishing Dream

Dear Amanda Ross,

I like to think of myself as a chap with his ear to the ground. Lately, I have heard rumblings to the effect that you are 'the most powerful woman in publishing'. If this is the case, I would like to talk to you.

I am on a journey to the heart of the Publishing Dream. You may well be the pulsing organ I am searching for. If there is a gap in your busy schedule, I would be keen to pick your fertile brains. I understand you are undergoing something of a taxing period PR-wise – let me reassure you, Amanda, that any written account of our meeting would portray you in a very positive light. Perhaps this is your opportunity for public redemption.

I eagerly anticipate your response.

Your friend,

Tim Clare

PS – For what it's worth, I have something of an 'in' with your pal Richard Madeley. Do pass on my fondest regards.

# 4

'All publishers are bastards,' said Mark Le Fanu, General Secretary of the Society of Authors. He flashed me an impish grin and sat back in his chair.

I smiled weakly. I'd been recording our conversation on a Dictaphone and the tape had just run out. As it turned out, he needn't have waited to deliver his off-the-record punchline. In yet another iteration of my apparently inexhaustible cack-handedness, I hadn't realised that the Dictaphone was voice activated. When I got home and tried to play back our conversation, I discovered that the tape had only recorded my loud, obnoxious braying, switching itself off during Mark's quieter, more civilised responses. Thus I got to listen to forty-five minutes of crass, stammering attempts to manoeuvre him into agreeing that a career in writing was a colossal waste of time.

I am not a natural interviewer. Indeed, I have a cluster of personality traits that combine to give me a negative capacity for any kind of verbal information gathering. I am opinionated, rabidly enthusiastic and I enjoy holding court. If someone brings up a topic that interests me, I'll interrupt them to say: *God, yeah, that's so fascinating, in fact I was reading an incredible article just last week...* blah blah blah and eyes glaze over and before I realise what I'm doing I've killed a great line of conversation to rattle on about stuff I already know. Silences make me anxious, and I feel compelled to fill them. On top of all that, I've inherited my dad's unfortunate speech rhythms – he runs the ends of his sentences together and leaves the pauses in the middles. It works fine for him because my mum steps in to finish off his thoughts, but I don't have someone on hand who can draw on decades of experience to guess what I'm about to say, which means people tend to wait, because it seems rude to interrupt someone mid-sentence – which would be fine, except they're waiting for a pause which never comes, and I end up monologuing ad nauseum.

I'd spent the previous week trying to learn about the history of authorship in an attempt to get a grip on the bigger picture. It was an exceedingly boring and fruitless task. While Joe phoned from London, telling me how writers across the globe were setting about translating his work into new languages, I blundered around libraries and the Internet, learning little except the fact that I was crap at research. In the end, I only found one book on the subject – a second-hand copy of Victor Bonham-Carter's *Authors By Profession, Volume 2* that I'd picked up for three quid in Hay-on-Wye – and it was over a quarter of a century old. Though my single battered tome only covered the years 1911-1981, its account ended with Mark Le Fanu taking over as General Secretary of the Society of Authors. When I went on to the Society website and discovered he was still going strong, I decided to get in touch, to fill in the missing two and a half decades. I shot him an email asking if we could talk and, within half an hour, he'd written back, saying yes, of course, and inviting me to London.

I sat waiting in the Society of Authors reception area. On the low table in front of me a solitary bourbon biscuit lay on a white china plate, surrounded by brown crumbs. To my left, shelves groaned under the weight of ring binders and intimidating legal tomes; each of the ten volumes of 'Entertainment Industry Contracts' was at least three inches thick, and their contents ran to over 200 chapters.

In my jeans and polo shirt, and with a maroon rucksack slung on the chair next to me, I felt decidedly underdressed. There was something quaintly archaic about the decor, a pleasant, quintessentially English sort of formality – all of the toothless charm of the old Empire, with none of the bombast or bigotry. Gazing down at the green spotted carpet, I felt myself coming over all patriotic, at which point a white-haired gentleman appeared, looking more English than a map of England tattooed across the Queen's face.

'Hello,' he said, extending a hand. 'I'm Mark.'

He ushered me into his office.

Rather than feign competence, I admitted to him straight off the bat that my only book on the subject of authorship came out in 1981, and I asked him to pick up the story from there, which, very obligingly, he did.

After working as a lawyer, Mark was looking round for something a bit different when he saw a vacancy for an assistant at the Society of Authors. 'All my friends said, "God, no

– stay away from there. Authors are nothing but trouble." But I ignored them.'

'Why?' I said. 'Were you a closet writer yourself?'

'No.'

'Really?'

'Absolutely,' he said. 'Writers need a strong tendency towards sado-masochism. Some years ago, we used to get letters from members along the lines of: "My first novel has now been rejected by twenty publishers – should I try writing a second?" We'd send them a polite reply but as far as I'm concerned, if you have to ask that question then you're not a writer. You choose if you're a writer. Skill doesn't matter – it's a powerful personal urge, and one which I don't have.'

'Is there a difference between calling yourself a "writer" and an "author"?'

'Well…' He shifted in his seat as he considered the question. 'I think "author" presupposes one has talent. I mean, I wouldn't discourage anyone from writing a book and getting it privately published if they really want to, but it seems a peculiar urge. For instance, I do some sketching in my spare time, but I would never consider my work worth reproducing. But if you've finished a novel, you end up thinking it's prize-winning.

'The problem is that all the publicity goes to the few happy stories of million pound advances or the breakthrough misery novel that changes its author's life. You're never going to read the headline: "10,000 authors rejected this week." But that's the more accurate reflection of publishing reality. Great Britain has a huge output – much bigger than America's per capita.'

'Isn't it something like over 100,000 new titles a year?' I said.

'Well, I think the number gets a little inflated,' said Mark. 'It's very easy to get an ISBN these days, what with the growth of self-publishing, but it's certainly a colossal number. When I started here publishers would complain that they were getting swamped with dreadful submissions. At first, I thought they were making unhelpful generalisations, but I quickly learned that there's an awful lot of total crap around.

'When we launched the Betty Trask Awards—' The annual awards for first-time novelists under thirty-five writing work 'of a traditional or romantic nature' '—we attracted over two hundred applications in the first year, and most of them were total rubbish. There's such a flood of manuscripts out there, and most of them are complete dross. I'm not sure that all good authors get seen – it's very easy for talented authors to die in the slush pile, and unfortunately, it's not always the good ones that are the most tenacious.'

A little background for those lucky enough to not be intimately familiar with the jargon and intricacies of publishing – the archetypal journey a first novel takes from brain to bookshelf is this:

Author is struck by inspiration.

Author writes masterpiece.

Author puts masterpiece in envelope along with covering letter and an SAE and sends it off to a publisher who publishes books of that genre.

This manuscript is 'unsolicited' – the publisher hasn't asked to see it – so it goes in the 'slush pile', a huge mountain of unread submissions. Manuscripts may take months to read, and typically, this task is given to the lowest drudge in the office pecking order. Nowadays, many publishers are not prepared to invest resources in maintaining a slush pile at all, and unsolicited manuscripts get sent back unread. Stories circulate of bestsellers getting plucked from the slush pile like emeralds discovered gleaming in a cowpat, but these tales are popular precisely because the events they describe are incredibly rare.

So, our archetypal author, duly chastened, sends masterpiece to a literary agent.

Literary agent recognises genius and accepts author as client.

Literary agent sends out manuscript to publishers. Manuscript is no longer 'unsolicited', but carries an agent's endorsement. How quickly it gets read depends on agent's clout and how busy publisher is.

Publisher recognises genius and offers author a contract, including an advance against royalties the novel is expected to earn. Agent takes slice, Inland Revenue takes slice, author gets the rest.

Nine months to a year later, novel appears on shelves. Probably bombs. Author never heard of again.

'Somehow the popular view of publishing manages to combine this image of publishing houses as a Byzantine, shadowy clique, whose members are very unbusinesslike and fickle, with this unrealistic, glamorous idea of the rich celebrity author. The fact is, for almost everyone involved, it's a very unpredictable, tricky industry. Promotions are focused on fewer and fewer titles and it skews sales accordingly – we did our last survey of members' earnings in the year 2000 and the statistics were frightful. Although the mean wage isn't bad, it's kept artificially high by a tiny percentage of incredibly big earners – the *median* wage for authors in the twenty-first century is awful.'

Mark was right – the figures made for bum-tightening reading. The survey found that, although three per cent of the Society's members had earned over a hundred thousand pounds in the previous year, three quarters of members earned less than the national average wage, two thirds earned less than half the national average wage, and half earned less than the national minimum wage.

'Our responsibility at the Society is to look out for our members' interests,' said Mark, and then added, with a heavy sigh, 'but there's only so much we can do. If you get a career with a fair wind behind it then maybe you'll do okay, but there's no guarantee it will last. Once sales begin to falter, it's often all over. It's often far harder to get a third or fourth novel published than it is a first. We do our best, looking over contracts and that sort of thing, but for the vast majority of people who want to be authors, it's rather a case of "don't give up your day job".'

For me, this final hoary adage carried an especial sardonic ring. I'd spent my whole academic career training to become a writer. I wasn't qualified to do anything else – and if I didn't choose my path soon, I never would be.

# 5

Mark Le Fanu's doomy prognostications concerning the lot of the professional author contrasted sharply with the almost continual barrage of good news coming from my friends. I started to dread phone conversations, knowing that they would inevitably contain updates on everybody's latest great achievements. The surge of jealousy that followed a call, then the shame at not being happier for my friends, was usually enough to ruin my mood for the rest of the day.

'So you know Joe's sold the movie rights to his book?'

I was in my bedroom, eating a peanut butter sandwich and talking to Luke on the phone. Up until then, we'd been having a nice chat, discussing neutral topics, cracking bad jokes. I dropped the half-eaten sandwich on to the plate. I'd lost my appetite.

'I did not know that,' I said flatly. 'How brilliant. I'm so pleased.'

'Yeah,' said Luke. 'I think it's going to be great. Hey, me and Joel were talking about you today.'

'You were?'

'We were going through the latest round of edits for our book, and there was this joke in there that I'd done, and our editor picked it out, and Joel went: "That's definitely a Tim line."'

'Really?'

'Yeah. And I was like, "Yeah, it's totally a Tim line." It was exactly the kind of thing I imagine you saying. I think I'd put it in there because I knew it'd make you laugh.'

I felt my wounded ego rally a little. 'Nice to hear I've been of help.'

'Yeah,' said Luke. 'We cut it.'

'Oh.'

'It didn't work.'

'Right.'

'Look, mate, I've got to go. Nice talking to you.'

'Oh, okay. Uh… bye.'

A moment later, it was just me and the sandwich. I stared at it for a few seconds, till I heard a knock on my door.

'Tim?' It was Dad.

'What?'

'I'm just making some lunch,' he shouted through the door. 'Do you want a sandwich?'

I hung my head. 'I think I'm all right, thanks.'

Back when I was at university, I looked upon the lives of my creative writing tutors with a many-flavoured yearning – a yeasty mixture of hope, jealousy and weary melancholy. *That* was the kind of life I wanted. To get paid in return for teaching creative writing seemed a rewarding, wonderful wheeze. It sounded like an absolute skive.

Soon, I came to know better.

Don't get me wrong – talking about writing is a piece of piss. I can pontificate for hours on the nuances of expository syntax, waxing lyrical about the 'plot' of a sentence, about the evil parasites called modal verbs, about how an author can use sub-clauses to delay gratification and set up juicy sucker punches. Mutter the word 'suddenly' under your breath and I'll launch into an extended tirade so drenched in vitriol you'll conclude that, long ago, an adverb slaughtered my entire family. I *care* about prose. When crap writing of any genre gets lauded by the critics, I'm a hair's breadth from rigging myself, nads to clavicle, with fertiliser bombs and marching into the nearest Waterstone's. If teaching creative writing just involved stridently delivering my opinions to a mute but appreciative audience, I would be superb.

Unfortunately, like most jobs, working as a creative writing tutor requires certain basic organisational skills, such as the ability to manage one's time, the ability to meet deadlines, and the ability to sit down and actually read the bloody manuscript instead of sticking it under a pile of magazines and playing *Pokémon Diamond* for six hours straight.

Since finishing my MA in Creative Writing, I had been doing part-time work for manuscript critiquing agencies. In return for a sizeable fee, these agencies would look at an aspiring author's novel, and provide a detailed report on ways it could be improved. As an additional carrot, the bigger critiquing agencies promised that, if a novel was good enough, they had the contacts to hook up the author with a proper literary agent or a publisher. Often, writers approached a critiquing agency after receiving a flurry of rejections.

I found the work difficult. Years of chasing writing stardom had brought me so close to success I could almost smell the freshly drying ink, and yet in actuality, I was no more a bona fide published author than the illiterate pilchards who bombarded the agencies I worked for with dire, slapdash hackery. My only tangible claim to superiority was that I'd poured my entire life into the creative writing sinkhole, whereas these dilettantes usually had families, social lives and successful careers. I desperately wanted to etch a distinction between the unreadable novels the wannabes dashed out in a matter of weeks and the Book that represented the culmination of my *entire life's work*. Surely I was better than them?

Wasn't I?

At fifteen, I had decided to attempt my first novel. I did so with the explicit motivation that, even if I didn't end up producing the last great literary masterwork of the twentieth century, I would at least create something that, in years to come, would give me some insight into what I had been like as a teenager.

Rereading the manuscript over a decade later, my primary insight was that I had been terrified of the opposite sex.

The novel tells the story of one Raymond Powers, a man in his late twenties who works in an 'import-export' firm. Despite the fact that over half the book takes place at his office, neither Ray nor any of his associates are seen to do any work, nobody ever discusses anything related to their job – aside from occasional, nebulous references to a 'big client' – and we never find out the name of the company he works for.

Rather than being a wry Kafkaesque commentary on faceless workplace bureaucracy, this almost total absence of detail stemmed from the fact that I had no idea what a real adult job consisted of. All I knew was that it was horrible, pointless, and soul-destroying.

In the first chapter, I expand Ray's predicament into a searing indictment of corporate culture:

> All the hopes and aspirations of youth had petered out within the initial week of real work, leaving him empty. Suddenly all the dreams that had still been possible died. Disillusionment with the repetitiveness and the inescapable system had dulled his soul and his drive. Now he was dying, losing another, irretrievable piece of his personality every day in his efforts to keep on working, to stay in the game.

From there on in, things only get edgier. Ray starts smoking 'drugs' and finds himself repeatedly visited by a bizarre female ginger-haired dagger-wielding gobshite, who giggles and chats intricate nihilistic bollocks. In a series of awkward quasi-S&M encounters, Ray faints, wets himself, lets her pin him on the floor and humiliate him. Eventually Ray shrugs off the shackles of his old existence, burns down the office, and sets off to wreak giddy havoc throughout the world, viciously amoral and liberated by his discovery that life has no meaning.

Rereading the entire manuscript was one of the most excruciating experiences of my life, not just because it was 95,000 words of dull, angsty adolescent toss, but because I could remember just how proud I had been, how intelligent, groundbreaking and *important* I had believed my work to be. Looking back at it was like watching my teenaged self enjoying a slow, self-congratulatory wank. I'd thought that I'd got the human condition sussed, and that my rare insight would dazzle readers the world over.

But without this insanely narcissistic level of self-belief, I doubt I'd have ever started, let alone finished it. I'd knocked it out in my spare time over about nine months, writing first in longhand, then transferring it from one notepad to a second, then typing it up on the computer. Over the next two years, I inflicted it upon a series of readers, listening to their comments and obsessively editing and refining, all to no avail. How did I manage to devote so much time and effort to writing without developing a realistic appraisal of my skills?

Growing up in a backwater like Portishead may be partly to blame – it's hard not to get an inflated sense of your intellect in a town where being able to read the text on the back of a Peperami wrapper earns you the nickname 'Professor'. But it's possible an even more fundamental principle was at work.

In 1999, around the time I finally gave up on my first novel (which I'd called, in all seriousness, *Psychic Rubber Nipples*), the American Psychological Association's Journal of Personality and Social Psychology published a study by Justin Kruger and David Dunning entitled 'Unskilled and Unaware of It: How Difficulties in Recognizing One's Own Incompetence Lead to Inflated Self-Assessments'. The study concerned itself with breaking down and explaining what has come to be known as the Dunning-Kruger effect, or what a layperson like me tends to think of as 'Pop Idol Syndrome' – the apparent inverse relationship between ability and self-belief that has brought so many tin-eared crooners caterwauling on to our screens.

The study's authors argued that: 'When people are incompetent in the strategies they adopt to achieve success and satisfaction, they suffer a dual burden: not only do they reach erroneous conclusions and make unfortunate choices, but their incompetence robs them of the ability to realise it... they are left with the mistaken impression that they are doing just fine.' The study tested participants in three fields – Humour, Logical Reasoning, and English Grammar – then asked them to rate their performance in each of these areas and estimate how their performance compared to the group average. The authors found that the least skilled participants grossly overestimated their ability in each of the tasks and rated themselves as above the group average, whereas the most skilled participants tended to possess the most accurate self-perception. Dunning and Kruger hypothesised that deficiencies in 'metacognitive skills' mean incompetent individuals consistently overestimate their ability and performance at certain tasks, and that they are less able than more skilled peers to recognise competence in others. Paradoxically, the report argued that the best way to get incompetent individuals to lower inflated estimates of their own ability is to help them improve at a task, thus improving their self-appraisal skills. In other words, one of the preconditions of getting good at something seems to be knowing how crap you are it.

Perhaps I had always been in denial, keeping aloof when in

actuality I was down there in the Publishing Dream's ugly gutter – a rancorous sawdust pit where dropouts and failures congregated with their delusions and resentment, brandishing poorly typeset self-published paperbacks and baying at the injustice of a system that refused to recognise their exquisite genius. The glowing sense of authorial destiny that had propelled me through my youth was no indicator of future glories. If anything, it portended the opposite – a dismal spiral of failure and denial, comprising a slow, grand estrangement from reality.

Not every manuscript the agencies sent me was awful. Some were merely poor. But the real surprise was what a colossal grind writing reports quickly became.

Reading discursive, poorly punctuated novel after discursive, poorly punctuated novel made the Norwich Union Death department's 'expected output' bar seem like loafing Huck Finn-style in the shade beside a stream, fishing with a bit of twine tied round one's big toe. I derived no pleasure from the process whatsoever; indeed, I suspect there is some flame-licked grotto in Hades where former literary aspirants are subjected to an eternity of this deliciously ironic punishment. Imagine being a diehard TV fan, and getting a job where you're paid (not terribly well) to watch abysmal amateur remakes of your favourite shows, and you have to note down every piece of bad dialogue or instance of crappy set construction and explain why the dialogue is bad or why the set is crappy, and then when you've finally finished watching the show and making your notes you have to put them all together in a lengthy report, pointing out every eye-wateringly obvious mistake while feigning patience and enthusiasm, and when you've finished *that*, there's another show waiting, one which makes all the same mistakes again, and so the futile cycle continues, cascading downwards into dark, stench-thick infinity.

What made it all so tragic was that these troves of diabolical pap occasionally represented years of sacrifice and diligent toil by pleasant, ostensibly intelligent people. Prospective authors might have acted diffident, but usually it was so much passive-aggressive manoeuvring. The result was covering letters that contained a bizarre mix of sardonic self-deprecation and roaring bushfire egotism: *Can you tell me if this story is salvageable or if I'm just wasting my time? Please feel free to be as harsh as you like – I can take it! I see* The Scorpio Contingent *appealing very strongly to the millions of readers who enjoy Tom Clancy-style thrillers. If popular I have ideas for five more novels, all of which would be suitable for conversion into Hollywood movies. I should very much like to devote myself full-time to writing, as I enjoy it and feel I have a natural flair for storytelling. Do you think there is a market for this?*

I'd sometimes receive an email along similar lines, fizzing with naked desperation:

Dear Tim,

I don't know if this email will reach you or not. (probably not!) Anyway, sorry to bother you but I read your article on the publishing industry. I've been writing a novel for about the last ten years – the trouble is, how do I know if it's going to make me millions and millions of pounds or if it'll result in public humiliation so grievous that I'll have to fashion a noose out of electrical cable and hang myself from the nearest railway bridge? My friends say it's good but I suppose the publishing industry might see things differently!! Could you give me some pointers on submitting my work? I really need this book to succeed so I can buy back the affections of my estranged wife and children. Don't worry if you haven't got time to write back – you'll probably read about me in the news, when my dangling cadaver bursts across the 10:15 from Stowmarket like a bolognese-stuffed pinata.

Thanks!!

I wanted to unpack this mindset and discover the motivations behind it, but I was merely a temperamental flywheel in the vast, clanking apparatus of manuscript critiquing. I dealt with cold, hard product, not the writers who produced it. I needed someone who confronted these forlorn creatures on a daily basis, who might have accrued some insight into their twisted psychological landscapes, and thus, by extension, my own predicament. I decided to go straight to the top, and approach my nominal boss – Helen Corner, founder of Cornerstones literary consultancy.

Helen emailed me directions. The directions were wrong. Had they corresponded with the route I ultimately took they would have gone something like this:

Leave the tube station and turn left. Keep going past the bus depot until you reach a bridge. The street that you need is on your left. Ignore it. Instead, walk over the bridge and follow a narrow, crooked road until you reach the high street. Stop for a moment, and allow yourself to feel the first troubling twinge of confusion. Continue on down the high street, past *Chick-o-Land, Mega-Kebab* and a hardware shop where the window display consists entirely of black glue traps hung like macabre bunting. When you reach the sweat-spattered workman cracking concrete slabs with a pneumatic drill, take a right. Proceed down a residential road lined with big, single-glazed houses.

Stop. Look around for a street name, feeling your perspiration-damp collar chafe each time you turn your head. Take out your mobile phone and dial the Cornerstones number. Listen to the engaged tone. Put your mobile phone back in your pocket. Look again for a street name, this time becoming aware of the weight of your rucksack and the ache in your lower back. Sigh, and begin retracing your steps.

Turn right, staying parallel to the railway tracks, until you reach a thickset olive-skinned man with sad eyes walking alongside an eight-year-old boy clutching a large daisy. Watch the boy as he sniffs the flower, then turns and thrusts it into one of the man's nostrils. Cross the road to the sound of their yelling.

Traipse down a narrow corridor of drab, slumped flats until you come to a bearded man in a grey hoodie sitting on the pavement with a three-litre bottle of Merrydown cider. Wait at the kerb until he coughs a bright poppy of blood into his white handkerchief then cross the road. Keep going past a boarded-up pub until you reach a chain-link fence and an empty netball court. Take out your mobile phone and dial the Cornerstones number. Listen to the engaged tone. Swear loudly. Wipe sweat from the clammy earpiece and put the phone back in your pocket. Wad up the hem of your shirt and wipe sweat from your face and hands. Take a deep breath.

Go straight on, telling yourself you're going to miss your meeting. Fantasise about becoming eternally lost in inimical, grime-smeared backstreets. Hang a left then follow a dogleg round until you find yourself on a street lined with concrete forecourts, garages and security blinds. Head onwards, dizzy now from the heat, past a gaunt man in a vest who is painting a windowsill battleship grey with slow, truculent strokes. Continue walking for some 200 metres. Stop, this time from sheer exhaustion. Take out your mobile phone and dial the Cornerstones number. Gasp with relief when it rings. Speak to Helen, and establish that the windowsill being painted grey belongs to the office you're looking for. Turn on your heel and retrace your steps until you reach the underfed man. Ring the buzzer, panting.

Although I'd worked for Helen for over a year, all the work was done by phone and post, so this was the first time we'd met. I'm not sure why I was surprised to be greeted by a young, smiling, energetic woman with a pixie cut – I supposed I'd assumed that everyone associated with the publishing industry was either a haggard, sallow wreck, or slow and thick-set with largesse. She took me straight into the downstairs meeting room, which was like an IKEA showroom, all stainless steel and laminate wood flooring. I'm prone to electric shocks (something to do with poor clothing combinations generating a surfeit of static) and seeing so much exposed metal in a single room made me edgy.

She put the kettle on. While it gubbled and steamed she told me: 'I think writing is something you're compelled to do.

If it's in you it sort of wells up and you have to respond. I think a lot of people would give up if they knew the real story. It's real hard graft.' She brought over our tea in chunky white mugs. 'Many, many published authors say that if they'd realised how tough and badly paid it is they'd never have bothered. You can't go in asking, "Does this make financial sense"? I strongly believe in managing one's expectations.'

Helen told me she'd started out as an assistant at Penguin. Her job involved overseeing the slush pile – the gargantuan, never-ending mountain of unsolicited manuscripts from eager literary hopefuls. Every now and then, she'd find a story that showed real promise, but wasn't quite up to scratch, and she'd have to turn it down. It was a real shame, she said. She could see the things that were wrong with it, but she just didn't have the time to coach individual authors through the redrafting process.

One day, she found a manuscript that she thought *was* ready. It was the first novel her boss had bought from the slush pile in ten years, and it turned into a number one bestseller. Cue mucho kudos for its lucky discoverer.

'But I thought that there was a gap in the market for editorial feedback – for shaping and teaching authors and providing a professional second opinion. For most publishers, it makes economic sense to just return all manuscripts that haven't come through an agent unread rather than employing someone to wade through them. Agents have largely taken over the editorial role, and even they don't have huge amounts of time to help an author through the tricky process of redrafting. When I founded Cornerstones there was just one other agency doing manuscript critiques.' She was referring to The Literary Consultancy, a larger, better-known agency. 'Now there are tons. I've spent about ten years carving out a niche and educating the trade. We started with five freelance editors – now we've got sixty or so. We choose them very carefully and monitor them continually.' She gave me a pointed look.

But given all its pain and disappointment, why on earth would she want to help introduce yet *more* feckless hopefuls to the soul-crushing world of publishing?

'Have you read my book, *How To Write A Blockbuster*?'

I shook my head. Perhaps this was where I had gone wrong.

'Well,' said Helen, talking rapidly as she launched into what sounded like a well-rehearsed promotional spiel, 'one of the case studies I cite is an author called Jane Yardley. She was the head of a pharmaceutical company and she had a sparkling imagination, so one night she started to write a novel, but she was savvy enough to realise that she couldn't just chuck it out into the ether and hope to get a deal, so she came to us. We had a look, and we told her, "There's something really good here, but the story's quite tangential and it's not quite ready," and she went away and edited it. Anyway, we normally put a stop at three reports if they're still not getting it. Otherwise it turns into vanity editing.

'Anyway, Jane rang up and said please please please can you look again. I've done loads to it. You'll see how much it's improved. So we agreed to do a fourth report and it *had* dramatically improved, but it *still* wasn't ready, and we told her so. So a little while later she came back again, and I said, "Listen, Jane, I *absolutely* can't do this anymore," and we ended up having a forty-minute phone discussion where she begged and pleaded, and so eventually I gave in... and it was amazing. A week later she got an agent, and two weeks later she got a really substantial five-figure deal with a publisher. I mean, five reports in two years is a steep learning curve.' *And a rather expensive one*, I thought. 'But she and I both know that her book would have been rejected if she hadn't gone through all those redrafts.'

*Well*, I thought, *that's not* necessarily *true*. Helen presupposed a causal relationship between Jane's five critiques and her successfully securing an agent, without demonstrating that the former had caused the latter. Had Jane sent out her manuscript in its original form, an agent might have taken it on and offered her free editorial advice to boot. It wasn't inconceivable that getting critiqued by Cornerstones could have *slowed* her journey to publication.

The problem with holding up anecdotes of this ilk as evidence is that there's no control group to compare them against. Every manuscript is different, and editors and publishing trends are always shifting. Superstition and magical thinking thrive in unpredictable environments. Something about turning a profit from prospective writers' desires and aspirations troubled me a bit. It wasn't that I thought that Helen was dishonest or that Cornerstones didn't provide a good service – it was just that I knew how desperately I had longed to become a published author and how vulnerable that kind of longing can make you. It's one thing to encourage a person to follow their dreams – it's quite another to offer to assist in the pursuit in return for a significant fee.

'Isn't the danger that writers will use stories like that as rods to beat themselves with?' I said. 'You know, like the ones about *Watership Down* or *Animal Farm* getting rejected by dozens of publishers and then going on to become massive successes? Stories like that are atypical, but they get disseminated as if they're representative. Isn't there a danger that people start buying into this myth of the long, hard struggle to publication without hearing about all the other writers who tried all their lives and didn't get anywhere?'

Helen picked up her mug and took a sip of tea. 'The thing about this whole process is you have to be really brilliant and creative and sensitive to actually write the story and get your feelings down on paper, then you need nerves of steel to push through all these barriers between you and publication. Look, I speak to agents all the time,' she said, 'and they all say that what they're after is something fresh and original.'

'Hmm.' I remembered what Steve Aylett had said. 'Do publishers *really* want originality? What do you mean by "original"?'

'Well, it's got to make someone sit up and say, "God, I've never seen this before." We see so much "timeslip" stuff – you know, a kid goes through a door, and suddenly they're in the Victorian era – and we get loads of Harry Potter-style stuff.'

I leant forward. 'But isn't Harry Potter a fantastic counter-argument to publishers wanting originality? It's a hodgepodge of poorly thought out pastiches of other people's work. There's bits of generic hocus-pocus in there, heavy echoes of Mildred Hubble and *The Worst Witch* books… Did readers really go to Harry Potter because they thought it was original?'

Helen hesitated. 'I think... I think it was the right time. Harry Potter was very marketable, a very easy read. So much of publishing is about luck and timing. Editors often go to agents and say, "We need stuff for six- to eight-year-olds, some ghost stories, and we're opening an erotica list," and agents have to scrabble around finding manuscripts that fit the bill. Twelve months later, the market slumps. It's extremely random.'

'So are publishers *actually* looking for original stuff?'

She nodded. 'I think they want a book that's got great characters and a fantastic plot, you know, something that's a thumping good read.'

'But none of those things are originality per se, are they?'

'Well... no, I suppose not.'

I felt like Helen was keeping something back. With all her emphasis on thankless slogs and randomness, I wasn't entirely clear how the book world could have ever held an appeal.

'Why did you go into publishing in the first place?' I asked.

Her mouth twisted into a smile. 'Well... I wanted to write.'

'Really?'

'Yes. I'd done a writing course but I felt I was still really naïve and I wanted to learn more.'

'Do you still write?'

'Well... no,' she said, then added quickly, 'but it's simmering away in the background. I've shelved it for a while. I'm just way too busy doing what I do. I think what creativity I have is continually used up by working with authors.'

'What did you write about?'

'When I took a sabbatical a couple of years ago I started writing a narrative non-fiction adventure story based on my romance in Africa.' She shuffled in her chair, as if confessing something shameful. 'I, uh… I nearly turned that into a book. Jamie Oliver's management company had me on their list but that, uh, I grew tired of that idea.' She let out a sigh, gazing down into her mug. 'And, uh, anyway… things sort of went belly up. The last thing I wanted to do was to dwell on the past, on stuff I wanted to move on from.' She looked up. 'So I shelved it.'

For a few moments, I wasn't sure how to respond. Could Helen and I really be kindred spirits? Was I looking at a fellow casualty of the Publishing Dream?

'But didn't you say that writing's something that you have to do?' I said. 'Didn't you say it "wells up and you have to respond"?'

Helen shrugged. 'I think you can switch it on and off though. It's like a tap, and when it's on words just pour out of you, and you have to write… but maybe… you can turn it off.' She took her mug by the handle and turned it through ninety degrees. 'And maybe, one day, you can turn it back on again.'

And then, as if reading my mind, she added: 'I'd never say I'm a failed writer and that's why I do what I do, because at some point I *definitely* want to pick it up again. I feel quite confident that I'll get back to it.'

I was poised to ask her another question but she went on, apparently rallying. 'Actually, that brings me on to my most important point. This is my driving ethos.' She steepled her fingers then pushed them forward across the table like a plough. 'It's a message of real hope.

'I *never* want to crush a writer's passion and ability. I might, uh, "manage their expectations", but I never say stop, because you never know where your writing's going to take you. I mean, my writing's brought me here.' She glanced around at the meeting room. 'If someone had said to me, you know, "Give up – you're a rubbish, rubbish writer," I might have, then I wouldn't be here. For all its difficulties and frustrations, I think writing is a good thing, and even if it doesn't lead you on the path you imagined it would, you never know where it might take you.'

Helen had been doing such a good job of trashing the Publishing Dream that this final optimistic twist felt like a betrayal. Sure, writing hadn't taken me where I had expected – the despair, impoverishment and humiliation had all come as complete surprises.

I left the office frustrated. Everybody I'd talked to so far had given me mixed messages. They hated writing but would never quit. I needed to give it my all but I shouldn't give up my day job. Writing was a compulsion that could be turned on and off like a tap.

Gah! I was more confused than ever. Meanwhile, the hissing fuse on my big black decision bomb was shrinking. Joe's big launch party was only two months away, and if I hadn't made my choice by then, it would be the final confirmation of my failure – both as an artist, and an adult. I had to make up my mind who I would be when I entered that room full of my friends.

Would I be celebrating with them as a fellow literary

high achiever, or feeling a flush of relief knowing that I'd permanently escaped from this stressful, parlous lifestyle?

I'd wasted too much time on mealy-mouthed ditherers. It was futile shaking down monkeys for wisdom while the organ grinders went on luring punters with their sour siren dirges. I had to cut out the middleman, quit shilly-shallying, and go straight to the dream-vendors themselves – the publishers.

# 6

It was late morning when I checked my inbox and found this:

Dear Tim

Thank you for your email, yes I am very tied up at the moment with Icstis, and so really pushed for time.

Could you please send me a brief email saying who you are and what you would like to talk about.

Best wishes

Amanda Ross

Managing Director

I shot back a reply:

Hi Amanda,

Yes, it's a frantically busy time at the moment, isn't it? Great to hear you're interested.

As I intimated in my previous epistle, I am searching for the heart of the publishing industry. I have spoken with authors failed and famous, high-flying agents and their bent-backed lackeys, cynical journos and big editors dripping with ill-gotten largesse. I have travelled to the past and gazed, squint-eyed, into publishing's hazy future. I have grovelled at the feet of Jeffrey Archer.

173

Yet for all my wanderings, I still feel there is some inner sanctum I remain disbarred from. A period of dedicated sleuthing has led me to believe that you may be that inner sanctum. I'd like to ask you about the Publishing Dream, the fantasy of the superstar author, and find out how you have coped with the untold power that crackles at your fingertips like the dark, eldritch magic of some malevolent sorceress.

If we could do it sometime in the next month, that'd be fantastic.

Toodle-pip,

Tim Clare aka 'the most wonderful man in pen-pushing'

PS – I'm sorry to hear about your suffering at the hands of Icstis and very much sympathise; the recent heatwave has made my lumbago flare up with the ferocity of a thousand buffalo. Get well soon.

# 7

So you're a young, ambitious writer, working on your first novel, and over a period of several months, some of the biggest literary agents in the UK travel across the country to meet you. They talk about what an agent does, how the industry works, and what you can expect when your novel gets bought by a big publishing house. They phrase it just like that – 'when' it gets bought, not 'if'. For the first time ever, important people seem genuinely interested in your work. You've spent so long working and hoping and dreaming, and now here you are, meeting all these high-up industry professionals who appear to take your dream seriously.

It must feel wonderful, right?

Well, maybe it would, if they weren't saying exactly the same thing to the fifty other writers with you at every meeting, fifty writers all with the exact same dream as yours.

During my second semester as a student on UEA's MA in Prose Fiction, I attended a series of 'informal presentations' from literary agents. The atmosphere at these meetings was one of slow-burning communal lust – it rose from the audience like steam from a pavement grille in winter. As the agent stood at the front of the room, talking of fat advances, international rights and film deals, amorphous notions of literary destiny hardened into a fierce sense of entitlement. The hunger was palpable – people sensed it in their neighbours and began slavering like beasts in a holding pen. More than once, I found myself bunching my hands into jag-knuckled fists; I had to physically look away to break loose from the group psychology.

In previous years, these visits had been compressed into a single frenzied day, students and agents slick with mutual desperation as they struggled to form meaningful bonds in the midst of a roiling human contraflow. By comparison, I had been told, the current proceedings were positively genteel.

Post-presentation Q&A sessions inevitably dissolved into a bizarre form of mating display. There were no genuine queries to be answered – we all knew how to submit a manuscript – so the only point of asking a question was to show off. Students often launched into meandering rococo disquisitions that were often not questions at all, just lengthy statements with a 'Do you agree?' tacked on the end. There was plenty of brinkmanship involved. If you were sly you could offer a tantalising hint of your novel's content – 'Do you ever take on detective stories with an historical-pastoral setting?' – but sometimes a person would go too far – 'I'm writing a literary thriller set in Kabul – are you interested?' – and we'd all cringe like prodded anemones. The agents, we had been told, were just there for a chat – this was not a recruitment drive.

But it was – of course, it *patently* was – and from thence sprung the pervasive tension. I remember being terrified, both of saying something unconscionably stupid, and of missing a potential tryst with fate.

In one of the first meetings, I asked what I thought was a well-judged question.

'Are there any events that you'd recommend aspiring writers visit?'

The agent smiled and replied: 'Ah. What a good question.'

I allowed myself a brief flush of satisfaction. We hadn't been introduced to many agents yet, so this well-dressed chap with auburn ringlets of hair and a big, important nose seemed to radiate stature, as if he were gatekeeper to a realm of impossible delights.

'Well,' he went on, 'there's the Hay-on-Wye Literary Festival, of course, and readings, things like that.' He glanced towards the ceiling and stroked his chin, clearly stretched by my uncommon verve as an interrogator. 'Also, there's the London Book Fair in April – I don't know if any of you have heard of that?' Heads bobbed in a slow palsy of affirmation. 'It's probably the biggest event in the UK publishing calendar. A really good opportunity to see how the industry works. All sorts of massive deals get done there – there's an entire floor devoted to agents and publishers arm-wrestling over rights.' His expression clouded over. 'I mean, it's not actually *for* writers. All the agents there are extremely busy negotiating contracts. It wouldn't be appropriate to approach them there.' To my horror, he looked straight at me. 'Absolutely don't go harassing agents at the London Book Fair,' he warned, his tone suddenly stern. 'It's not appropriate. I'm serious.'

*But I never mentioned approaching agents!* I wanted to protest. *You brought up the London Book Fair, not me! I just posed a brilliant and incisive question!*

But it was too late. He was already fielding somebody else's query, and I was forever embossed upon his memory as an aggressive stalker prepared to gatecrash important negotiations in an attempt to foist my tawdry wares on an unwilling industry.

As if.

Since then, the London Book Fair had always felt like the incredible party I wasn't welcome at. As if it wasn't enough that the Book had never gone on show there, beautiful and buzzy like the mysterious debutante in the diaphanous gown, the LBF rendered my agent uncontactable for weeks afterwards. Those three little letters had made me sick with jealousy.

But I was a changed man. No longer did I sit and curse the darkness. I had lit not a candle but a blazing torch, and I was marching with it deep into the dank catacombs of my sickness. Perhaps the agent had warned me off to keep me from discovering the truth – that the London Book Fair was not a dream-factory, but an abattoir.

Surely, if anything could cure me of my desire to be the Big Author, it was seeing literature with its guts hanging out. All that greed and panic and novels squealing as they died on the slab. I pictured blood-stippled aprons and cleavers clad in skirts of gore. This had to be it – publishing's dark heart.

On the other hand, if the LBF really did represent the industry's exciting, vital nerve centre, that meant it was full of important, well-connected people who had it in their power to finally make my life's ambition a reality. If I could track down just one sympathetic editor and convince him or her I was worth taking a punt on, I'd be laughing. Wasn't this, after all, how the cynics said it was done? Wasn't the road to a book deal meant to be cobbled with licked arses?

Surfing the net in a red-and-blue striped flannel dressing gown some time after two in the morning, I felt uncharacteristically shot through with purpose. I clicked through to the London Book Fair's online registration form and began to fill in my details. The first section was easy enough, consisting of the standard biographical stuff – name, date of birth, address – but the second page stopped me in my tracks.

There it was – a pithy single-word summation of my life's failings thus far:

*Profession.*

Putting 'unemployed' just wouldn't cut it – the Book Fair was reserved for industry professionals, not disaffected layabouts fresh from a three-week stint of getting up mid-afternoon, slouching on the settee in their boxer shorts and watching *Columbo*. I considered putting 'author', but that seemed wrong too – I'd never had anything published and, more importantly, it might tip off publishers that I was lugging round a grudge the size of an infant whale. I imagined them affecting their best hypocritical leers as I strolled past, or else rolling down their stall shutters and pretending to be closed. No, no, I had to go incognito. I needed to blend in, so they would relax and revert to their true forms, like strippers on a fag break.

'Ex-author'? Well, that remained to be seen.

No, I needed these people to accept me as one of their own.

All at once, the right answer became clear.

*Name: Tim Clare*
*Profession: Publisher*
*Role: Chairman/President*
*Company: Fabulous Books Inc*

And that's how, in the space of thirty seconds, I became founder, chairman, owner and sole employee of Fabulous Books Inc – British publishing's best-kept secret.

A thick, oppressive heat and constant low rumbling from somewhere far off gave the London Book Fair the feel of some doomed ex-pat community in the tropics, rumple-suited middle-agers shuffling about uneasily as the mother of all storms drew nearer. As I entered I saw a poster promoting future events – the following week, the massive hangar-sized area would be given over to the WWE Royal Rumble. My resolve hardened at the knowledge that, no matter how frenzied proceedings got seven days hence, they would never match the action going on right at that moment. Somewhere in the building, dozens of sweaty men and women were grappling over a prize far greater than being crowned WWE Intercontinental Champion – the honour of bagging publishing's Next Big Thing.

The ground floor was arranged like a giant department store, stalls laid out in numbered blocks and crosshatched with walkways. Garishly coloured banners promoting various publishing houses, distributors and printing companies hung from the ceiling, each one ten, twenty metres long. Four escalators rose out of the throng, transporting punters up to a similarly crowded mezzanine.

A little groggy from having risen at six to catch my train into the Big Smoke, and with several hours to kill, I decided to embark on a wander. Most of the stalls on the ground floor belonged to publishing houses – shelf upon shelf upon shelf of big glossy kids' titles, fat bland educational textbooks, middlebrow issue-led novels adorned with pastel-shaded treescapes in soft focus, gold-embossed self-help tomes, gorgeous coffee-table collections of art and photography, sassy chick-lit, dour reference books and aurora-splattered 'Mind & Spirit' paperbacks. The big players like HarperCollins, Random House and Penguin had forked out for expansive display spaces, replete with multiple meeting tables, and vast, elaborate promotional hoardings adorned with book covers or the smug, gurning phizogs of star authors. On my first few circuits, I kept expecting to turn a corner only to see Joe's giant face beaming beneficently down at me. It felt like a small victory that he hadn't progressed to the rank of massive-visaged literary posterboy quite yet.

For smaller publishers it was a different story. Where the large stalls bustled with handshakes and genial introductions, the little ones squatted in the cracks like one-man hotdog concerns wedged between skyscrapers. Often, they were just a table-width across – some were scarcely deeper than a wardrobe. Lone representatives sat at empty tables, nervously fingering the handles of their coffee mugs, glancing up with a kind of weatherbeaten desperation whenever someone seemed to linger in front of the stall for more than a couple of seconds. The sadness in their eyes took me back to a press junket that had ended in the narrow alleys of Amsterdam's red light district, and the Filipino midget I'd seen waiting cherry-lit and babydoll behind glass, her brittle smile twitching at the edges as over and over she met punters' gazes, watched them appraise her body in a glance, wrinkle their noses, move on.

By half past ten I was coated in a caul of perspiration. It wasn't just the humidity – my assumed identity was beginning to make me feel nervous. A few days prior, I'd received a plastic-walleted badge that read, in large block capitals:

**MR TIM CLARE**
**PUBLISHER**
**FABULOUS BOOKS INC**

Back in the nocturnal snug of my bedroom, such flagrant deceit seemed like a harmless wheeze, but now I was out in public it became an entirely different proposition. Fellow attendees glanced at my badge before they glanced at my face. Were they judging me? What was my status here? I couldn't help but notice that most of the other fair goers' badges were plain white – mine was a sickly turquoise-green. Why had I been singled out? Was my badge colour some secret publishing code for 'fraudulent twat'?

Desperate for moral support, I began phoning friends. I tried to convince them to come down and join me, claiming somewhat improbably that the London Book Fair would be 'a great laugh' and we'd have 'an amazing time'. Eventually, I got through to Luke, who was on his way to a meeting with some trendy media company in London.

'Come on, mate,' I said, over a crackly line, 'it'll be brilliant. There's a bar and everything.'

'But why are you there?'

'Uh…' I didn't feel ready to 'fess up about my quest, so I settled for a half-truth. 'Research. You know… journalism and stuff. *I'm undercover*,' I added, in a stage whisper. 'Go on. You know you want to.'

'Do I?'

'Sure you do! The place is crawling with bigwigs. We'll get a few bevs, then schmooze. Come on, you're a pro now. You need to be doing this kind of thing. You can help me with my reportage. We'll have a great time – I guarantee it.'

There was a long silence. At first, I thought Luke's train had gone into a tunnel.

'Hello? Luke?'

'All right,' he sighed. 'I'll come.'

'Nice one! See you later.'

I snapped my phone shut and slipped it back into my pocket. All I had to do was avoid people until Luke arrived. Travelling up to the mezzanine, I dipped my head and did my best to affect the demeanour of an unapproachable misanthrope. No sooner had I stepped off the escalator than some plucky swine rushed the machine-gun nest.

'Excuse me.'

I pretended not to hear but he stepped out from behind

his Perspex lectern, moving as if to block my path. I halted, met his gaze.

*Remember,* I told myself, *you're supposed to be here. You're not a failed writer. You're Tim Clare, President of Fabulous Books Inc!*

He was a sinewy guy in his early thirties, done up in blue pinstripes and tie, his hair slicked into perky spikes that only emphasised his receding hairline. He flashed a grin and cocked his head.

'Hi!' He beamed. 'Do you use traditional litho-printing in your projects?'

The question took a few seconds to feed into the Batcomputer and come back blank. During this process I performed a kind of exaggerated double-take.

'I... I'm sorry?'

'Do you use traditional lithograph printing for your books?'

Fuck fuck fuck. I was a publisher. Publishers have books. In a single, crashing instant, I realised that I hadn't thought this through at all. I'd done no research for my role – I hadn't bothered to work out even the most rudimentary backstory. What type of books did Fabulous Books Inc publish? What the fuck was traditional lithograph printing?

'I, uh... well.' I shrugged, staring off to one side. 'You know, we tend to deal with stuff like that on a, uh, on a project by project basis, depending on the, uh, project... you know?'

There was an awkward pause.

'Right... okay. Have you ever thought much about digital printing?'

I felt myself turning turtle under his gaze. He saw straight through me, I was sure of it. Any second he'd alert the guards and I'd be given the bum's rush.

'Well, you know…' I opened my body language, forced myself to make eye contact. 'We like to think of ourselves as pretty cutting-edge. Embracing and adapting and, uh, all that.' I flashed him a smile and he nodded like I was making all the sense in the world.

'Right,' he said, brightening, 'that's great, because what we're about is providing quality digital printing alternatives – digital printing has come on in leaps and bounds in the last few years, and it means you can combine the flexibility of digital technology with a finished product that's as good as, if not *better than* what you'd get on a litho press.'

As he talked, a second, shorter colleague appeared alongside him, all chubby and eager.

'What sort of print runs are you doing?' he said, rubbing his palms like a carnival weightlifter.

'Ooh…' I stroked my chin and tried to look like I was doing tricky mental arithmetic. Meanwhile, the first guy had ducked down behind the lectern, where he was assembling a fat, multicoloured selection of samples. I shook my head. 'Again, you know… it varies from project to project. I mean, we do all sorts, really. Everything you can imagine.'

The first guy stood and slapped the samples down on to the top of the lectern. 'Here's some examples of the kind of quality you can expect. It's well worth a look.'

His colleague nodded vigorously. 'Absolutely.' He picked up a gecko-green flier, wielded it importunately. 'You really have to look at this – it's really impressive.'

I reluctantly accepted the flier, made a show of turning it over, testing the veneer with my thumb.

'Lovely,' I said.

'Isn't it?' said the first guy, tickled pink. I could see his dumpy colleague reaching for a second sheet. If I didn't bail out now I was going to be stuck faux-cooing over print samples all day. What would a real publisher say in a situation like this? Well, for starters, they'd be too busy attending actual meetings to wander aimlessly amongst the stalls.

Meetings! That was it!

'Look,' I said, 'I've actually got an eleven o'clock. Do you have anything I could, uh, take away?'

The two men's expressions wilted to frowns. They began shuffling through the samples.

'Well,' said the first, 'we're not really…'

'We don't really have anything to give out, exactly,' said the second. 'Uhh…'

I took one of the glossy A4 brochures from a box on the lectern. 'How about this?'

'Ah.' The shorter, fatter guy exchanged a glance with his colleague.

'We're not really supposed to give those out.'

I allowed my grip to slacken slightly. 'Well, you know, I *am* interested, but I don't want to get you chaps into trouble or anything…'

The taller guy sluiced air in through his teeth. He glanced at my badge.

'Okay, go on then.' He hunched forward and whispered: 'Just don't let our boss know we let you have it!'

I tapped the side of my nose and chucked the pair of them a cheeky wink.

'Don't worry, boys – your secret's safe with me.' Slipping the brochure into one of my plastic bags, I began to walk away.

'Our phone number and email address are on the back if you need to get in touch,' said tall guy.

Shorty leant over the lectern and called after me: 'Feel free to ring if you've got any questions!'

I turned and gave them a camp little half-wave over my shoulder, adrenaline coursing through my system.

All at once my thirst was unbearable. Reeling from my lucky escape, I took the escalator back downstairs, towards my eleven o'clock with some beer.


Behind the bar, progressively larger champagne bottles were lined up left to right like babushka dolls – the smallest was about thirty-five centilitres, enough for two glasses, and from there they trended up towards a final, gargantuan megabottle the size of a diving bell. Each gold-foiled neck wore a red ribbon tied in a bow.

After hammering out an agreement, it seemed editors and agents could come down here to sign and celebrate. I wondered about the politics of picking a bottle – did different sizes correspond to different magnitudes of deal? Would supping from the second-smallest bottle feel somehow meagre if the folks next to you were supping on the third-smallest? And no matter which you chose, the megabottle was always there, squatting huge and obscene like a toad king, reminding you that your deal might be big, but it wasn't *mega*.

Luke hadn't showed and he wasn't answering his phone. Adhering to the fair's unspoken booze hierarchy, I opened my throat and chugged a frosty pint of Carlsberg Export. My shirt was damp with sweat and the beer went down at Slide Factor 10.

One of the biggest obstacles to my acceptance into refined social circles is that I grew up drinking with working-class people. Where I come from, it's perfectly acceptable for a fully grown man to guzzle cider until his eyes roll back in his head and he thrashes around on the floor like a randy elephant seal. Back home, a friend and I once resolved to settle a dispute over who knew the most about wine by dint of a competition – whoever drank the most bottles by last orders was the expert. I kicked off proceedings with a beautiful, buttery Sauvignon Blanc and awoke the next day supine in the grounds of a comprehensive school. Needless to say, when faced with selecting an apt aperitif, he now defers to me.

I wiped the froth from round my mouth and ordered a second pint.

The bar was certainly packed for eleven o'clock on a Monday morning, and not with tentative juice-suppers, either. Guys with the sharp, parsimonious features of eighteenth-century scriveners muttered terse responses into mobiles between long, luxuriant sips of Merlot. A few yards down the bar a skinny woman with a laptop bag was ordering a double gin and tonic. I could understand why a canny distributor might take a client for a couple of jars to soften him up but most of these people were drinking on their own. Perhaps they were pulling exactly the same ruse as me. Maybe there was a whole subculture of unemployed depressive polymaths who slunk from trade fair to trade fair, posing as cruise operators one week, restaurateurs the next, boozing in the dire womb of bland corporate anonymity.

I withdrew to the far end of the bar, finding a measure of privacy behind a large potted fern, and settled down to observe the Book Fair's ebb and flow.

With stands for all the major publishers in plain view, I couldn't help but think back to the agent's warning about not hustling for business. Naturally it held true for members of the general public, but I was different, wasn't I? I was no crackpot. I understood the industry. I had a *degree*. What if I were to sidle over to one of the stands and strike up a conversation? Nothing too forward, just a casual 'Hey, how's it going?' Then maybe, once we'd developed a rapport, I could mention my book, see if they'd like to read it. What if I implied it wasn't mine? That might be even better. I could act like it had been submitted to Fabulous Books Inc: *'But we're far too small fry for a killer title like this. We could never do it justice. You know... I suppose I could let you have a peek. That is, if you'd like.'*

As I pictured the buzz about this hot new manuscript spreading round the London Book Fair, my eyes began to close.

'Excuse me. Do you mind if we join you?'

The voice jerked me out of a teetering half-doze. I glanced up to see a guy turned out in a black pinstripe suit with a white shirt, red braces, and a red silk handkerchief poking from his left breast pocket. The fierce lights above the bar caught the sheen of perspiration coating his bald head and made it gleam. He was the best-dressed person I'd seen all day and his confident air had big cheese written all over it.

I straightened up and tried to look sober. 'Oh, of course. Please do.'

He came over to my table with two halves of lager, followed by a rotund, flush-faced lady with sprawling bladderwrack hair. I looked back down at my fair programme and pretended to read. The two of them took genteel sups of their drinks, smiling, saying nothing.

The man gazed off towards the café. 'Yeah. It's been all right, hasn't it?'

The woman, mid-sup, nodded vigorously. 'Mmm. Mmm.'

'Yeah.' He arched his back, then took another sip of lager. I could feel his eyes on my pale green 'PUBLISHER' ID badge. He coughed politely. 'So how are you enjoying the fair?'

I looked up. *Shit!*

'Oh fabulous, fabulous.' I flashed a deferential grin. 'You know, I've been around, had a few meetings... just snatching a quick break. It's a bit, uh, humid in here, isn't it?' I fanned my cheek with the programme and pulled a 'cor what a scorcher' grimace.

'Yeah,' he said, tutting and rolling his eyes.

I couldn't see his badge. 'So, uh... how have you been getting on? Busy busy busy, no doubt.'

'It's been quite successful actually.'

'Oh really? Good, good.'

'Yeah.' He gave a single-shoulder shrug. 'I've not been to the London Book Fair before.'

I hoisted an eyebrow. 'Have you not?'

'No. She convinced me to go.' He thrust a thumb towards his female companion. 'I've been promoting my book, trying to find a publisher who's interested in taking it on.'

'Your book?'

'Yeah.' He reached into his bag and pulled out a glossy paperback. The title read: *The Buccaneers Fight Fat Cat.* 'I'm an author, see.'

'Oh.' My grin hardened into a wonky rictus. 'Oh.'

'Hollis Brown,' he said, extending a palm.

'Tim Clare.' I pumped his arm with as much enthusiasm as I could muster. 'Fabulous Books Inc.'

Hollis Brown's journey towards the Publishing Dream began with the end of the world. It was 1988.

'I looked around, and I saw that global warming was coming. Right then, I realised that one of two things was going to happen – either we could all say "let's stop burning fossil fuels", in which case the whole global economy would collapse, and there'd be anarchy... or, the other route, we just ignore it, in which case the oceans would rise and continents would get flooded and the whole global economy would collapse anyway. It had to. So I looked at the facts and I saw that's where we're heading.'

But for Hollis, the world had already ended. His realisation of humanity's cataclysmic fate coincided with the breakdown of his marriage. Suddenly, the future he'd relied on for all those years was gone. Deciding that he was best off living for today, he quit his job in engineering, cashed in his insurance policies and went travelling.

'My job had always tied me to one place. I wanted to find what I could do while still going wherever I wanted to.'

He was browsing in a bookshop when he found his answer. At the time, he was preparing for a year-long trip to Thailand.

'And I picked up this Famous Five book, only it wasn't by Enid Blyton – it was a "cover version" written by some Danish bloke. I read the first page and it was total crap. I thought: "I could do better than this."' He bought the book and gave it to his daughter. She was seventeen, and had just quit doing her A-Levels to look for a job. 'Three or four months had passed and she was still unemployed so I said, "You've read a couple of these, surely you can do better than this. You're doing nothing – why don't you start writing Famous Five books?"'

About two weeks later, she gave him the opening two chapters of a book she called *Five Go To London*. 'And it was just like Enid Blyton's Famous Five. So I said, great, I gave her a thousand pounds and I said, "Forget about work, and get on doing this book."'

'Really?' I said. 'You handed her a thousand quid?'

'Yeah,' said Hollis. 'I just thought it was so good… and I was really involved in the story. It was quite powerful.' In *Five Go To London*, Anne, Dick, Julian, George and Timmy the dog were to confront a gang of thieves who steal the crown jewels. In addition to the generous writing bursary, Hollis decided he would protect his investment by personally coaching his daughter through every step of the creative process. 'Because I said to her, "If you're going to do this, you've got to do it right. First thing, how are the crooks going to steal the crown jewels?" And she said to me, "I don't know." So I said, "Well, then we're going to have to find that out." So we went to the Tower of London, and I had a look around, and I had a bit of a think and I worked out a way that someone could steal the crown jewels.'

The more he thought about his daughter's project, the more excited he became, and the more he chivvied her along, checking how much she'd written and suggesting ways the story might develop.

'And she never wrote another word.'

Not one to squander an opportunity, and with his Thailand trip looming, Hollis asked her to give him the two chapters she had written, and said that he would finish the adventure himself.

'Before then, I never knew I could write,' he said, with the grateful astonishment one might feel after hoisting oneself up on to the parallel bars for the first time and discovering an ability to turn triple somersaults in midair. 'I'd never written anything. If you'd told me to write a letter I wouldn't be very good at it. But you sit down, and you just... you get into the "mood" of it... and you're somewhere else.'

Hollis finished the book, and retitled it: *The Famous Five: The Final Adventure*.

'Wasn't attempting to end one of the most popular children's series of all time a little audacious for a first novel?' I asked.

He shrugged. 'Yeah, but it was brilliant. You can't go

better than stealing the crown jewels, can you? The whole point of calling it "The Final Adventure" was to stop other people from writing crappy ones.'

However, when Hollis tried to get it published, he discovered that the people who owned the rights to the Famous Five were not overly keen to release a book that cut off one of their most lucrative revenue streams.

Undeterred, Hollis switched tacks and created a new set of characters, the Buccaneers, who, like the Famous Five, consisted of four children and a dog. Freed from copyright constraints, he began to write adventures for them.

'I sent my manuscript to agents and editors but I just got it returned. It's very difficult to get anything read. The way the modern industry works, it's all about self-promotion. The thing is, you're asking people to put their money into your work. So to convince them you've got to show that you know how to sell a novel, so they know they'll get their money back.'

While he was in India, he had decided to pay to have over two thousand copies of the book printed. He handed me one.

The cover was a lurid combination of orange, blue and red, decorated with a pair of pencil crayon drawings – one of a cat's head, the other of a boy wielding what appeared to be a pool cue. The pictures were transcendently execrable. I mean, *God* they were bad. On the inside back cover was a grainy black-and-white author photo, and underneath, the legend: *HOLLIS BROWN – Film Star and Sausage*.

'Ooh… very nice,' I said.

Hollis had been trawling the LBF, trying to woo publishers. 'Since I got here this morning I've met three very positive people who took my book and said that they'd read it and get back to me.' He smiled. 'And you, of course.'

I felt my cheeks prickle with heat. 'Oh yeah. I'll definitely have a read.' I didn't have the heart to tell him that Fabulous Books Inc do not accept unsolicited submissions.

'I mean, this is Phase Two of promotion,' he said. 'I've been round posting copies through the letterboxes of people in the neighbourhood.'

'What, friends?'

'No, just, you know... local letterboxes.' He picked his bag up off the floor, and rummaged around inside until he found a ring-binder. He slapped the binder down on the table and began flipping through a thick selection of plastic wallets. He stopped on a piece of lemon-yellow A4, speckled with flowers. He prodded it with his index finger. 'This one's from the daughter of a guy at work.'

It read:

*Dear Hollis,*

*Thank you for letting me read your manuscript. I am nine years old and I really enjoyed the book. I like the book because it is sort of modern. I can tell it is modern because of the cars, phones, animals and places. My favourite person in the story is Elké and my favourite animal is Sheba. I also liked Skin. I chose those characters because they are all clever. My favourite bit in the story was when they were fighting with the bull. I read a lot of books and I really enjoyed yours.*

*From Clare Johnson*

Hollis began flicking through the binder and I realised that it was full of letters from children who had read his book. 'I've sent out about five hundred copies.' He stopped flicking and pointed to a pastel-pink letter. 'Look, here's one from Canada. God knows how it got over there.'

In the back of *The Buccaneers Fight Fat Cat*, Hollis asks the reader to send a letter of endorsement 'so that I can convince any publisher or agent to take me on to their books freeing my time to write many more adventure stories'.

'I just want to write more books,' he told me. 'I don't need lots of money. If I go back to India I can live on three quid a day.' Indeed, at no point during his pitch to me did he espouse the merits of the book, or even provide a rudimentary synopsis – his focus was on the fact that he really, really wanted to be an author, and it would make him really, really happy.

'For me, writing means freedom. If you can write, you can go and write on a beach. You just sit there, and you go, "Oh, this is nice, I'll write a book here." It's the best life in the world, if you can do it.'

I felt my lower lip curling in a weird fusion of dismay and contempt. I was remembering Helen Corner's credo of 'expectation management'. Here was a guy utterly bewitched by the promise of becoming a Big Author. He didn't temper his references to tropical idylls with self-deprecation or a know-ing smirk – for him, they constituted a sane and accurate appraisal of an author's life.

Of *course* they did. He had lived with these fantasies for almost twenty years. He had nurtured them, filling them with rich, vibrant detail until they were as real and as palpable as any memory – more so, in fact. He had spent so long amongst them, hiding from reality's mess and unpleasantness, that he could feel the warm, fine sand beneath his toes, see the sunlight glint firegold on the blue-green ocean, hear gulls wheel and cry against a cloudless, infinite horizon.

I knew how it felt to live like that – sweet ecstasy, for a while, but oh the crash.

Hollis finished his half-pint. 'D'you fancy a drink?'

'Um, no thanks,' I said, not wanting to get any more booze-raddled than I already was.

He turned to his companion. 'You?'

She nodded.

'This is another of my fans,' said Hollis, beaming. 'She's from the industry.'

The woman looked embarrassed and rocked her head from side to side. 'Well, not really anymore but I know a little bit.' She had a clipped German accent and her words came out in a sort of quavering half-chuckle.

'And what do you think of the book?' I said.

She glanced at Hollis. 'Oh, I think it's just so great.'

Hollis left to go to the bar. His friend told me her name was Ruth, and that she had worked in printing for about thirty years.

'So how did you come across the book?' I asked. 'Email?'

Ruth shuffled uncomfortably. 'No, my, uh… well, my ex-boyfriend actually was a colleague of Hollis's. He had been given a copy and he said would you like to read it and I said I would. I think Hollis is trying something so difficult. He needs some help. If I can help him, I'll help him, because I know a little bit about publishing.'

'What do you like about the book?'

Ruth looked up towards the ceiling. 'Oh, you know... the story. The characters. Everything.'

'Do you write yourself?'

'I'm trying, I'm trying.' Her ruddy complexion seemed to deepen and she concentrated on worrying at a white spot on the table with her thumb. 'It's very hard. That's why I have so much respect for Hollis. Writing a novel is the most compli- cated art form, I think. Lots of people can think of a story but to make it work and use characters and put it all together is very hard.'

I glanced over at Hollis, waiting by the bar. 'Are the two of you, err... going out?'

'Oh no, no.' She shook her head in a convulsion of denial, turning redder still. 'I just said I would help him out in any way I could.'

'Do you think he'll be successful?'

Ruth hesitated for a moment. 'Uh... yes.'

'What per cent chance would you give him?'

She frowned. 'Definitely, uh... fifty. If he, maybe, gets a good editor. I would change a few things. I don't know. He puts too many paragraphs in. They disrupt the flow. And some of his sentences... they are not quite right.' As she went on, her awkwardness seemed to leave her. She straightened up, made eye contact. 'And I would put more obstacles in, you know, because I think the characters need to meet difficult things which they overcome. In the story they just go from here to here to here and they do everything too easily. They need to face more obstacles. I think there is not so much plot.'

'Have you mentioned these things to Hollis?'

'Umm... we talk,' she said. 'We talk.'

At that moment, Hollis returned with the beers. 'All right there?'

I stepped back from the table.

'I'm, uh, actually going to have to go now. Very nice to meet you.'

Hollis held out a copy of the book. 'Take it and have a read. Let me know what you think.'

I accepted custody and forced a smile. 'Sure. Thanks. I'll be in touch.' Hollis's enthusiasm was endearing, but he had even less chance than me of seeing his literary dreams realised. He was just a really nice guy – too nice, in fact, so happy and genuine that no one had had the heart to tell him: *Mate, have you ever thought that writing might not be for you?*

I was trudging round the mezzanine, lost in thought, when my phone buzzed in my pocket. It was Luke.

'Tim!' he yelled over a burble of middle-class chatter. 'Are you here?'

'Yeah. I'm up on the first floor, by the Google stall.'

'Thirty-five fucking quid to get in! This better be amazing!'

I plucked an electric blue Google yo-yo from the box next to me and threaded the string loop round my index finger. 'Umm... yeah. I mean, it *is* a trade fair, so—'

'Where are you?'

'By the Goog—'

'I'll meet you by the top of the escalators.'

'Okay.'

*Click.*

I really wasn't up for it. Earls Court was packed, humid and dull, and it was scarcely midday. There was nowhere to sit down and my feet ached. I made my way towards the escalators, part-sozzled and grumpy.

And then, as I rounded the corner, I saw it – a long partition constructed from white canvas stretched across metal poles, and a sign that read: *International Rights Centre.*

This was it.

This was the place the agent had been talking about, the place he'd been so terrified I might find, the fabled arena in which publishing destinies were ripped asunder and remade in cold, hard profit-and-loss statements.

No, it couldn't be.

But it was.

The London Book Fair's International Rights Centre.

The Heart of the Publishing Dream.

# 8

*Come to the London Book Fair,* I'd told Luke. *You'll have an amazing time.*

The weird thing was, I'd been right. Luke had.

The same, sadly, couldn't be said for me.

It was late evening. Music pounded through the bar as I stood holding an expensive glass of red wine, surrounded by some of the biggest names in publishing. The whole pub had been hired for an exclusive party, and it was rammed. Guests had to shout in each other's ears to be heard. Monstrous potted plants in huge urns were surrounded by heaps of bags and coats. At the door, two bouncers stood with their arms folded, checking invites.

Just a few metres away, on the leather settee, Luke and Joe were engaged in enthusiastic conversation with bestselling author, Orange Prize winner, Booker nominee and – according to a list compiled that year for the *Observer* – fortieth most powerful person in UK publishing, Zadie Smith.

It had happened yet again. My friends had upstaged me. I tried to beat back my rising envy and disappointment, but I couldn't. When I gazed down into the surface of my drink, I saw a sour, scruffy failure glaring drunkenly back. No wonder no one wanted to talk to me. I was an outsider, and clearly bitter about it. At last, I was coming face to face with the ugly truth – not everyone gets to go into space. We can't all be astronauts.

Earlier, that afternoon, I'd scrutinised the octogenarian stewards from a distance, trying to project an air of patrician disdain rather than the razor-edged terror I truly felt. There were two openings in the canvas wall – one read 'Green Badge Holders' Entrance', the other 'Orange Badge Holders' Entrance'. So that explained the colour coding on my ID – publishers were verdigris-green, agents a garish lifejacket-orange. The white badges were for visitors, assistants – low-rung industry detritus, basically. Two check-in desks played host to sizeable queues – both bore signs that warned 'Pre-arranged Appointments Only'.

Sure there were meetings going on downstairs but they were all too safe, too damn chummy. It was exhibitors showing off their wares – superficial rapport-building, fluff talk, maybe pleasant discussions about the marketing and distribution of current titles.

But the International Rights Centre was different. It was closed to the rabble. It stank with mystery and purpose, the kind of place an agent might whip out the Next Big Thing.

Mindful of being clocked by the veteran guards, I departed for another circuit of the nearby stalls, pretending to be entranced by books with titles like *Gnomeworld* and *I Love Crochet* as I came round for another sweep. I returned just in time to see a cluster of suited punters getting turned away – and they had legitimate business within, no doubt. Holy shit.

One of the guards chucked a bushy-browed glance my way and what little remained of my nerve dissolved like an Alka-Seltzer. I slunk off to meet Luke.

He had been waiting. When I rounded the corner Luke stood posing in black suit and polished shoes, a cherrywood pipe hanging at a jaunty angle from the corner of his mouth. He removed it with a practised insouciance and affected a taut-jawed 'mah mah mah' laugh. At first, I thought he was doing an impromptu Popeye impersonation, and stared in mild confusion – along with several bystanders – until he gripped my shoulders and, pipe stem clenched between teeth, barked, 'We can't stop here, this is bat country!'

'Oh,' I said. 'Hunter S. Thompson. Right.'

Luke stepped back. 'I've put a lot of effort into this.' He gestured at his smart attire. Compared to me, Luke *always* put a lot of effort into his appearance. He knew the names of different fashion labels. He 'liked to spend on jeans'. He did his hair in front of the mirror, using styling products. I was the diametric opposite. My hair was a tousled thicket. Clothes freaked me the fuck out. I wore whatever was in reach and got dressed as if wrestling an invisible bear. 'I better appear in whatever you end up writing about this.'

'Oh, absolutely, mate,' I said, safe in the knowledge I'd never have to go through the tedious rigmarole of committing any of this nonsense to paper.

'So how have you been getting on?' We stood in the middle of the walkway and let people shuffle round us.

'Fucking hell… it's been a nightmare.' I patted my badge,

then leant forward sternly. 'I've nearly been rumbled,' I muttered. 'Some guys cornered me and—'

'Do you fancy a drink?' Luke glanced back towards the escalator. 'We can talk about this at the bar.'

I shrugged. 'Yeah, all right.' I looked at the clock. 'It is nearly lunchtime, after all.'

Back downstairs, Luke ordered two pints of Export and two double gin and tonics. As usual, I let him get the round in because as far as I was concerned he was the grown-up and I was the kid – that is to say, although he was a year younger than me, he had a wife, a mortgage, and a full-time career as a writer and stand-up poet, whereas I was the errant jobless lunkhead who still lived with his parents. And of course, with his writing partner Joel, Luke had that all-important book deal. The Publishing Gods had favoured him and I'd be damned if I wasn't going to weasel a little drinkypoo or three off the back of his good fortune. Besides, the temperature at the Book Fair was still rising and without a regular supply of cool beverages we both faced the very real possibility of heat exhaustion and physical collapse.

'I saw it,' I said, still a little awestruck. 'I saw the heart of the Publishing Dream. It's up there, behind that partition.'

'So let's go in,' said Luke.

I shook my head. 'Luke, Luke, Luke... one does not simply walk into Mordor. They have guards. *Old* guards.'

'But we've got ID.'

'The sign says you need an appointment. I saw them turning people away. Real people, with real jobs in publishing. What'll we say if they try to stop us?'

Luke snorted like it was the most obvious thing in the world. 'That we've got a meeting.'

'With who?'

'Whoever we do business with. What have you been telling people?'

'Uhh...' I took a bashful chug of my pint. 'I've tried to avoid that conversation actually. I've just kind of stonewalled.' I told him about my close call with the printing salesman.

'So you haven't even worked out a backstory?'

'I didn't expect anyone to call me up on it. I just thought... I don't know.'

'So who are we then?' Luke was also wearing a green badge – his fake ID proclaimed him director of Eggbox Publishing, a real small press set up by our (published) friend Gordon, who was also somewhere at the fair, meeting contacts.

'Fabulous Books Inc.'

'And what type of books do we do? We've got to figure this out.'

I pulled a face. 'I don't know. I mean, we must be a start-up, otherwise people would've heard of us.'

'Okay.' Luke focused on the swirling froth atop his beer. 'So we're a new, dynamic publisher...'

'A small press,' I said.

'Yeah, but we're trying to do something different...'

I nodded. 'We're two ambitious, young guys with big ideas...'

'*Really* big ideas...'

'Because usually, small press outfits end up being so...'

'...small?' Luke said.

'Exactly! And we want to be, uh...'

'...big?'

'Yes!'

'Really big! Fabulous Books is all about just producing really, really big books. You know... *big* books.'

'Big books.'

'Really big books. Literally. That's our schtick.'

I raised my plastic pint glass. 'To big books.'

'To big books.' We clinked pints then necked the rest of our lager. 'Get a couple more in, Tim.'

I wiped the froth from my moustache and beckoned the barman.

Several drinks later we set off into the guts of the Book Fair – our mission, to blend in and move amongst the genuine publishers until their inky funk rubbed off on us. Then we'd try for the inner sanctum.

I felt strangely at ease as we bustled past fellow fair-goers, and Luke appeared similarly comfortable in his new role, beaming with unlit pipe in hand. My gut buzzed with percolating booze and the colour and noise of the fair seemed just a touch more wondrous than before our pit stop.

We hung a left and I stopped dead. Lined up on the shelf in front of us was copy after copy of a book by none other than Steve Aylett – it was *LINT*, his faux-biography, but with a totally new cover involving a buxom maiden wailing in the clutches of some sort of snarl-faced merman. I stared, experiencing the faintest tickle of a reality crisis. I was used to Steve's work being weird marginalia – he was like the imaginary friend that only I could see – but here, it looked suspiciously like he was being published and promoted in a competent, exciting way. I glanced up and saw the title above the modest stall – Snowbooks.

'What is it?' Luke was frowning at me.

'Check it out,' I said, pointing to the shelves. 'Steve fucking Aylett.'

Luke picked up a copy of *LINT*. 'Oh, this is the guy you like, right?'

A chap stepped out from the stall. He looked even younger than us, and was wearing some crazy kind of hybrid suit jacket-cum-hoodie.

'You all right?' he said.

'Mmm,' I said. 'Just checking out *LINT*.'

He gave a slow nod of recognition. 'Have you read it?'

'Yeah,' I said. 'I'm a massive fan. I think he's fucking brilliant.'

'Oh, me too,' he said. He held out his hand. 'James.'

I took it and shook. 'Tim Clare. Fabulous Books Inc.'

'Yeah,' James went on, 'I've been reading his books for years and then I got to interview him for this online magazine I edited. I found out he didn't have a UK publisher for *LINT* and I signed him up for Snowbooks.'

'How's it been going?' I asked. 'He's had a bit of trouble finding an audience.'

To my surprise, James replied: 'Oh great. We got a big *LINT* window display set up in the Oxford Street Waterstone's, and it's in the Borders three-for-two. People have been talking about it like crazy on the Internet – the weird thing is, they've started claiming to have read novels by Jeff Lint, and they talk about his movies and stuff as if he's real. There's a whole Lint mythology that's started springing up spontaneously. It's really exciting.' He glanced at our badges. 'So anyway – what do you guys do?'

'Fabulous Books,' said Luke, tapping the air with his pipe stem.

I looked down at the floor. 'Yes.' Unfurling my fingers, I released the blue Google yo-yo, sending it spinning down towards the linoleum before a masterful flick of the wrist brought it back up into my palm. 'We do big books.'

Luke looked at James solemnly. 'You know... *big* books.'

James stared at us in a way that suggested he did not know.

'The thing is,' I began, then paused to send the yo-yo on another slow circuit, 'we thought to ourselves, modern books are getting smaller.' I realised I was slurring my words a little, tried to play it off as a kind of lackadaisical hipster drawl. 'Novels are slimming down, we're seeing little gift books, and what with computer technology you can fit hundreds of books in your pocket.' I glanced up to check he was getting this.

James nodded, his eyes flickering with barely suppressed fear.

Luke took up the baton. 'So we thought, you know, why not go the other way?' As he talked, his accent gradually climbed through the social echelons until he was affecting a kind of lilting, plummy purr with hints of posh Scot. 'Why not make "big" books? Not big in the sense of pumping a ton of cash into them or bringing in some celebrity author, but, you know, *big*. Literally big.' He spread his palms like a fishing boast.

'Mmm, mmm,' I muttered in sonorous concurrence. 'It's like–' I paused to spin the yo-yo again, mainly to buy a few seconds' extra thinking time '–we want to have the biggest books.'

'Sure,' said Luke. 'We've been looking round the fair today and, I mean, we've seen some pretty big books, but not *big*, you know? The biggest was maybe... *this* big?' He indicated a size of a few pitiful feet.

'There's this tradition of producing beautiful, glossy art books to sit on your coffee table,' I said, 'so we thought, what if the *book itself* was the coffee table? You know?'

James gripped his chin with thumb and forefinger.

'Yeah, yeah.' Luke closed his fist around his pipe and thumped the cherrywood bowl against his breastbone. 'We're looking at making books that take maybe two or three people to turn the page. Nobody else is doing it.'

James exhaled slowly.

'What authors have you got?' he said, after a pause.

I sighed. 'Well... that's not really our focus. I mean, our strategy is to concentrate on making the books big.'

Luke closed his eyes and nodded. 'Big books.'

'And then we feel that the authors will come to us. A lot of publishing revolves around the cult of personality, you know, and we want to bring the focus back to the book. That's where we want to invest our energies.'

'Right,' said James.

The rise and fall of the yo-yo was making me feel a little dizzy.

'Look,' I said, 'we've got to chip, but it's been fantastic chatting to you.'

James smiled, seeming a little punch-drunk. 'Likewise,' he said. 'Have you guys got cards I could take?'

Luke and I grimaced. We hadn't thought of that. We began to make a show of rifling through our bags.

'Think there's one in here somewhere...' mumbled Luke.

'I've given so many out today,' I groused. 'Might have run out.' I shook my head. 'Yes. Would you look at that. Damn shame.'

Luke looked up from his bag. 'Me too.'

'Not to worry,' said James. 'Here, you can take one of mine.' He handed us both a card. 'Get in touch, yeah?'

'Absolutely,' said Luke.

'Will do,' I seconded, and gave James a tip of the brow salute.

And with that, we strolled off, Luke chewing on his pipe, me attempting a 'Round the World' and nearly braining a PR girl with my yo-yo.

Back at the bar an hour or so later, we were in celebratory mood. We had glided through the Book Fair like carp, spreading the word about 'Big Books', creating a high-voltage buzz. Our new personae had left us brazen and elated – people listened patiently as we spouted patent bullshit. So this was what it was like to be a publisher!

Luke had the fair programme spread out on a table,

a fresh pint next to it. 'Hey – it says here there's a party on this evening.'

'We should go.'

'It says it's invitation only.'

I nudged him aside to get a look. 'Who's running it?'

'Canongate. So it'll be Jamie.'

Jamie Byng had recently been voted the thirty-fifth most important person in British publishing (by a panel that included his wife) and when I first met him, he was in his underpants.

It was the Hay Festival 2005, and I was filming the series for Channel 4. Early on Sunday morning, the film crew bustled me into a car and we drove off into the countryside. The director had decided that she would keep some parts of our schedule secret from me, so that I'd react with 'genuine spontaneity and surprise' to each of the key encounters she had planned. Unfortunately our caffeine-addicted soundman, Dai, a fantastic chap who looked like a craggy, Welsh Paul Whitehouse, kept blowing the surprise by talking in all-too-decipherable 'code', asking her things like 'So what time are we scheduled to meet, ahem, "Terry P" then?' on the same day that Terry Pratchett was speaking at the festival. On this occasion, however, Dai had forgotten the name of who we were off to see, so I remained clueless.

We pulled up in a field of swaying oilseed rape (which I happen to be fiercely allergic to), Dai miked me up, and I was instructed to creep towards a farmhouse at the end of a rutted dirt track, occasionally mugging to camera as if nervous and/or excited, rather than knackered, hay-feverish and baffled. For the purposes of the series, the story was that I'd received a 'tip-off' that a 'big cheese' was staying outside town, and I'd resolved to track him down. To this day I'm not sure what was more imbecilic – the stagey twists and turns of the supposed 'documentary', or the fact that I cheerily played along. I mean, I *assumed* that the participants had been briefed in advance and knew that none of these encounters were my idea. I assumed that they'd been told I was coming.

So it was that I crept up to the house and rapped on the door. I waited. No response. I knocked again. Out the corner of my eye, I saw my director tilting the camera up towards a top window. I stepped back from the house and followed its gaze, only to see a groggy Jamie Byng staggering out of bed in his underwear. In the few minutes it took him to dress, come downstairs and answer the door, he had transformed back into his usual debonair, unflappable self. With his long, curly hair, watchmaker spectacles and constant convivial swagger, his appearance brought to mind celebrity chef Hugh Fearnley-Whittingstall after a heavy night on the juice.

All through the interview that followed I desperately wanted to say, *Look, I'm sorry for invading your privacy, I swear to God this wasn't my idea, it was those twats behind the camera, I'm not some creepy literary stalker, honestly, and besides, you know, you look very good bollocko, you've got some lovely abdominal definition, seriously, fan-bloody-tastic, you must tell me about your workout regime,* but no, the camera was constantly on me, and thus I had to stay in character as a borderline-psychotic scrawler wannabe prepared to shatter all boundaries of common decency in a pathetic bid at recognition.

Luke, in his own parlance, knew Jamie 'to hug'. They had met at a couple of Luke's poetry performances and, now that Luke had a book deal, they tended to move in similar circles.

'We'll get invites, no trouble,' said Luke.

We decided to sidle conspicuously past the Book Fair's Canongate stall in the hope that we'd catch Jamie's eye and he'd call us over full of classy bonhomie. As we neared we saw that he was locked in an intense conversation with some thickly moustachioed dude in a tweed jacket. Luke looked uneasy. 'Uhh... I don't want to interrupt him. Maybe we should go get something to eat.'

I nodded. 'Mmm. Soak up a bit of that booze.'

'Yeah.' Luke glanced over at Jamie. 'We'll come back. Let's get some fresh air.' And we sloped off, out into the sunshine.

On our way back from getting sushi (crap sushi, as it turned out) we ran into Luke's publisher (and Joel's, and Joe's) smoking a fag on the Earls Court steps.

'All right, Simon,' said Luke.

'Hello, Luke! How are you?'

In the recent poll of British publishing's most influential players, Simon Prosser was twenty-eighth, an impressive seven places above the Byng-meister. His appearance was equally distinctive – a charming meld of Andrew Lloyd-Webber and Jarvis Cocker . Whether by accident or design, I seemed to be bumping and inconveniencing my way up the literary food chain.

'Good, I'm good, thanks,' Luke said. 'Me and Joel have been working on our rewrites for the book.'

'Oh great, great. Hey, you know I'm sure we'll be able to find some room in the promotional budget to sort out a great little launch party. You know, maybe get a gin company to sponsor it or something so they sort out all the drinks.'

I blamed the churning in my guts on the warm, stringy tiger prawns I'd just eaten. The mention of a launch party reminded me that time was running out. The London Book Fair would probably be my last chance to make that all-important breakthrough.

'That sounds fantastic. I've been thinking of some promotion ideas...'

As their conversation continued, I stood and listened politely, pretending not to care. I was torn between affecting a cool indifference and looking for an opportunity to say something urbane and striking that might impress Simon. Much as I resented the success he had conferred upon my friends, I craved that kind of recognition for myself. If I was really serious about my make-or-break mission, perhaps I ought to be vying for his favour. I fantasised about discreetly slipping my manuscript into his briefcase, then receiving an excited phone call several days later: 'Tim? I found your novel. It's absolute genius! The book of the decade. *So* much better than Luke and Joe's pedestrian efforts. I simply have to publish it. Please – name your price. Whatever it is, I'll double it.'

'Are you going to the Canongate party later?' Luke asked.

'Mmm, yes, I should think so.'

'Cos we were going to see if we could come.'

'Mmm.' Simon peered over his glasses sceptically. 'It's pretty heavily subscribed. Strictly tickets only.'

The conversation expanded to cover our friend Gordon,

whose first novel had come out the previous week, and John, whose non-fiction book Simon had just been reading.

'Tim's going to be writing something about the Book Fair,' he said.

'Oh, are you doing an exposé?' Simon laughed, turning to me. 'Am I going to appear in it? I'd better watch what I say!' He took a drag on his cigarette, grew suddenly pensive. 'You know, your friendship group... the talent among you all...' He exhaled. 'I mean, I don't think there's been a group with such talent in, oh...' He circled his cigarette, building up towards something big '...at least four years.'

I confess I felt a twinge of disappointment at this unexpectedly modest estimate. Still, being part of the most talented literary group since mid-2003 – that was something, wasn't it?

'Wow,' I responded, not wishing to appear ungrateful.

'All of that creativity's great,' Simon went on with Bunterish enthusiasm. 'All of you sparking off each other and inspiring each other.'

'Glad-handing each other up the greasy pole, you mean,' I said.

Simon laughed. 'And *I'm* the greasy pole!'

I suppressed the image rising unbidden from the recesses of my mind and smiled politely.

Back inside the Book Fair Luke and I did another conspicuous fly-by of the Canongate stall, but Jamie was nowhere to be seen.

'Maybe he's gone to lunch,' said Luke. 'Let's get a beer.'

\*

Fear crackled in the pit of my stomach. All my senses were heightened; I felt an almost preternatural connection with my surroundings. The alcohol had stripped away the restrictions of my socially conditioned conscious mind, unleashing something atavistic, instinctual – a kind of second-sight.

I took a deep breath. 'Are you ready?'

At my shoulder, Luke nodded. 'I'm ready.'

We were up on the first floor, our gazes trained on the entrance to the International Rights Centre. 'Remember,' I said, 'we have every right to be here. This is the most normal thing in the world for us.'

'Nice and cool,' said Luke.

'It's now or never.'

'Let's do this.'

We discreetly bumped knuckles, then began to advance with what I hoped looked like composed professional intent. I tried to avoid making eye contact with the elderly bouncers without appearing to be doing so deliberately. As we closed the distance I felt my heart bang and my lungs burn. Sweat collected round my collar. If they stopped us, we'd say we were late, that we had an appointment. Who with? Fuck it, we'd angrily blurt out a random name and hope they'd back down.

Two metres from our target, an eight-strong Japanese delegation appeared from nowhere and swarmed towards the entrance. On impulse I accelerated and attached myself to the back of their group, ducking slightly. The guard to our left was busy giving directions to some lanky streak of piss with a gel-slick centre parting; the guard to our right cast a cursory glance across the advancing throng. He frowned as we began funnelling into the entrance. He peered at the badge of the Japanese woman closest to him. I held my breath, creeping forward inch by inch, the yo-yo tight in my clammy palm.

Someone standing by the reservations desk said: 'Excuse me.'

The second guard turned to respond.

Luke and I shuffled past.

We were in.

We stood at the back of the IRC, sipping at steaming black Americanos we'd bought from one of the many 'Coffee Points' situated around the floor. I had asked for a shot of caramel in mine, drunkenly quipping: 'I can't make big deals without my caramel.' The server had smiled politely, as if she dealt with this type of asinine twattery every day of her life.

Row upon row of tables spread before us in a pale geometric vista. Numbered pillars marked the domains of various agencies, people from Spain, Germany, France, Australia, Japan, America and Great Britain, wall-to-wall stiff, grey suits.

This was where the fair's low rumble emanated from. This was where the magic happened. This was the sharp end of the industry, the place where destinies were forged and false hopes came to die. This was the sick nexus of truth I'd been jonesing for. This, surely, was the Heart of the Publishing Dream.

'This is shit,' said Luke, slurping his coffee.

'Err...' I gazed out across the ocean of dull negotiations, trying to think up an objection. I could not. 'Yes. I suppose it is.'

'It's just a bunch of business people in suits.'

'Fuck,' I said. 'I think you're right.' I blew on my coffee, went to drain it then changed my mind and flung it into the bin. 'Let's get out of here.'

We marched towards the way out. I was suddenly very tired.

Riding the escalators back down I felt the strange throb of disappointment. The IRC was supposed to be my break-through moment. I had expected to see something amazing, or horrible, some arresting revelation that would force an irrevocable shift. My self-imposed quest required an inspiring denouement or repugnant, traumatic encounter, but the IRC had simply been dull.

We were heading for the exit when I heard a cry of 'Luke!'

'Jamie!'

I looked up to see Luke and Jamie Byng locked in a manly embrace. They disengaged, and Jamie and I shook hands in the conventional manner. I'd bumped into him once or twice since the TV interview, and each time I'd felt hugely awkward. I could never work out whether he remembered me.

'How are you doing?' said Jamie.

'Oh great, great,' said Luke. 'Busy day?'

'Absolutely manic.'

Luke made his play. 'I, uhh, hear you're having a party.'

'Yeah, yeah,' Jamie said. 'I'll be doing a bit of DJing, like I did at Port Eliot.'

The Port Eliot Lit Fest was a small festival that took place every year down in Cornwall. The previous summer, Jamie had appeared in an evening slot as 'DJ Jamie Byng', working the decks in the main tent.

'I remember that,' I chirped up. 'As I recall you needed help slotting the records on to the spindle.'

Luke shot me a dirty look.

Jamie shrugged. 'Yeah. I was pretty smashed.' He turned back to Luke. 'So, look, are you guys going to come?'

'Sure – where is it?'

'The Fat Badger. Starts at eleven.' Jamie reached into his pocket and retrieved three fliers. 'Here you go. You're very lucky. These are my last ones.' He handed them to Luke. 'Anyway, I'd better go.'

'Okay, see you later.'

I gave Jamie a friendly nod then Luke and I continued towards the exit. We waited until we were outside the building, glanced back to check that we weren't being watched, then high-fived and started boogying wildly.

We stood outside the Fat Badger, waiting for Joey D, who we had offered our spare ticket to in exchange for a sofa to crash on. He had decided to come by bike. As we teetered out on the pavement, somewhat sullied by several hours in the pub, we saw at least ten people without tickets get turned away by the door staff. One very important-looking, crisp-suited guy got out of a taxi, brandishing his ticket.

'My colleague doesn't have one,' he said, pointing to the chap next to him, 'but that's not a problem, is it.' He inflected the end of his sentence as an assertion rather than a question.

The woman on the door shook her head. 'Sorry. No entry without a ticket.'

The man's nostrils flared. He swatted at the air with his

ticket. 'But we've just come all the way across London! Jamie invited us personally!'

The female bouncer shrugged. 'Sorry.'

The man folded his arms. 'So you're absolutely refusing to let us in, despite the fact that we've been invited?'

'*You* can come in,' she said, then nodded at his colleague, 'but he can't, unless he's got a ticket.'

'Right.' The man spun on his heel and marched back to the taxi. 'Fuck this. This is absolutely ridiculous.' He clambered into the cab, beckoned for his ticketless companion, and the two of them sped off with what remained of their dignity.

Naturally I felt a delicious flush of *Schadenfreude*. As Luke and I stood huffing curls of water vapour into the streetlights' amber glow, a notion took shape in my stout-and-lager fuddled brain. Maybe I'd been concentrating on the finger instead of the moon. Sure, the International Rights Centre *facilitated* the Publishing Dream, but that didn't mean I could expect to find said Dream within its boundaries – that was like trying to find the essence of rhythm inside the hollow of a drum.

And now, here we were, with invites to the hottest literary party in town. I mean, this was how it was supposed to be, wasn't it? Swank, wine and intelligent chatter leavened with a judicious helping of blag-proof exclusivity. If I was really set on schmoozing my way into print, tonight was my best bet.

But why would any of these people want to speak to a nothing like me? My vision blurry, I regarded the partygoers with a boozy, cynical swagger. Look at all these cliquey upper-middle-class freeloaders with their skiing holidays and old-school networks and parental handouts. Publishing, a meritocracy? Heaven forefend! Why, without the class system people would rise and fall based on ability alone! Perhaps this would be exactly the shock I needed – a ringside seat at an ugly publishing mafia love-in. It would be conclusive proof of what I'd spent years denying – that the industry was a grubby self-satisfied cartel echoing with the haw-haws of crapulent philistine toffs.

I was on the point of breaking out into a mumbling tirade when Joe turned up on his racer.

'All right, chaps?' He chained his bike to a lamppost and Luke doled out the tickets. Brandishing them, we strolled past the bouncers with smug insouciance, and entered the party.

Inside the Fat Badger the air was a torrid stew. I spent a few awkward minutes twatting passers-by with my backpack until Joe very sensibly suggested I take it off. On the far side of the room, past the bar, Jamie was in deck-spinning mode as promised, and, judging by the dance floor throng, he was doing a sterling job.

Joe and Luke had started chatting to people they seemed to know, so I began to edge through the crowd towards the bar. Glancing back, I saw Simon, Joe and Luke's publisher, making his way outside. I looked again and – Christ on a billy bike – was that Zadie Smith?

Sure, I'd never read any of her books, but as far as literary parties went she was a primo zeitguest. I tingled with excitement, and imagined Joe and Luke doing the same. It felt bizarre – just a couple of years ago we'd all been penniless students, swapping our modest scribblings, chatting about how great it'd be to see our work printed in a poetry magazine or in some local anthology. I remembered Joe's story of sitting at a table in Hay-on-Wye with his parents, glow-cheeked at the mere *presence* of Ms Smith nearby. Buoyed up with a sense of occasion, I pushed the boat out and bought a bottle of Merlot.

When I turned back round, Joe and Luke were sitting on a red leather sofa in the far corner, happily chatting away to Zadie like old chums.

Which, as it turned out, wasn't a million miles from the truth.

A bit later, when they were done, I got the chance to question them on it.

'Oh my God,' I gushed. 'That was so ballsy. What did you do? Did you just go up to her and say "hi"?'

Luke frowned. 'No. I've met her before, at one of my poetry gigs.'

'Really?'

'Yeah.'

I turned to Joe. 'What about you?'

'I met her at a drinks thing a while back. We chatted for a while then. She's really nice.'

My mouth worked for a few seconds without making words. Eventually, I blurted: 'Why didn't either of you tell me?'

Joe shrugged. 'Yeah. I suppose it never really seemed that unusual to me.'

Both he and Luke seemed surprised that I found it at all noteworthy. I couldn't believe it. I stared back at them, part of me thinking they were winding me up. *We used to write poems together in my student bedroom!* I wanted to yell. *How can you look so bored when you're living our dream?*

I didn't want to admit it, but another part of me was scared. I felt stupid and gauche for getting so excited. Joe and Luke seemed so natural and at ease in this environment, but I felt like I was back in the party tent at Hay-on-Wye, staggering from gaffe to gaffe, a pissed, needy pariah who evidently did not belong.

'Hey, how you doing?'

I turned around and it was James, Steve Aylett's publisher.

'Oh... hi,' I said. *Oh shit*, I thought. 'Nice to see you again.'

James leant in so I could hear him above the music. 'You know that stuff you were saying earlier... about the big books?'

'Uh... yes?'

He narrowed his eyes. 'Were you winding me up?'

'Umm...' I no longer had the intellectual resources to sustain a lengthy charade. 'Yeah, pretty much.'

He nodded, totally unsurprised, and I felt like a complete tit.

'Why?' he said.

I shrugged. 'Now that you mention it, I'm not sure.' I scratched my head, embarrassed. 'I guess... I guess we just wanted to fit in. I've been looking for the "heart" of the publishing industry. We snuck into the IRC. I thought we'd see all these huge deals going down... but it was crap.'

To my relief, James seemed to find this funny. 'Yeah – people don't really do that many big new deals at the Rights Centre anymore. It's mostly meeting international publishers, talking about established deals – bookkeeping, really.'

'Oh.'

'Well, you know, you guys should stay in touch anyway. Let me know what you're up to.'

I told him I would and, feeling like I'd had a lucky escape, wandered off to find somewhere to sit.

So it was that I found myself perched on the arm of a sofa, as far into the corner of the room as it was possible to get, supping meekly on a glass of red while my friends schmoozed and chortled. Watching people chat, joke and dance I felt myself regressing back through adolescence until I was twelve again, lingering clumsy and stutter-gobbed on the fringes of the school disco while sporty boys strutted and peacocked and pranced.

I was crap at a lot of things, but I'd always thought of the book world as the one place where I fitted in. Surveying my surroundings I realised that, here too, I was an outsider. I didn't work in the industry, and I didn't have a book coming out. I was no more a part of this world than Hollis.

I thought back to our meeting. I recognised so much of myself in his vainglorious aspirations, and that frightened me. Worst of all had been the misgivings Ruth had dared not share with him – she made me realise that, in all probability, most of my friends who had responded to the Book with praise and optimism had also been harbouring a whole raft of clandestine doubts. The feedback had always been vague: 'Yeah, I enjoyed it. It's really good fun.'

The more I thought about it, the more I recognised my complicity in the transaction – I'd deliberately solicited opinions from the people I knew were least critical and most likely to lavish me with cockle-warming compliments. I'd made it plain that the Book was my Big Project, that I'd staked a lot on it, and that the Book and my self-esteem were lashed together in a do-or-die three-legged race. When I'd pushed people for constructive criticism, I'd felt secretly resentful when they actually provided it, even in its mildest form. When my agent had got back to me suggesting changes, on some level I'd felt betrayed. Where was her old enthusiasm? Why didn't she believe in me anymore?

Was this sinking feeling the beginnings of an answer to my big question? Were my efforts paying off? During my travels, I'd seen avarice, unhappiness and idiocy, and recognised these tendencies in myself. The publishing industry was not the resplendent Sugarcandy Mountain I had spent so long fantasising over. I was not the preordained literary megastar I had imagined.

Yet these realisations made me no happier. Indeed, I felt worse. A lot worse. Even during my bleak crack-up with Dad in the car, some hived-off section of brain had been fighting back, stridently asserting that things would come good, because they had to, didn't they, because that was the plan for me. Now I had seen, *really* seen, that thousands of people nursed similar delusions – only the nature of a delusion is that you never recognise it as such, you never even see it as a dream or an ambition, it's just something that is *going to happen* sooner or later, like the kettle boiling a minute or so after you flick the switch, or *EastEnders* being on TV when you get home from work.

A dream is like a tool for helping someone live their life. It has a whole bunch of assumptions and expectations about the way that the world works hardwired into it, and you make decisions on what to do and how to invest your time based upon that framework. Finding out that your assumptions and expectations are wrong can be unpleasant, traumatic even, because from there it's a logical step to discover that – probably – all your efforts have been misguided too. Most people filter the information all around them to exclude feedback that doesn't fit with said expectations. Confirmation bias is a short-term way of feeling safe and in control.

The problem with the truth is that it's got no obligation to set you free. It is what it is, and those who pursue it do so without knowing whether they're peering into a pretty kaleidoscope or the gob of a loaded cannon. Ignorance might not be bliss exactly, but the right kind of stupidity can be a damn sight more palatable than a tête-à-tête with stark, unvarnished reality.

Back at the start, I'd known my dream might be absurd, but I hadn't thought about what I would do if my mission to renounce it proved successful. I'd imagined things would just, sort of, work out. Another incorrect expectation. Another jolt of unpleasant feedback.

It's said that the closer you get to the light, the bigger your shadow becomes. Perhaps I felt bad because I was nearing my goal. Maybe my delusions were digging in, in preparation for their Last Stand.

I thought about the IRC, about what Luke and James had said – how it was 'just a bunch of business people in suits', just 'bookkeeping'. All my life I'd been running away from the grey vacant world of paper-pushing, clock-watching monotony, petrified that one day I'd wake up and find that I'd turned into my dad. I looked at the world of work and nine-to-five routines and imagined myself in a scratchy suit, doing the jaw-jaw-jaw of mindless office politics and really believing that it was important, that any of it mattered, Christmas parties and lunchtime pints, evenings in front of the TV with the missus and kissing the kids goodnight on their clammy foreheads before settling down to break the back of the perennial paperwork mountain, promotion, missed promotion, yearly holiday allowance and a gym membership and finding the time to paint the garage and a gradual estrangement from joy and amazement and frivolous stuff like the wonder of being alive because that doesn't pay the mortgage, does it, slow death and occasional unwelcome insights into the futility of it all, late-blooming regret, chronic back pain and waking up at 3 a.m. to piss, gazing into the out-of-focus toilet bowl wondering where all the time went, wondering what the lesson was supposed to be, wondering why I never just ran off into the fields to play.

Was trying to become an author just a different colour of hamster wheel?

'Excuse me.'

I blinked out of my glum reverie.

'Excuse me.' An attractive girl with long, wavy brown hair stood in front of me, trying to get my attention.

'Me?' I pressed a palm to my chest.

She nodded. 'Yes.'

I brightened. 'Oh. Hi.' Perhaps I had been too hasty.

She looked past me. 'Can you just move for a second so I can get my bag?' She pointed to the heap of coats and handbags next to the sofa.

'Oh, right.' I got to my feet. 'Sorry.'

She nudged past me, looking annoyed. Bass thumped through the soles of my shoes. The Fat Badger rang with laughter.

# 9

I woke to find a mug of tea on my bedside table. The mug had a cartoon picture of a startled hen on it. I dragged myself upright and took a slurp. The tea was cold. Dad had probably left it there for me hours ago.

I checked the clock on my mobile phone.

12:20 p.m.

Afternoon already, and I wasn't even out of bed.

I pulled on my jeans from where they lay puddled on my carpet, grabbed the top T-shirt from the pile Mum had washed, ironed, folded, and left in my wardrobe. Stomping downstairs, I found a note on the kitchen worktop:

*Hi Tim*
*Gone to Weston*
*Back around 3*
*Half a scotch egg in fridge*
*Love Dad x*

I heard mewling, then Jonesy padded in from the lounge.

Jonesy was the family cat. He'd come to live with us as a kitten, when I was in sixth form. Knowing that I got pretty nervous around dogs and worried that I'd kick up a fuss, my parents brought him over from his birthplace, my auntie's house, in secret. I think they hoped that even a temperamental curmudgeon like me wouldn't have the heart to expel a lovely little soot-black kitten once I'd seen him padding clumsily around the living room.

The truth was, I was pleased to have a new addition to the family – but I took pains to milk the scenario for all it was worth, insisting that I didn't mind Jonesy's arrival, but I was 'saddened' that my parents hadn't felt able to be honest with me. Their guilt had earned me at least a fortnight's worth of lifts and lowered expectations.

As it had turned out, on the day he came to stay with us, it was me who spent the best part of half an hour sitting on the cork-tiled floor of our kitchen, patiently coaching the shivering kitten out from his hiding place behind the dishwasher. Over the years, his list of aliases had expanded until it sounded like the roll call for a brutal, prolific hip-hop collective: Jonesy, Wonesy (pronounced 'wonze – ee'), Bonesy, Jonesymon and Wonezachu (both oblique references to popular pseudo-bloodsports cartoon franchise *Pokémon*), the derivative forms Wonesymon, Bonesymon, Bonezachu, Flonseymon and Wonesyflon, moving on to more outré constructions like Wiggy, Wid-wid, The Wig, The Kitty, The Kit, The Mog, Moggo, Mr Chub and Lovely Boy, to name but a few.

'You all right, Wiggomon?' I said, scooping him up in my arms like a baby. I stroked the arch of his back, while he glanced placidly around, purring. Things seemed all right for Jonesy. He just pottered about the place, sleeping in warm patches, occasionally regurgitating a shrew carcass on to the settee. I remembered reading somewhere that domestic cats never reach full psychological maturity – behaviourally, in most ways, they remain kittens their entire lives.

Jonesy began to wriggle. I put him down. He strolled over to his bowl, pushed his face into the mound of dry food, and began munching contentedly.

I thought about making myself a sandwich, but it seemed like a lot of work. I put on a coat, a scarf, and one of Dad's woolly hats, and headed out for a walk.

The day was overcast, but muggy. Soon I was sweating, and I had to take off all three and carry them under my arm. I walked past my old secondary school, down into the high street. I didn't like to admit it, but the London Book Fair debacle had hit me hard.

My quest was based on a lie. I'd kidded myself I was a pragmatist – that whatever the outcome, I'd be happy. But now the pendulum was starting to swing towards giving up, I could feel myself resisting. I still clung to the fantasy that I could turn this spectacularly round, and part of the reason, I realised, was that if I *did* quit my dream of being an author, no one would see it as an achievement. I craved recognition, and as much as I was beginning to see how unhealthy that addiction was, I wasn't sure I was capable of surviving without it.

And was it really so bad to want the approval of my peers?

Walking through town, I passed a Costa Coffee, a *Big Issue* seller, a McDonald's, all new additions since I'd been away at university. I wandered past the leisure centre into the brand-new marina development, a bizarre collocation of twee, maritime-themed terraced houses and huge luxury flat developments that made it look as if a defunct seventies cruise liner had run aground in Disneyland. There were multi-storey apartment complexes, underground car parks, even neon-lit wine bars full of leather sofas, laminate wood flooring and chrome.

I stood at the end of the quay, watching the grey Severn heave and plunge. Even my backward, knuckle-dragging yokel hometown was doing better than me.

The night before, sitting in my bed with only my Nintendo DS and a half-eaten box of choccy fingers for company, I'd phoned Joe.

'All right, mate?' I'd said. I could hear from the noise of traffic and wind that he was outdoors.

'Yeah – just on my way to the pub. What you up to?'

'Oh, you know...' I brushed biscuit crumbs from a valley in my duvet. 'Just chipping away at stuff. And you? Any more news on the book?'

'Uh-huh. Sold the film rights.'

'Yeah. I'd heard. That's... great.'

'Thanks. Also had some nice chats about potential covers. I'm looking forward to seeing what they come up with.'

I gazed down into my lap. 'That sounds really fun.'

'Yeah. Be nice to see you at the launch party, mate.'

'Right.' I was too drained for jealousy. Just the thought of being resentful made me feel knackered.

'Hey, look, I've just arrived, so I'd better go. Speak to you soon.'

'Yeah,' I said. 'Bye.'

But really, what I'd wanted to say was: *help*.

*

Since I'd been back living with my parents in Portishead, my social life had withered like a limb in a cast. Occasionally, in a half-arsed attempt to stop myself going stir crazy, I'd venture out the house and go to the local pub, to sink pints with old schoolmates who'd never left in the first place.

But what started out as ironic, self-aware parochialism soon metamorphosed into a crushing routine of booze and booze and booze and nothing to say to each other. I discovered, to my surprise, that it was possible to be too drunk to walk or see, yet still feel utterly bored.

At first, I blamed my hometown friends. We'd be sitting around a table, slurping cider while the Sky Sports News tickertape rolled silently by on the plasma screen behind us, and I'd go: 'So yeah, I've got a few poetry gigs coming up in London,' or 'You guys ever watch many Akira Kurosawa movies?' or 'Man, I made this kick-ass lamb risotto last night,' and there'd be this long, stodgy silence, so I'd repeat myself, like I was talking to an elderly relative: 'Guys? I said I've got a few poetry gigs coming up in London,' and maybe, eventually, I'd get a few nods and the odd 'Oh right,' in return, then somebody would change the subject to Jean-Claude Van Damme movies or Nu Metal bands or tits. I told myself these people were insular cretins who had no concept of the world outside the valley, who'd probably fade like spectres if they strayed beyond the town limits.

But after a while, I started to listen to what was exiting my mouth, and I realised that even *I* wasn't interested in most of the crap I came out with. I didn't pick topics likely to be of mutual interest and I didn't ask how my friends were doing –

I chose areas in which I had expertise, then did my best to show off. It became obvious my main goal in any conversation was to emphasise how *different* I was to the people around me.

I was an author. I had a destiny. I was *better* than this.

Later on the day of my walk to the marina, I called my old school mate Jukesy and suggested a night on the cider. We met down the Red Lion, occupying a table parked between a fruit machine and the gents' toilet we'd both thrown up in on numerous occasions. When I arrived, I was wearing my yellow-tinted aviator glasses and a brown corduroy jacket.

Jukesy looked me up and down. 'All right, mate? Nice to see you're still rocking the "Fear and Loathing meets supply teacher" look.'

'All right, Jukesy.'

Feeling chewy and nihilistic, I drank to an efficient rhythm while we played pool. I don't even like pool, but it gave us something to do between gulps. Soon, we were both plastered.

As I've explained, in secondary school we both thought of ourselves as insouciant geniuses in a slough of boss-eyed thickies. However, in sixth form, our arrogance caught up with us. We found the jump in difficulty tough, having spent so long skiving off homework, and both dropped to E grade students. But while I eventually knuckled down and rallied, Jukesy seemed to give up. He barely scraped through his A-Levels, took a year off to work shifts in a factory and drink, then went to university, where he did lots more drinking but very little work until at last he dropped out. By the time I moved back to Portishead, he was living with his mum and doing shifts behind the bar in a pub two minutes' walk from his house. He had no money, no plans. The only areas in which he excelled were boozing and playing *World of Warcraft*, an online role-playing game, in which he invested about forty hours a week. Every so often, he would be offered a job opportunity – a chance to move away, to try something new – but he always seemed to find an excuse not to accept, often at the last minute.

I'd never asked him about it because it had never seemed my place to question his life choices, especially given my own disastrous run. But seven or eight pints in, my despondent, booze-addled brain decided that now was a perfect time to get to the bottom of things. It'd be fine. I knew how to be tactful.

'Mate,' I slurred, 'I never asked you.' I looked down at the table, using my fingertip to draw strange glyphs in the thick film of grease. 'You know, like, how you used to be clever, but then you sort of gave up and now you don't do anything? Uhh... what happened?'

He took a sip of his pint. I expected him to respond with a 'What the fuck are you talking about?' or at the very least a jokey 'Nah, I'm fine – uni was bullshit' brush off.

Instead, he thought for a moment, then said: 'The thing is, the difference between you and me was you always knew what you wanted to do. Yeah, I was clever and everything, but I never knew what I wanted to do with it. I never knew what I was supposed to be doing with my life.'

'Uh, right.'

His answer stayed with me all through the clammy tremors of the following day's hangover. I felt a bit guilty about reducing one of my oldest mates to a cautionary tale, but still – was I setting myself up for disaster? Just like those high-achieving kids I'd read about, Jukesy had rebelled against the weight of expectation. He had chosen to stop trying rather than be seen as average. But it hadn't killed off his need for recognition and achievement – that desire had just been sublimated into trivial, non-academic tasks. He was an accomplished stunt-drinker, notorious for being unable to refuse a challenge when faced with an audience – I once watched him down an entire 70cl bottle of Sour Apple Funky Monkey just because someone said he couldn't. And online, in his alternate persona as a gnome mage in *World of Warcraft*, he was a powerful and successful member of the community, wealthy, skilled – someone to call on when you needed help. He put as much time into the game as most people invest in a full-time job, and it seemed to have become an important part of his identity.

What would I do with myself if I quit trying to be a writer? Would I really be able to follow a career in something else, to *be* someone else, and throw myself into that role with zest and aplomb? Or was I about to cast myself adrift from the only thing that stopped me from spending my days slouched in front of a computer, racking up imaginary achievements in exchange for imaginary money and imaginary acclaim?

# 10

Being stuck in Portishead was giving me a nasty case of the jibbers, so I did my usual routine of upping sticks and heading off to London, to crash on a succession of friends' couches for a few days. Doing so only made me feel more fraudulent and unreal. Everyone had jobs, social lives, routines. By contrast, I didn't seem to have a purpose anymore – my life felt like a botched experiment that had got its funding cut partway through. My quest for resolution had tanked. What was I going to do with myself?

Surfing the net on a mate's laptop in the wee hours, I stumbled across an ad for a comedy night in central London. To my surprise, one of the acts was Steve Aylett. He'd never struck me as the kind of person who'd relish live performance, but there it was.

A thought began nuzzling its way into my brain like a grub. Maybe I should go to the show. Finally, it'd be my chance to meet him face-to-face. Perhaps he'd offer me some sustaining (yet characteristically sardonic) pearl of wisdom. Perhaps he'd shuffle uncomfortably, wary of the wild-eyed, hand-wringing stranger who seemed to have nominated him as some kind of personal messiah.

But as I sat there in my boxer shorts and curry sauce-stained Powerpuff Girls T-shirt, my face bathed in the blue glow of the laptop screen, I knew there was no chance of my being mistaken for an unhinged stalker. After all, we had a relationship now. He was my friend. And I was his biggest fan.

The gig was in a hard rock/metal bar just off Tottenham Court Road called The Crobar. As I sat in the poster-plastered interior, nervously fingering my wine glass, my fevered, nerdy mind worked out that the name was an anagram of 'Orc Breath', an epithet I supposed the heavy-set clientele, with their frayed Def Leppard T-shirts and animus towards personal hygiene, might be rather satisfied with. Besides myself, there were ten, maybe twelve other punters in the bar, and I began to realise that my nerves weren't solely to do with my upcoming encounter – I was also anxious for Steve. Stand-up seemed a bit of a departure for him. What if my literary hero was shit?

All throughout the compere's awkward, shambling introduction and the weak, feedline-punchline routine of the first act, I tried my best to laugh in the right places and look like a normal audience member, all the while feeling exposed and ludicrous. I wanted to pass this off to myself as a caper, another scrape that my apparent inability to plan ahead had gotten me into, but the joke was wearing thin. This was my life – my actual, only life, and I was utterly at a loss for what to do with it. I had nowhere to go, nothing better to do really than set myself picayune errands whose pointlessness always became manifest barely minutes in.

'Ladies and gentlemen, Steve Aylett!'

The announcement snapped me out of my self-pitying fug. I glanced up to see Steve up on stage, wearing an old-man latex facemask. He balanced his round, mole-spectacles over the mask then attempted to take a sip of beer through the mouth. Then, in a reedy, faltering voice, he launched into a long monologue about being a guest star on *The Muppet Show*.

The premise of the entire routine was that his character, Lord Pin, didn't understand that the Muppets were just puppets.

'What people don't realise,' he wheezed, 'is that as soon as the cameras were off, it was as if all the life drained out of them.' He recounted sneaking into a broom closet for a sly nap, only to step on the head of a spare Kermit puppet. 'His skull burst with a terrific report... It was rather like when you tread on a light bulb.' He went on to describe his hysterical panic at believing he had accidentally killed the star of the show.

On paper, the gag seems a little thin, but I'm sorry, I really am... I know I'm an horrendous fanboy, I know it's nauseating and predictable, but I loved it. His halting deadpan delivery made the material seem all the more silly. I laughed until my lungs ached, and the more I tried not to make a spectacle of myself, the worse my convulsions became. Maybe the strength of my reaction was partially due to relief. Maybe you would've sat there stony-faced.

After he'd finished the monologue, he reached for his throat and peeled off his face. Perhaps my expectations were too high, but the mask lifted away to reveal what must rate as the Most Normal Face in Britain. In fact, his face was so incredibly normal as to be almost unsettling. With his neat hair and circular glasses, he looked like a stereotypical cowed bank clerk.

To finish his set, he did a reading from one of his books, this time, not in character. As himself, he was less assured, but still entertaining. He finished, the small audience clapped, and the compere announced a fifteen-minute break.

This was my chance. With one of his books in my hand, I rose from my seat and navigated my way through a maze of chairs to his table.

'Uh, I... hi,' I started, promisingly. 'I, uh... I really enjoyed your performance.'

He looked up from his chair, his expression a study in terrifying neutrality. He said nothing.

'I, uh... I was wondering if you'd sign this book.' I brandished a copy of *The Inflatable Volunteer*. 'Um, yeah – my name's Tim Clare. I wrote to you? You did an interview for me?'

'Ah yes.' Though his words implied recognition his face remained fixedly neutral. 'You said you were going to send a finished version back to me to edit.'

I didn't remember ever saying that but I didn't want to displease him so I said, 'Oh, yes, of course.' There was an awkward pause, then I handed him the book. 'So.'

He took it, got out a pen. 'I think this is a really good one,' he said.

'Is it the one you wrote in like ten days or something?'

'Uh... no.'

He handed me back the book. 'Thanks,' I said. 'I'll, uh... I guess I'll be in touch then.' And with my teeth clenched, I shuffled back to my seat. At my table, I opened the book to see what he'd written. There was no message, just a biro picture of an apparently furious pig. I glanced back across at his table. The rumpled mask lay before him like a flubby pancake. Above slamming drums and crunching power chords, I heard him say to a friend: 'Actually, I feel a lot more comfortable with the mask on.'

The music faded out and the compere was back on stage, introducing the night's final act. The guy was a replacement for the advertised headliner, who'd pulled out at the last minute. He clutched the mic and regarded us all with an insouciant, mildly drunken grin. He got about two minutes into his scripted material before mentioning that he had a one-year-old daughter and his wife was in the process of divorcing him. We waited for a punchline that never came. This, apparently, was not a 'bit'. Sensing an atmosphere, he departed from his set entirely, and started chatting to members of the audience, attempting ad-libbed gags about menstruation, while returning ever more frequently to the subject of his impending divorce, often with a heavy sigh, then a silence. Twenty long minutes passed in toe-curling intimacy.

I left the bar feeling weird and drunk.

I was disappointed I hadn't managed to impress Steve with some witty remark, but the more I thought about it, the more I realised I'd genuinely expected that our encounter would trigger some kind of epiphany. I'd convinced myself that meeting him in real life would have a power and immediacy that would finally decide me.

It was less than a month until Joe's big launch. Clearly, I was getting desperate.

Not watching where I was going, I stepped straight into a whirlwind. A crowd was blocking the road, and because I wasn't paying attention I got sucked into its slipstream. People seemed to be shifting in some kind of weird spiral. I realised there had to be an epicentre, and craning my neck, I saw it.

In the middle of the road, hemmed in by jeering gawkers, Amy Winehouse was cowering, alternately swiping at the air or shielding her face. She looked confused, appalled. Cameraphones flashed, and as she tried to turn away from her tormentors so the crowd rotated to follow her, some moving clockwise, others widdershins, wheels within wheels, studded with faces trying to catch her eye and yelling: 'Oi! Amy!' It felt like she was an axle turning huge, fleshy cogs in slow motion.

Caught in her orbit, I could only watch, pretending I wasn't complicit in the ugly ritual. Somebody with an arm on her shoulder was vainly trying to appeal to the mob: 'C'mon, guys, leave her alone. She's just someone trying to get home.'

It was a dismal scene to witness under the influence of two glasses of dirt-cheap Vino Collapso, so I can only imagine how horrific it must have been on a shitload of crack – probably like a musical choreographed by Hieronymous Bosch. Eventually, as my part of the circle rotated past the bit of road I needed to be on, I broke free.

I spent my walk to the Tube thinking about what I'd just witnessed, pondering Amy Winehouse as a fascinating cipher for the Faustian vagaries of fame, without once considering the possibility that she might have been a human being who just wanted to be left alone.

As I made my way through the tunnel towards my platform, a skinny, long-haired busker sat cross-legged, knocking out a really solid George Harrison cover on a tatty jumbo acoustic. I walked past thinking 'nice one', and respecting the guy for having the humility and commitment to his craft to still be out there, performing for indifferent punters late on a Sunday night. He'd looked happy – like he wasn't bothered that this wasn't a stadium vibrating with ardent fans, like he didn't care that the *NME* wasn't carrying a six-page spread asking him about the state of the music industry, like he was just grateful to be able to sit and play guitar for people, and sometimes come away with a bit of beer money.

Almost at the end of the tunnel, I stopped. Why didn't I ever support people like him? Why did I always grouse about injustices and my own lack of recognition, while rarely making the effort to praise and reward the bands and writers and artists that I liked? How was *he* supposed to know that I thought what he was doing was cool?

So I turned around, walked all the way back to where he was playing, bumping into a couple of people on the way, and I chucked a two quid coin into his guitar case.

He looked up, and smiled – a big smile that included his eyes. 'Cheers,' he said, and nodded.

'No worries,' I said, gave him the thumbs up, and strolled away.

Taking my seat on the Tube, I felt a weird elation rise within me. *This* was what I'd been doing wrong. I'd spent so long asking what the world could do for me, agonising over what *I* was owed, what *I* needed, I'd never stopped to think about the hundreds, thousands, tens of thousands of other aspiring writers, musicians, performers and artists out there who needed help, too. Why had I wasted so much time thinking of them as rivals? These people were my allies. We were in it together. We shared aspirations, values – we could help each other.

And by that simple act of giving two pounds to that busker – *two* pounds, mind, the biggest denomination of coin – I'd made a substantial deposit in my karmic bank account. What goes around, comes around, I told myself. This was just the beginning. I had a new attitude now – an abundance mentality. Every day, in innumerable small ways, I would give back to the artistic community, nurturing and supporting my fellow creators, and, sensing this, the cosmos would support me. Things would start to fall into place. A newfound positivity would guide my actions. I'd write a masterpiece, I'd sell it, then during a witty, self-deprecating TV interview I'd recount the moment where I stopped, turned round, and gave two pounds to a busker, the moment where I reconnected with the universe and healed my old jealousies, the moment that led me to international stardom.

As the train sped up, so my excitement ramped. I'd made up my mind! But of course, if I was going to be a success, I'd need a new novel to sell. I'd start as soon as I got home! What would it be about? I had to get this right. Maybe I needed to exploit my new sense of interconnectedness to ask the artistic community for inspiration. It wouldn't do any good to be selfish about this. I had to genuinely want other artists to do well. There was no faking out the universe.

But did I *really* want other people to do well? After all, I was already thinking about my *own* problems, my *own* triumph. How would I start giving back? How would I know if I was sincere or not? What if it turned out I was wrong? What if I got home, and tried to write, and nothing came out? What if I never managed to write another word again?

By the time the train reached my stop I was sweating and my heart was palpitating. How the fuck was I going to produce a bestseller? What if I messed this up?

I clutched at my hair and let out a snarl of frustration. Nice one, indeed.

I was back to square one.

# 11

A week later, I was slumped in front of the television, flicking through channel after channel of drab, imbecilic wallpaper, when I happened upon a *Panorama* documentary. Imagine my surprise when I discovered that one of the subjects was none other than the most powerful person in publishing, Amanda Ross! My eyebrows shot upwards like a pair of electrocuted caterpillars.

The documentary focused on the now infamous controversy over television quizzes that used premium rate phone numbers, claiming that winners had been selected before lines had closed, allowing service providers and production companies – such as Amanda's Cactus TV – to reap a hefty profit from unwitting punters. Richard, Judy and Amanda had all publicly disavowed knowledge of this 'irregularity', but the public relations firestorm was continuing. By the end of the programme, I finally understood what Amanda had meant by 'Icstis' – ICSTIS is the Independent Committee for the Supervision of Standards of the Telephone Information Services, and I could only surmise they had been giving Amanda and her cohorts a proper bollocking, hence her misinterpreting my sympathy with regards to her 'taxing time PR-wise'. (ICSTIS later fined the show's phone service provider a then-record £150,000, citing a 'reckless disregard for viewers'.)

I thought this might be a good time to get in touch:

Hi Amanda,

How are you? All systems go, no doubt! I just watched that Panorama documentary – what a lot of rot! Some of these crackpot socialists can't stand to see free enterprise at its most prosperous! Well, I suppose there will always be some nay-sayers trying to make mountains out of molehills. Don't let the buggers get you down! Of course I realise now what you meant about 'coping with icstis' – apologies for my awful gaffe! I suppose I'm just not as media-savvy as a 'big noise' like yourself!

Anyway, I just wanted to wish you all the best and try to chivvy you along in making arrangements for this brief chat we talked about in our previous correspondence. I'd love to be able to include some of your expert thoughts and opinions in the project and, as I said, I'd be sure to paint you in the most flattering light possible. Let me know when you've got a spare half hour coming up – I'll buy the coffee! Chin up!

Your friend,

Tim Clare

I hadn't heard anything from Amanda for ages, and I doubted that my mischievous show of moral support would reignite our correspondence. Still, feeling as low as I did, it was nice to lose myself in ludicrous fantasies about suddenly becoming 'well in' with the most powerful person in publishing, and having her sort me out a massive, life-changing book deal.

Days passed. Still no word from Amanda. At last, I cracked. Bollocks to it. I had nothing left to lose, so I went all out, in one final bid for attention:

Hello Amanda,

Long time no email! Haven't heard from you in an absolute age – I suppose you've been maintaining radio silence while this whole silly mess about 'ripping off viewers' blows over.

In my darker moments, I worry that you may be getting cold feet about our meeting. Am I being paranoid? Or perhaps this is how the 'top dogs' in media operate, eh? Making me sweat a bit, maybe!

I realise that your job requires you to maintain a cool, professional distance at all times, so let's cut the shilly-shallying and get down to brass tacks. The benefits of meeting me for a brief interview are as follows:

1) Your public image will undergo a 'nip and tuck' (sorely needed, I'm sure you'll agree!) – I can promise to slant any written content so that you come out smelling of roses!

2) You will have the opportunity to impart your incomparable expertise to the indifferent, swineish multitudes – God knows they could use a kick up their collective backsides!

3) You will get valuable one-on-one interview experience – the dog's never too old to learn new tricks, I always say!

4) I will buy you a hot beverage of your choice, plus a cake or pastry of your choice, up to a total value of five pounds sterling.

I'm sure your keen entrepreneurial acumen is telling you this deal sounds too good to be true. Let me assure you, this is a genuine offer!

Have a quick peek in your diary then let me know when you'd like to
meet up. I can't wait!

Your friend,

Tim Clare

Her reply came quickly.

Tim

I haven't arranged a meeting because in all your long correspondence you haven't actually told me what it's about or if it's an
interview, who you would be writing for?

Yes I am mad busy, so can't proceed unless I know what I'm
letting myself in for.

With best wishes

Amanda Ross

Her response put me in an awkward position. After all, I rather
felt I *had* told her what I wanted to talk to her about – yet it
would hardly do for me to accuse her of being obtuse. More-
over, I wasn't convinced that the truth – the actual, unvarnished facts – would prove all that palatable. I wanted to speak
to her because, well, I hoped that either I could use her to
blag a publishing deal, or she'd put me off writing for ever.
She picked the 'authorised' Robbie Williams biography *Feel*
as one of her recommendations, for God's sake. Meeting her
would either finally secure me the leverage I needed to make
my dream a reality, or it would confirm what I desperately
needed to believe – that the publishing industry was a soulless
cartel, and that literary stardom was, at best, completely

random, at worst, proof that you were writing empty, toothless pap.

But in these uncertain, postmodern times, what *is* truth?

Hi Amanda,

Terrific to hear from you – but enough of my drool-gobbed sycophancy, here's the skinny on our meeting: I'm writing a book[1]. Excerpts will undoubtedly appear as syndicated articles[2] (in 'quality' dailies only, of course!) and it's being adapted for radio[3]. A TV series has been mooted[4] but I'm not sure I can handle the fame – I mean, I love the limelight as much as the next guy, but getting papped scratching my arse in the privacy of my own bedroom via telephoto lens? No thank you!

Various entities have chucked their cash-stuffed hats into the ring[5] – as you can appreciate it's all very sensitive so if you're keen to find out details I'll need you to sign an NDC[6]. Not that I think you'd snitch, Amanda! Business is business, after all.

---

1 Well, I *had* written a book. But more than that, I wondered if, with a contribution from Amanda, I might have enough material for another one.
2 This was an opinion, rather than an actual genuine full-blown bona fide fact. Nobody had read anything I'd written – but I felt convinced that her involvement would change all that. Well, okay – not convinced, exactly. Hopeful?
3 By me. In my head.
4 See above.
5 Well, as good as. I'd chatted to lots of publishers, agents and editorial assistants throughout my journey. Most of them smiled, shook my hand – if that's not a tacit way of saying, 'Let's do business, big shot,' then I quite genuinely don't know what is.
6 This was a piece of media jargon I picked up when I edited the English script for a Hungarian computer game. It stands for Non-Disclosure Contract, a document companies use to prevent freelance staff blabbing about a project before it hits the shelves. If Amanda asked to sign one, any chance of meeting her was over, because, of course, there were no secrets for her to keep undisclosed. I hoped that by floating a term like NDC, I could imply a big media-business style buzz while making further investigation slightly too inconvenient to be worth her while.

My book's about authors, getting published, and the industry that surrounds this dream. I've interviewed many people in the book trade, and let me tell you, you cut quite a controversial figure! One editorial assistant described you as 'the Pol Pot of publishing'[7]! Utter balderdash, I'm sure. Tell you what – when we meet up, I'll pass on her name and you can make the necessary phone calls. She'll be out on her ear before you can say Waterstones three-for-two[8]!

In any case, as I've said before, I'd like to set the record straight vis-a-vis Amanda Ross, i.e. your good self. Just a brief chat so you can give your side of the story. I think people will really like the real you! I know I do!

Also, my offer of the hot beverage and cake or pastry up to a total value of five pounds sterling still stands. But it won't last forever[9]! How are you fixed for this Wednesday? We could get this thing in the can!

Your friend,

Tim Clare

Sure, I had been creative in my presentation of the facts, but I didn't care anymore. I had made my final bid. There was nothing to do but wait, and pray.

An hour later, I received this:

---

7 In my job writing manuscript critiques, I was essentially working as a freelance editorial assistant. I was the one who had described her in this way. Little did I realise how significant this five-word epithet would become.

8 I mean yes, strictly speaking, I'm not a 'she' – but surely, in today's enlightened society, we've gone beyond reductive notions of gender essentialism. Tim Clare is at once a 'he' and a 'she', and neither; emotionally, intellectually, politically and spiritually, I am a hermaphrodite. Aren't we all?

9 In this, I was utterly sincere. Start backing down in front of these big media types and they'll piss all over you.

Hi

I have to do it now just to get that name! How about tomorrow at 11am at Cactus?

Ax

I was blown away. Somehow, my reckless stupidity had paid off. Across a series of emails, we had progressed from the frosty officiousness of 'Dear Tim', through the straightforward 'Tim', to the breezy, almost affectionate 'Hi' – and to think I now merited the signoff 'Ax'! As far as I could tell, she was ending her email with the shorthand for 'Amanda, kiss' – the kind of kiss you'd use to greet a *well-liked associate*.

I had made it. I was in.

Without stopping to consider the consequences, I shot back a jubilant reply:

Amanda, it's a deal!

# 12

'So what are you doing in the Big Smoke, Timmy C?'

Me and Joe sat in the American-style diner, scoffing break-fast and drinking knee-tremblingly strong black coffee.

I drizzled maple syrup in a loose figure of eight over my pancakes and bacon. 'Oh, uh... Kind of like an interview.'

'New job?'

'Err... something like that.'

My meeting with Amanda was in a couple of hours. Already, the huge amount of caffeine I'd consumed was making my hands tremble. I still didn't have the guts to admit to Joe what I was about to do. Back when I'd tried to get my novel published, everyone had watched me fail. All of my friends knew how much I'd wanted it, knew that I'd given it my best shot, so there had been no pretending that I was fine, no sparing my blushes. This time, if I crashed and burned, I wanted to do it in secret.

'What's the latest on the book?' I said.

'Review copies have gone out,' said Joe. '*GQ* is going to print an extract. I've been doing a few interviews. All very exciting. Launch party's going to be fun, I expect.'

I flinched. 'Yeah.'

I sawed through my breakfast, pushed a syrupy swatch of

meaty pancake into my gob. There was no sense in kidding myself. I *really* wanted what Joe – and Luke and Joel and John and Gordon and all my other friends – had. I wanted to make a living doing what I enjoyed. I wanted other people to read the stuff I'd come up with and think it was cool. I wanted to be interviewed on the radio and serialised in magazines and photographed for newspapers.

But so far, my best had been nowhere near good enough. And as Hollis had shown me, you can want something with all your heart, you can try with all your might, but that doesn't mean you'll get it.

Meeting Amanda Ross was going to be the single biggest opportunity of my life. If I could only charm her, get some mark of approval or piece of advice, I might finally be able to join my friends and hold my head high once more. But if she took a dislike to me... well, it sounded like she had the clout to get my name blacklisted throughout the entire UK publishing industry. Even if I wanted to struggle onwards, a bad encounter would salt the earth so heavily I'd never work in this town again.

Amanda was number one – if she couldn't help me, no one could. This time, it really was make or break.

# 13

Sheltering beneath the awning of the Divaani Mini-Market, I gazed through shifting walls of drizzle across the road towards the entrance of Cactus TV. What the hell did I think I was doing?

Her email had said 11 a.m. It was twenty minutes to. I wanted my arrival to be punctual, but not so early that it was clear I had nothing better to do. My stomach was churning. I had woken at half-five that morning with a terrible clutching sensation deep in my gut. I tried to tell myself it was the curry I'd made the previous evening, which had contained five bird's-eye chillis and an entire garlic bulb, but deep down I knew it was old-fashioned nerves.

I wiped a film of rain from my brow and flicked moisture from my hair. On the Tube journey from breakfast with Joe, I'd scribbled down some questions in my spiral-bound note-book. I hoped my notebook and pen would add a much-needed air of legitimacy to the whole ludicrous enterprise.

I belched and tasted bacon. Oh God. I couldn't greet the most powerful person in publishing with a waft of porky breath. I ducked into the mini-market.

Inside, it was warm and dry. Nag Champa incense burnt in a polished bronze dish above the counter. The man at the till beamed as I entered. I grabbed a roll of Trebor Extra Strong Mints and smiled back.

I wondered if I ought to bring Amanda some kind of tribute. Though I doubted she would ask me to make good on my 'hot beverage and cake' offer, I felt it might be safest to have a jokey gift on hand just in case things got hairy and I needed a humorous means of placating her. Unfortunately, in the field of impromptu presents for publishing industry big shots, the Divaani Mini-Market seemed conspicuously understocked.

As I searched, a far graver concern nuzzled its way to the top of the heap – a scenario that, in my gleeful reverie, I'd not even considered. What if Amanda was serious about my revealing who had called her 'the Pol Pot of publishing'? What was I supposed to say?

I'm a rubbish liar at the best of times, but this was a high-pressure situation. I feared that I'd panic under cross-examination and blow the whole ruse. If the London Book Fair had taught me anything – and it seemed likely it hadn't – it was that when undertaking an elaborate, pointless deception, I needed to work out a story in advance.

Thinking fast, I devised a contingency plan. I would tear a page from my notebook, and on it write a name. Then I would fold the page into quarters, and place it in my pocket. If Amanda brought up the question of who had slandered her, I would nod, reach into my pocket, produce the folded paper, and place it on her desk. I'd smile archly and say: 'Now, I'm going to put this here… and it may turn out that when I leave, I forget to take it with me. Furthermore, it may turn out that there's a name written on it. But I don't know anything about that, right? It's just a bit of paper I accidentally left behind.' At this point, I would wink conspiratorially, and she would laugh at my silly bit of pantomime, and drop the subject.

But what name to write? I'm not a particularly vindictive person and, even after all my rejections, there was nobody in the publishing industry I wanted to stitch up. My eye drifted to the heaps of newspapers next to the freezer section. The headline on the back of one sports section read: JEWELL JUMPS AS PEARCE IS PUSHED.

*Do a Keyser Söze!* I urged myself. Thus inspired, I wrote 'JEWELL PEARCE' in block capitals, tore off the page, folded it over on itself once, twice, and shoved it into my pocket.

Buoyed up by my ingenuity, I quickly solved the gift problem as well, deciding to purchase a Kinder Egg. It would offer Amanda a toy, a surprise, and some chocolate – that's three gifts in one, all for under sixty pence. Shrewd, Mr Clare. Very shrewd.

As I bought the mints and egg, I glanced at my watch and realised it was quarter to eleven. The wait was finally over. It was time to get busy.

'Hi.' The tanned receptionist's taut-grinned greeting came with a flotilla of implicit statements. In a single syllable it said: *I'm here to help. I hate my job. Who are you? I'm very busy. I'm very tired. Do you have an appointment? Please don't turn out to be a nutjob.* And, of course: *Hi.*

'Hi,' I replied, then added, as insouciantly as possible, 'Yeah, I've got an eleven o'clock with Amanda.' I elided the words 'appointment' and 'Ross' because, *yeah, you know, I*

*have so many appointments these days that saying 'appointment'
gets kind of boring, and we all know who Amanda is, right?*

'Okay.' The receptionist did not look startled or incredu-
lous. She glanced down at the appointments book on her desk.
'What's your name, please?'

'Tim Clare.' Sounding casual about your own name is
particularly easy.

'Okay. Would you like to take a seat?'

I went and sat down on one of the two sofas. To my left, a
large TV was showing an episode of *Trisha*. A woman was
sobbing and Trisha was looking concerned and sympathetic.
The caption beneath them read: *My daughter had a baby with
child murderer Ian Huntley… aged just 16.* I couldn't make out
what either of them were saying but there was lots of quiet,
serious speaking punctuated by ripples of audience applause.

The receptionist was on the phone. She too was talking
quietly – I couldn't discern anything from her conversation
beyond: 'Yes… yes… okay.' She put the receiver down and
rose a little to look at me over the desk. 'Would you like something to drink?'

'Oh, yes please.'

Moments later a second, equally tanned assistant appeared
from the far door. She stopped in front of me, placed her
palms on her thighs then bent at the waist, as if stooping to
address a toddler.

'Can I get you anything?' she said, smiling. She was rather
attractive, and this made me nervous.

'Just a tea, please.'

'How do you take it?'

'Um, milk and one sugar, please.'

She straightened up, turned on her heel and left the room. I leant back into the sofa and waited.

And waited.

Outside, in the forecourt, large goldfish swum through long tanks. I could see through a glass door into an empty adjoining room. It had bare breezeblock walls and a concrete floor. It was full of large objects under dust sheets, the only exposed item a red plastic pedal car. The reception area itself was sparse and rectangular, with white walls and a very high ceiling. Potted cacti stood sentry in the corners while irides-cent, multicoloured cylindrical lampshades hung from the ceil-ing, shimmering like weird jellyfish. On the glass coffee table in front of me stood a huge glass bowl full of individually wrapped mint chocolate éclairs. I did a quick scan and estimated that there were at least three hundred. I do not like mint chocolate éclairs. I think they are a bit of a fringe pleasure.

I checked my mobile phone for texts, then switched it off. I took out my notepad and reread my questions. They weren't very good – just fluff talk, really, but I couldn't even take in the words. My pulse was racing. I took a deep breath through my nostrils, and thought I could smell BO. I glanced up at the receptionist. She seemed absorbed in her work. I took a surreptitious sniff of my armpit. It reeked. Though the room was cool, I was perspiring heavily.

At last, my tea came. I accepted the striped mug and saucer with clammy fingers. I blew on my tea. This was ridicu-lous. What was I so afraid of? She was just a person. I had to calm down.

Yet, in the back of my mind, I was envisioning an elaborate sting. I had not won Amanda over at all. She had invited me here to prove a point. Any moment the phone call would come through and the receptionist would announce that Amanda had cancelled on me.

I sipped my tea. I am very fussy about tea-making – I am prepared to start arguments if certain principles are not adhered to – but this particular cup was very good. I expect I would have found the piping hot beverage soothing, if it weren't for the fact that there were no soft furnishings to soak up noise, and so every time I returned my cup to its saucer a loud *chink* echoed through the room.

I wondered if Amanda had made a mistake. Perhaps she thought I was someone else. Perhaps she would take one look at me and realise I was a time-wasting fraud. I really needed the loo, but I didn't want to go in case I missed our meeting. I couldn't imagine the crushing humiliation of arriving late because I'd disappeared for ten minutes to take a dump. No, I'd just have to clench my buttocks and cope with it – the very definition of professionalism.

I picked up my notepad and again tried to reread my questions. The TV was showing advertisements for loan companies. I found the white grins and swirling colours vaguely hypnotising, and had to force myself to look away. Loan ads were for the unfortunate and the indolent. They were meant for people in dire financial straits, people who had no real job. I was at work. I was an adult, with skills, aspirations and prospects.

My tea was still too hot but I finished it in a single slug. Moments later, the door opened.

'Tim?' The assistant addressed me at the respectful distance one might afford a minor electrical fire. 'Are you ready?'

'Yes,' I lied. 'Absolutely.'

I stuffed my notepad into my coat pocket then stood up. I followed her out of the room and along a narrow corridor lined with doors. Above our heads was a series of identical bulbs in identical conical lampshades. As I passed underneath I indulged in a spot of creative visualisation and told myself that they were beaming self-confidence and charisma into my body, and thus with every pool of light I walked through I grew stronger, more assured, *Come on, son, you can do this...* and at the same time I was thinking: *No matter how bizarre or brilliant or horrific or terrifying this turns out to be, after today it'll just be part of my life, just something that happened.* My heart slammed against the walls of my chest.

We walked up a steep flight of stairs then turned right. The assistant opened the door to an open-plan office and stood to one side.

'Just go straight through to the room at the end,' she said, nodding towards a door on the opposite side of the room. In my peripheral vision I saw several people clustered around a computer, and realised that I had no idea what Amanda looked like. God! What if I introduced myself to the wrong person, or worse, ignored her?

Leaking sweat in copious, stinky rivulets, I thanked the assistant and marched across the office, staring straight ahead lest I catch anyone's eye. Immediately a pair of tousled yappy dogs scampered from beneath one of the desks and started circling my ankles, barking.

Though the majority of characters in my failed novel were humanoid canines, including the protagonist, I'm not a dog person. In fact, after being chased by a dog when I was very young, I spent most of my childhood petrified of them. Though dogs and I have now achieved something of a rapprochement, I still get nervous around them under certain circumstances – like when I'm seconds away from the biggest meeting of my life and they burst out from behind a waste-paper basket.

I knew that the optimal reaction was to drop to one knee and enthusiastically ruffle the fur on either pooch's mischievous head while play-growling things like: 'Hey! How are you? Eh? Eh? Are you pleased to see me? Are you pleased to see me? Grrrr! Come on, you! Grrrr!' But as soon as I extended a tentative palm the dogs began hopping up on to their hind legs and I jerked away, grinning, scared shitless. I wanted to pet them, just to prove I thought they were adorable, but I knew if I tried and one went for my hand I'd shriek like a pitchforked banshee.

In the end, I affected a slow, shuffling retreat, all smiles, mumbling: 'Uh... hey, uh... boy?' Eventually, I managed to back into the room at the far end of the office. Someone snapped a command and the dogs retreated. I looked up and saw Amanda walking towards me.

I'm not sure what I expected. She'd been so built up in my mind as a legendary, elusive powermonger, I'd half imagined her whirring out of the shadows attached to some kind of Davros-style mobile life support unit, her scalp adorned with a complicated array of electrodes while plastic tubes pumped preservative into her horribly ruined throat. As with the moment of Steve Aylett's unmasking, I was almost disappointed. She was slightly shorter than me, with shoulder-length blonde hair and a big smile. She seemed *normal*.

'Hi,' she said, and extended an arm. 'Tim, is it?'

'Uh, yes,' I stammered, momentarily unable to remember. She walked into the room and closed the door.

'Take a seat,' she told me. 'I've got half an hour and then I really have to go. Things are mad busy.'

'Yep, yep.' By now I was shaking. I sat down at a small table. Paperbacks filled the shelves on either side of the room and sat in heaps on the floor. Richard & Judy Book Club posters adorned the walls like long medieval tapestries, proudly displaying a roll-call of authors catapulted to megasales and literary stardom. Next to the door lay two dog baskets, mercifully empty.

Amanda sat opposite me. 'So remind me – who are you writing this for?'

'I, uh...' My hands quivered as I tugged my Dictaphone from my pocket and set it down on the table. 'Well, I'm on a sort of quest. I've been speaking to editors and agents and writers and failed writers and, you know... all sorts of people involved with the Publishing Dream, and people who've been let down by it.'

Amanda looked perturbed. 'Oh dear...'

'No, no.' I found myself shaking my head, suddenly desperate to please. 'It's not an exposé or anything. I, uh...' As I spoke I tried to get the Dictaphone to start recording. It refused. 'Sorry. I can't get this thing to...' My fingers were slick with perspiration and kept slipping off the buttons. 'God. It was working earlier... It just doesn't seem to want to... Oh sugar... Sorry...' I fiddled and tapped, rattled and tinkered, but the Dictaphone was suddenly unresponsive as a pebble. 'Of all the times...' I smirked apologetically but Amanda seemed genuinely concerned.

'Are you okay?' she said. 'Is there anything I can do to help? Do you want me to go into the office and see if I can find you a battery?'

I glanced up, my face a mask of stricken anguish. Amanda was smiling.

And that was when I realised the most powerful woman in publishing was a nice person. Bit of a letdown, really.

I dumped the part-dismantled Dictaphone on to the table, tugged a pen from my top pocket, and prepared to do the interview the old-fashioned way: I'd write it up later using memory and a welter of inaccurate notes.

'I find all the criticism really annoying,' she told me. 'I don't care about the politics of choosing one person over another – I mean, authors make millions out of the Book Club, publishers make millions out of the Book Club, but I don't make a penny. There's no incentive for me to choose one book over another unless it's something I like. We get sent over seven hundred submissions a year, and a lot of them are rubbish. A lot of publishers try to chase trends – like we had a book on the list set in China,' *Empress Orchid*, by Anchee Min, the story of an ambitious concubine, 'and after that we had all these publishers coming up to us going, "Take a look at this – it's going to be the next *Empress Orchid*" and we're like, "But we've already done *Empress Orchid*, we don't need another one."'

Amanda explained that she had reading assistants who helped her whittle down the huge number of submissions. She said that, while lots of stuff was obviously inappropriate, by the time they reached the final fifty titles the process became incredibly painful.

'The last fifty are always great. Any of them could be fantastic successes – they all deserve to be on the list.' Though it sounded like the usual glib 'the standard of entries was truly astonishing this year and it was terribly hard to pick a winner' schtick judges come out with when they announce the winners of big literary competitions, the difference was that Amanda claimed nothing more for the Book Club titles than they were books that she had really enjoyed, and that she thought *Richard & Judy* viewers would enjoy them too. 'I just try to get a good mix. A few sun-lounger novels alongside one or two more challenging ones. It makes me so happy when a book I've chosen goes on to be a big success. It was amazing to help Kate Mosse,' author of 2006's bestselling title, *Labyrinth*, 'and she turned out be really, really lovely. All the people I've picked have turned out to be really lovely.'

'Of course,' I said, 'we can't really discuss the *Richard & Judy* Book Club without acknowledging the five-hundred-pound gorilla in the corner – the *Oprah* Book Club.'

A look of confusion colonised Amanda's face. Her eyes flicked over my shoulder to the corner of the room.

'Sorry?' she said. 'The five-hundred-pound gorilla?'

'You know,' I began, 'it's…' A creeping realisation snaked into my guts. 'Oh… hang on a minute… no, no… I'm not… I wasn't… oh *God*…' I gritted my teeth. 'It's an expression. It means a conspicuous thing that nobody talks about – like if you were, uh… I mean, God… I wasn't calling Oprah Winfrey a… no, no… Christ, no… I mean, that'd be… you know… that wasn't what I meant *at all*.' I shook my head vigorously.

Amanda looked even more baffled.

'It's just an expression,' I persisted. 'I wasn't making reference to… because… well…' I laughed nervously. 'Because of her problems with her weight and everything… but no… no, no. That would be *deeply*… Anyway.' I took a breath. 'The *Oprah* Book Club.'

'Sure,' she said. 'We were very much inspired by that. I've never made a secret of it. The *Oprah* Book Club had been a fantastic success in America and I was aware that we didn't have anything similar here.'

'I suppose the major difference is that, so far at least, you haven't run into any of the scandals that Oprah has.' I was referring to two major PR disasters – in the first, author Jonathan Franzen reacted with marked ambivalence towards the nomination of his book *The Corrections*, slating some of Oprah's choices as 'schmaltzy' and 'one-dimensional'; his appearance on the show was cancelled and, for a time, there was speculation that the Book Club might collapse in on itself under sheer weight of embarrassment. Franzen, of course, did fantastically well out of the publicity, coining it in a gargantuan way. The second, more recent scandal concerned the supposedly non-fiction memoir *A Million Little Pieces*, which sold millions and millions of copies before it transpired that its author, James Frey, was a giant bullshitter who'd simply made whole sections up. He appeared on *The Oprah Winfrey Show* and acted suitably contrite while the host expressed her disappointment in him, before he doubtless headed home to bathe his slapped wrists in chilled champagne.

'The one book I wish I hadn't picked is *Brick Lane*,' said Amanda. 'It's the only title I've ever put in the Book Club that I didn't like. I read it, I didn't enjoy it, but it was getting all this attention and I felt really pressured to stick a "serious" novel on the list. I was really insecure. I thought people would start laying into me if I left it out, saying: "How could you ignore this?" It turned out to be a massive lesson. Monica Ali didn't want to know and she snubbed us. Now we ask long-listers if they're happy before we go ahead and choose them.'

'But no one says no, right? I mean, you'd have to be smoking a year's supply of crack to turn down that much money.'

'A couple of people have said no, actually. There was one well-known female novelist, quite literary, who didn't want to be on TV. She said she was too shy.'

I felt a scoop coming on. 'Who was it?'

'No, I can't say.'

'Really?'

'I can't say. You'd have heard of her.'

'Oh. Okay then.'

'The thing is, I get incredibly nervous about the books I pick. When I choose "difficult" books like *Arthur and George* by Julian Barnes or *Cloud Atlas* by David Mitchell–' she later described both authors as 'lovely, lovely people' '–I think critics are going to say: "Who does she think she is?" I try my best not to meet authors if I think I'm going to pick their books. I sat next to William Boyd at the Costas and we were going to do his book on *R and J* the next day, and I was really, really nervous all evening. I just desperately wanted him to like the film we'd done, and be pleased with the experience. I mean, this isn't something I was trained to do – I've got no formal background in books. But it's turned out to be the biggest success of my career.'

I couldn't help finding it weird that someone with the power to radically change an author's fortunes almost overnight, helping them earn tens of thousands (sometimes millions) of pounds, should feel so worried about what broadsheet critics thought and so anxious that the writers she selected would approve. But in a way, it was exactly those insecurities that made her such a good judge of what would go down well with the *Richard & Judy* audience. The Book Club was designed for people who felt lost when they walked into a bookshop and who worried about expressing opinions about things they've read in case they betrayed their ignorance and ended up sounding stupid. The whole setup was supposed to be as unintimidating as possible, with congenial mainstream celebrities chatting about the books on the list in a loose, informal manner. In a way, pundits who accused the Book Club of 'dumbing down' were simply stating the obvious – of course its approach was simpler than highbrow literary supplements. It was *meant* to be simple and accessible.

I mean, don't get me wrong, I love old-fashioned elitism as much as the next pig-ignorant unreconstructed Thatcherite, but Amanda Ross wasn't strutting round talking smack about complex, intellectual fiction; I got the impression that she was just doing her best to promote books that she really liked – and, not unreasonably, a *sine qua non* of her liking something was that she understood it.

But then one could achieve the same thing with a monthly magazine or website full of appropriately unpretentious, straightforward reviews, deliver a selection of fifty, or a hundred, or two hundred novels a year, and let readers choose for themselves. For all its salt-of-the-earth chumminess, the *Richard & Judy* Book Club was just as elitist as the highbrow literary establishment, ring-fencing a handful of books each year and declaring them masterpieces, inevitably at the expense of other titles. Its net effect was to polarise publisher resources round a relatively minuscule cluster of authors, while leaving dozens of others out in the cold. Amanda Ross might very well be a 'lovely' person, surrounded by a coterie of 'lovely' authors, all slapping each other on the back and being 'lovely' together, but she was still utterly in bed with the Publishing Dream and all its grim corollaries. No matter how supposedly benign its aims, the Book Club was all about transforming writing from a profession into a lottery.

I put it to Amanda that, for the struggling author, she was nothing less than a zap-fingered demigod.

She threw her head back and hooted with laughter. 'I don't think that's true. By the time a book reaches me it's already gone through so many stages of approval, being picked up by an agent, accepted by a publisher... lots of people have had to say it's brilliant before I get to see it.'

But wasn't the whole enterprise built around making literary stardom seem rare and glamorous? Weren't viewers – many of whom doubtless had financial worries – supposed to see these authors adorned with praise and riches and think: *God, I wish that was me?*

'Absolutely,' said Amanda. 'Of course. The aspirational side is a big part of the appeal.'

'But surely that's bound to create a lot of suffering and disappointment in the long run,' I said, a little put out at her apparent lack of contrition. 'For every success story there's going to be hundreds and hundreds of failures.'

'Yes. It was really depressing going through the submissions we got for our writing competitions. When we ran the "How To Get Published" competition we got over 46,000 entries. We had to hire a team of readers to get through them all. And there were so many good ones. We ended up choosing five unpublished novelists, and they all got twenty-grand advances with Macmillan. Actually, there was so much good stuff they started a new imprint called Macmillan New Writing, so they could publish some of the others.'

'Ah right.' Beneath the table, I felt my knee jerk. 'You mean the imprint that offered virtually no editorial input, and gave its authors really crappy contracts with no advances?'

'Oh. Was it a bit controversial?'

'A bit.'

Amanda shrugged. 'I just think we need some alternatives nowadays. It's so difficult for an unknown author to get their work read by an agent, let alone a publisher. Most of it gets sent back without even being read.'

She seemed to feel such genuine anguish for literature's poor, undiscovered souls that I decided to voice a suspicion that had been nagging at me since the beginning of the interview: 'Have you ever tried writing something yourself?'

Amanda's body language instantly became awkward, apologetic. 'I started a couple of novels, actually. I tried doing something about my time in university...' She glanced away, embarrassed. 'And then I read *Starter For Ten* by David Nicholls. It was brilliant – so I chucked what I'd written into the bin. I also made some notes about my second house in Italy.'

'Was that going to be a memoir, then?'

'No.' She smiled, looking down at the tabletop. 'It was really cheesy fiction. But, you know, it wasn't really any good. I don't think I could write fiction. It's so hard.' The assertion seemed to help rally some of her confidence. She straightened up in her chair, re-established eye contact. 'There was a really lovely editor at Pan Macmillan called Maria Rejt who was very encouraging. She told me that I understand how fiction is constructed. She said I'd be really good at writing it. She wanted me to submit something, but... I don't know.'

I flashed Amanda a conciliatory grin. 'Well, maybe you should have a go. You never know...'

Amanda smiled weakly, and I felt a surge of something close to vertigo as I realised that, in spite of all my wanderings and everything that I had learned, I was sitting in a room with the most powerful person in British publishing, encouraging her not to give up on her literary dreams. It was like Richard Dawkins coaching the Pope through a tough patch of agnosticism.

'Maybe,' she said.

I thought about slipping my own novel into the conversation. Wasn't that why I'd come here? To try to woo the biggest name in the industry? I was about to say something, when Amanda got in first.

'So... your book,' she said.

Christ! She could read minds! 'I... I'm sorry?'

'You're writing about people who want to be famous authors, right? You said in your email.'

Oh... she meant *that* 'book'.

'Yes, right, right. Sorry.'

'What sort of things have people been saying?'

'Um...' I scratched my head, thinking back over all my encounters. 'Same as you, I suppose... That it's really hard. But no one can quite let go of the dream. And I think the holding on... that's what makes it tough.'

'It sounds a bit like a book I chose for the Book Club,' she said. 'Have you read *Moondust*? It's about a guy who tracked down and interviewed the nine remaining humans who've walked on the moon. They all seem traumatised by the experience. I think being an astronaut seems very lonely. It makes you into a, well... a bit of a freak, I suppose.'

And just like that, I found myself asking a question I'd never planned to.

'Are you happy?'

For the second time, Amanda hooted with laughter, then she looked at me as if I were a bit mentally ill. (Not an entirely unfair assessment.)

'Well... I don't know.' She laughed again, but nervously.

'I suppose I'm... okay.' And she looked to me as if waiting for approval.

'Cool,' I said.

Despite her insistence that she was very busy, the interview ran over time by about fifteen minutes. Amanda would glance at the clock and say, 'Ooh God, we've really got to stop now,' and then something else would occur to her and she'd start off on another tangent.

'I do wonder sometimes what'll happen to me when the Book Club finally winds down. Richard and Judy have got a few years left in them yet, but, you know... publishing isn't my world. I wonder sometimes if they'll still want to know me when my power's gone. Will they still be interested or will they not want to know?'

At last, I pulled on my coat and rose to leave. I hadn't quite plucked up the courage to pitch my novel to her, but I had been surprised at how nice Amanda had turned out to be and how much I had enjoyed her company. She was nothing like the out-and-out hardass some people thought they had seen in that first email. Maybe, I thought, I could drop her an email when I got home, saying thanks and slyly asking if she fancied a look at my novel. Perhaps that was the smart play.

Amanda stood up and walked to the door. Then she turned to me.

'So who was this person who called me Pol Pot?'

Oh shit. 'I, uh...'

'Was it a man or a woman? What do you think they meant?'

I tried to laugh it off.

Amanda was smiling but insistent. She was also – quite by accident, I'm sure – positioned between me and the door.

I decided to put the contingency plan into effect. I reached into my pocket and withdrew the crumpled note.

'Now,' I began, launching into my carefully prepared speech, 'I'm going to put this—'

Amanda reached for the note. 'Come on. You have to give it to me.'

'I, uh... I...'

'Give it to me.'

I held my hand out and meekly let her take it from me. 'But now, you can't open it until—'

'Yes I can,' she said. 'It might be blank. You might be scamming me.' She fixed me with an insistent stare, clutching the note like a wrapped present. 'Do I know the person?'

I felt my face prickle with heat. 'Oh, I... I don't know. I doubt it. You know, I think they were probably just—'

She unfolded the paper, smiling and frowning simultaneously. She read the name.

'Jewell Pearce? Is that a boy or a girl?'

'A girl,' I said.

'I don't think I've heard of this person at all.' She looked up. 'Who do they work for?'

'N-now,' I stuttered, wagging a limp index finger in a desperate attempt to lighten the mood, 'I never said I'd tell you the company.' Suddenly, after all our friendliness, we were back to negotiating. She really *was* hardass.

Amanda glanced at the note, then at me, then back at the

note. 'No, that's true,' she conceded. She opened the door and stepped out into the office.

Following her, I tried to disguise my feral terror with a feeble attempt at banter. 'Oh well. I'm sure you can make a few phone calls and find out. Then you can have her sacked.'

'No,' said Amanda, deadpan. 'I wouldn't do that. It just interests me how personal people can be about someone they've never met. But I suppose we're in the public arena, and it's right that people can say those things and have opinions and engage in debate.'

'Quite,' I said.

I never sent Amanda my novel. After the jarring awkwardness of our parting, I doubted I'd find a sympathetic ear. Besides, something inside me had finally shifted. I don't know if it was all her talk of award ceremonies and press gossip, or even, weirdly, the mere fact that Amanda seemed normal and nice, but the urgency that had been thumping inside of me had melted. I had made up my mind.

I could live with not being an author.

On the train home, I examined my Dictaphone and discovered that the battery had been in the wrong way round. As I thrust it back into my coat pocket I felt something round and hard, and realised I had forgotten to give Amanda her Kinder Egg. I decided to award the gift to myself for bravery in the face of extreme peril. I got a jellyfish in a baseball cap. It glows in the dark.

# 14

The pub was packed with my best friends. Drinks at the bar were free. Everyone was laughing, chatting, boozing.

It was Joe's book launch. And I was having a great time.

His novel had been released to huge acclaim. *The Times* said his teenage narrator was the best since Adrian Mole; the *Independent* said he was the best since *Catcher In The Rye*. Joel and Luke's book had come out too, Gordon had just got a multi-book deal, John's was due out soon – I was surrounded by success.

Maybe it was the vast amount of free lager, but my overwhelming feeling was not jealousy but pride. Everywhere I looked, there were people I knew and cared about. I could barely walk a metre without somebody clasping my shoulder and exclaiming: 'Tim! Hi!'

In the weeks that had followed my meeting with Amanda, I had felt myself beginning to unwind. Realising that I'd probably be okay without a book deal had helped me to relax a little.

But there was more to it than that. I'd thought that coming face to face with all my successful friends in one room would make me feel claustrophobic and shameful. I'd thought it would bring my myriad inadequacies crashing home.

In reality, it had the opposite effect. Seeing them all there brought home just how many good friends I had. I remembered what Helen had said, about how, for all the difficulty and frustration, writing was worthwhile, because even if it didn't work out exactly as you'd hoped, it would lead you to places you'd never expected. I looked round the room at all my mates and realised that, if I had never tried to be a writer, I would never have met any of them. They had supported me through some really rough times. I couldn't be that much of a loser if so many lovely people liked me.

Finally, I was somewhere I belonged.

Most of my fears had been unfounded, anyway. Nobody treated me differently for not having a book published. Nobody even talked about their careers – we all just shared stories of our time back at uni or talked about movies we'd seen or tried to make each other laugh with crap jokes. I started to realise that what I'd been dreading hadn't been humiliation, so much as losing my friends. I'd been afraid that, with all the new horizons opening up to them, they'd no longer have anything in common with me, and we'd eventually drift apart. Not topping the international bestseller lists I could cope with – but I'd be lost without my mates.

We drank and laughed and stuffed our faces with snacks. Joe stood behind the bar and read an extract from his book, and everybody cheered.

Late in the evening, he came over and threw his arms around me.

'Hey mate, great to see you,' he said.

'It's great to see you too,' I said, and meant it. Whenever

I'd gone through difficult times in my life, Joe had always been there for me. Sometimes he'd just had the bad luck of being the closest person to hand, or the only friend with a spare couch for me to crash on, but whether by accident or design, he'd helped me through some of my toughest moments. I was really proud of him. I was proud of all my friends – and very grateful for them too. 'Hey… congratulations.'

'Thanks, mate. You've been a massive support.'

'Oh fuck off.'

'No, seriously.'

I felt like a sickening luvvie, but I was too pissed to care. 'Come here, you.'

Later, I got to read his book's acknowledgements section. He thanked all the friends who'd helped him out, then added: 'Particular thanks to Tim Clare, whose patience, enthusiasm and friendship have been invaluable.'

I'd got my name on a hit debut novel after all.

# ACT THREE

# DEATH
# OF AN
# AUTHOR

# 1

Look. Sorry for breaking through the fourth wall here but you'll have noticed something. Something that rather undermines the whole premise of the story.

I told you that I'd always dreamed of being a published author. I told you that, when I realised I might fail – that I would *probably* fail – I felt the atavistic terror of a preacher who, gazing up at the stars, is suddenly gripped by the conviction that we are utterly alone in the universe. I told you that, bludgeoned by disappointment, I decided to have one last shot at making my dream come true, or else, for the sake of my sanity and bank balance, I would walk away, once and for all. And I told you that, after meeting the most powerful person in publishing, I decided that, well, maybe giving up writing wouldn't be so bad after all.

And, because neither you nor I are psychic, to tell you these things, I had to write them down. In a book. A published book. Which I authored.

You see where I'm going with this, don't you?

But I'm getting ahead of myself. First you need to know about death, a man with one eye, and mutton pies.

# 2

One of the advantages of being a disorganised, intermittently jobless itinerant is that, at any given time, you can piss off on holiday and nobody fires you.

Of course, you can't afford to go very far or stay anywhere that costs money, or eat anything more extravagant than ramen noodles and Space Raiders, but providing your mooching skills are in fine fettle, you can let your friends absorb the financial burden and invite yourself along as a kind of parasite-cum-team mascot.

So it was that I found myself riding shotgun in a hire car with my friends Chris, Ross, John and Joe, on the long northwards journey to Joe's grandmother's cottage in Dumfriesshire. The official title of the trip was 'writing holiday', which, to any normal person, sounds like a perfectly serviceable euphemism for a week of drinking, opining loudly about contemporary music, drinking, kicking plastic footballs into rivers, drinking, forming an uneasy (platonic) truce with the local sheep, drinking, consuming an entirely meat-based diet, drinking, playing cack-handed covers on a battered jumbo acoustic guitar, drinking, scrambling up hills to get a phone signal then sending irritatingly smug messages in ironic faux-textspeak – *HEY M8, SOZ I MISSED UR CALL!*

*HAVING A GR8 TIME IN SCOTLAND (LOL!)* – drinking, affirming one's masculinity by building a log fire, and drinking.

But no. Though the 'lads on a holiday' stereotype provided us with a convenient cover story, the sad truth was, we arrived, brewed some tea, opened our jotters and laptops, and wrote. We wrote poems and short stories, scenes for films and snatches of diary entries. One afternoon, I sat on the bare floorboards of the room that had once been a little schoolhouse, leafing through the pages of a complete set of encyclopaedias from 1934, looking up things like 'pangolins', 'Adolf Hitler', 'Papua New Guinea', 'voodoo', 'snipefish', noting down any facts or turns of phrase that particularly tickled my fancy. Another day, we wrote poems using only one type of vowel, then wrote 'translations' of these poems that used every letter except the original vowel – and all of this, dear reader, we did for *fun*. Ah, to be young.

But maybe that was the point. It was one of the least competitive, least stressful environments I'd been in for years. On the first day, the fields and mountains surrounding us were covered in snow, and we got to run amok, pelting each other with snowballs like idiots. Over the course of the week, snow gave way to brilliant sunshine. I'd sit out in the garden with my notepad and a cup of tea, feeling, well, peaceful.

It'd been almost nine months since my meeting with Amanda. I'd expected that final push to break me somehow – that our talk would either hurl kerosene on to the fire in my belly, pushing me to churn out my long overdue magnum opus, or that, finally, I'd be able to make peace with the monkey on my back, leaving it in Amanda's gentle custody, perhaps as a novelty playmate for her dogs.

But in the end, I felt neither – just a strange, lingering sense of... meh. I realised that part of me was even a little disappointed that Joe's launch party had proved so anticlimactic. At least disaster provides a closure of sorts.

I suppose I was more my father's son than I cared to admit. Dad had thought a clankingly fake suicide pact would somehow force upon me a Damascus-style revelation. It had been a transparently crackpot scheme but, now I thought about it, my whole make-or-break ultimatum had been based on much the same premise.

In fact, now I *really* thought about it – a sizeable wedge of my *life* had been based on much the same premise. A bloody-minded, all-or-nothing tantrum writ large. I'd got in the car with my big, crass dream, locked the doors, then accelerated towards a concrete verge, yelling out that, if God really gave a shit, he'd pull one or both of us clear before impact. Because, if I was honest, it hadn't been so much that I didn't *want* to live if I failed – it was that I didn't think I'd know *how* to live.

Wanting to be not just a writer, but a famous, successful writer, had given me a sense of purpose. It had pushed me to work hard in school, driven me through night after night of scrawling in jotters and poring over style manuals, filled me with a love of the well-poised sentence, the slick rhetorical move, the old-fashioned story, well told. I really wanted to be good – not just good, *exceptional* – and I wanted to make sure I didn't waste the chance I had to do something unique and lasting and important with my life. All the religious and

motivational books I read said it again and again: *Purpose.*
*Purpose. Purpose.* A sense of purpose was what divided the
Great Statesman from the destitute sot.

Purpose gave your life meaning.

Purpose made you happy.

So, as I tucked into my first-ever mutton pie – fresh from
the butcher's that morning and a snip at 69p – it was a little
odd to realise that all of that might be claptrap. What had
purpose got to do with eating a lovely pie? Absolutely fuck all.

In fact, having some huge destiny looming in the background was pretty distracting. It's hard to achieve mutual
orgasm when your mind keeps wandering off to tweak the text
of your Nobel acceptance speech. Believing that I was
supposed to be a great writer had closed me off to all the
wonderful, exciting, perilous, stupid non-writer stuff the world
had to offer. It was as if, the moment I decided my purpose
was to be a great writer, a million doors had been slammed
shut and padlocked.

Labelling myself in that way, I'd ended up with a
constrained sense of my own humanity. I'd denied myself a
whole host of states, reactions and interests, and yoked myself
to a story that I thought I already knew the ending of. Success
had become a matter of fidelity to the template.

But it was okay. I realised that now, and not just intellectually – I felt it, too. Over the months since I'd met Amanda,
some tight spiral inside me had unwound. Sure, I hadn't got
the grand explosive YES/NO answer I'd been fiending for,
but still. The whole dilemma seemed less urgent – making an
absolute decision, less important.

And yet – a little voice at the back of my mind still whispered: wasn't this what I'd feared all along? Wasn't this exactly the kind of woolly compromise I'd wanted to avoid?

Here is a joke:

A young, rising star businessman (or businesslady, for these days there are corporate high-flyers of either gender) visits the company psychiatrist.

'What seems to be the problem?' says the psychiatrist, stroking his long, fastidiously groomed beard (or her long, fastidiously waxed legs, for these days there are skilled psychological professionals of either gender).

'Well, doctor, I'm terribly shy,' says the businessman. 'Every time I'm asked to give a presentation, I get so nervous that the moment I stand up in front of everyone to speak, I wet myself. It's incredibly humiliating.'

'I see,' says the psychiatrist, and suggests the businessman cuts out caffeine, signs up to yoga classes and undergoes a course of hypnotherapy sessions. 'Come back and see me in three months.'

Three months later, the businessman is back in the psychiatrist's office.

'So,' says the psychiatrist, 'did you give up caffeine?'

'Yes,' says the businessman.

'Did you start going to yoga classes?'

'Yes,' says the businessman.

'Did you visit a hypnotherapist?'

'Yes,' says the businessman.

'And how do you feel?'

'Great!' says the businessman.

The psychiatrist types some notes into his laptop. 'If you don't mind my asking, how soon into the treatment did you stop wetting yourself?'

'Oh,' says the businessman, with a big smile, 'I still wet myself. It's just now, I'm not embarrassed.'

(rim shot)

Sure, all my feelings of guilt, self-hatred and panic had faded away, but I was just as unsuccessful and directionless as when I'd started. Yes, it was possible that I'd matured to the point where I realised my all-or-nothing quest was childish and unnecessary. On the other hand, it was just as possible that I'd wimped out. Now that I'd moved back into my own house again, now that I had a social life, I didn't feel the pain of failure so keenly, so I'd stopped asking myself the hard questions, like a short-sighted glutton who goes straight back to the kebabs and fried chicken the moment the chest pains stop. My ambition had burnt itself out, but nothing had grown in its place. I felt happy scratching a living from bits and bobs, writing when I had time, drinking with my friends, playing video games, but was that really a victory?

Had I found contentment, or just apathy?

I tried to cook up the old feelings of dread, tried to picture myself as a wilfully blind, temporarily happy imbecile plodding gamely towards his all-too-inevitable doom, but my heart just wasn't in it. There was half a hot mutton pie to eat, and banter to trade, and speed poems to write. The future, however crappy, would take care of itself.

About half an hour later, I received the text. It read:

hi tim. just to let you know
pa has been taken very ill.
we are with him in the hospital.
didn't want to spoil your
holiday but thought you would
want to know. love dad. x x

# 3

'Now please, you two, take this.' Omi, my grandmother, shuffled to the fridge. 'He won't listen to me at all. He's being so pigheaded and stubborn.' She opened the fridge door, stooped, and with some effort retrieved a small, yellow carton. She straightened up, turned, and held it out, waiting for Dad to accept custody. 'It's a vitamin drink. He's not eating in there. He needs *something*. How can his body fight if he refuses to eat?'

Dad took the carton, turning it over to read the back. After a moment, he looked up.

'Okay, Mum.'

'You, Tim.' Omi advanced on me, urgently shunting her walker across the pale kitchen tiles. 'Will you make him drink it? He doesn't care what I say but he'll listen to you.'

I tried to smile. 'Okay, Omi. I'll do my best.'

Omi also tried to smile. 'I know you will, my love. I know you will.'

A week had passed since I had received the text. I hadn't cut short my holiday in Scotland, partially because I was reliant on my mates for transport, but mainly out of cowardice. Rushing the length of the country to visit a gravely ill relative sounded stressful, upsetting. I wanted to fill my life with easy, pleasant things, and over the years I had learned that, if I kept my head down in times of trouble, other people would deal with problems for me. I suppose I had thought that Pa might simply get better, negating the need for a visit altogether. Unfortunately, he was still in hospital, so I made the trip westward to see him.

Dad told me the story. Pa had fallen late one evening. The fall meant he had to be admitted to hospital. His tracheotomy made him very vulnerable and he had caught a chest infection on the ward. On the same evening Dad had sent me the text, the doctors told him that Pa would not last the night. However, defying all expectations, Pa had rallied. He was weak, and only intermittently conscious, but he was alive.

We had stopped off at Omi's house on the way to the hospital. Dad asked her lots of questions about whose name certain bills and insurance documents were in. He said that Pa would probably never get well enough to live at home again – that he would have to go into residential care. Besides the infection, he had incurable prostate cancer, so it was only a matter of time. Dad told Omi she needed to visit some of the care homes with him, so she could decide which one her husband should go into for the rest of his life. Dad said there weren't many places so they needed to decide quickly.

The hospital was about five minutes' drive away, all downhill. Dad and I did the journey in silence. I hadn't been to a hospital for several years. I wasn't sure of how things worked and I found myself shadowing Dad, looking to him for cues on where to go, how to behave. I felt that I had done the right thing by coming, but that didn't mean I wanted to be there –

I took a deep breath and quietly tried to shut down all but my most basic mental capacities, hoping I could remain in a sort of standby mode until we left.

Dad took us to a lift, then along a corridor until we came to some double doors. To the left of the doors was a chunky push-button antiseptic foam dispenser and a sign that said 'PLEASE WASH YOUR HANDS' with a diagram beneath it. Dad squirted some foam into his cupped palm, rubbed it all over his hands, then tore off a big blue paper towel and wiped his hands clean. His actions were quick, almost automatic – I felt reassured by his familiarity with hospital protocol. I stepped up to the dispenser and tried to do the best job I could of washing my hands – I squashed the foam between my palms, pushed it into the webbing between my fingers, massaged it into the hair on the back of my hands, rubbed it underneath my fingernails. Then I took a paper towel and spent a full minute wiping down each of my fingers. The ritual helped me wrest back a little control, as if I was somehow contributing to Pa's good health. Just as importantly, it delayed my entry to the ward.

Then it was time. We went through the double doors, along a short, wide corridor, and then Dad turned to the bed on his right.

'Dad?' he said.

Pa lay asleep beneath powder-blue hospital sheets. His right wrist was connected to a static intravenous drip while an elasticated strap held an oxygen mask around his neck, feeding air into his tracheotomy hole. The inside of the mask was frosted with condensation. The crimped pipe coming away from it had partially filled with water, so a steady *scush-scush-scush* accompanied his breathing. It sounded like a cross between Darth Vader and a Soda Stream. I couldn't remember ever seeing him without his glasses before. With his teeth out, his head seemed about half its normal size.

I waited with my hands behind my back. Dad leant forward.

'Dad?' He placed a hand on Pa's shoulder. 'Dad? We've come to visit you.'

Pa came round quickly, blinking and staring wide-eyed. Like me, without his glasses he couldn't see detail more than about three inches away, so it took him a few moments to register where the voice was coming from.

'It's me, Dad,' my dad said. 'Tim's here too.'

Pa blinked, nodded slowly, then took a deep breath. 'Hello.' His croaking, substitute voice was far quieter than normal.

'Here, Dad, do you want me to help you?'

Dad moved Pa's pillows around and helped him to sit up a little. On a small, rectangular tray table that could be swung across the bed were a packet of wet wipes, a box of tissues, a history book about the Second World War and a folded copy of the previous day's *Financial Times*. A very intense smell hung around the bed, like milk and urine. I waited for Dad to bring over a chair, then I took one myself and sat down. Dad pulled the plastic curtain a little way round, so we couldn't see the person in the bed next to us.

I threaded my fingers, stared down at my hands. Dad sat down to my left.

'So, how are you, Dad?' Dad was smiling. He seemed almost chipper.

Pa seemed to think about this. 'All... right.'

'Mary Daniels! Mary Daniels!' A cry came from the opposite side of the ward. 'Please, I can't see you! Please! Mary Daniels!'

I looked across to where the voice was coming from. The man in the bed opposite Pa's was sitting up. Tufty grey newsreader hair covered his head. A mottled knot of scar tissue covered his left eye socket; his right eye was half closed, and it was hard to tell if he could see out of it. He didn't look particularly old, but he was obviously distressed, his slack jowls set in a permanent expression of open-mouthed dismay.

I glanced at Dad but he was acting as if he hadn't noticed. It was probably impolite to spectate on someone's suffering. I turned back to Pa, and tried not to hear.

'So... what have you been eating?' said Dad. 'Anything nice?'

Pa let out an indifferent sigh.

Dad picked up a slip of paper from Pa's tray table. Breakfast, lunch and dinner choices were laid out in green ink, next to tick boxes. Dad saw me looking and handed the menu to me.

'It's good, isn't it, Tim? They've got a good selection here.'

I looked down the list. Lunch was a choice between penne pasta or a tuna sandwich on white bread. Dinner – what I was brought up to call 'Tea' – was either casserole, shepherd's pie, or a vegetarian option, cauliflower cheese.

'Dad?' My dad was trying to get Pa's attention. 'Did you hear that, Dad?' Pa opened his eyes a little wider, to show he was paying attention. 'I said, they've got a good selection here. I'm tempted to stay over just so I can get some myself!'

Pa raised his eyebrows, let them drop, then, eventually, nodded.

'Mary Daniels! Mary Daniels!' yelled the grey-haired man.

Pa reached out a hand, his fingers opening and closing like the mouth of a baby bird.

'What is it, Dad?'

'Can... I... have... a tissue?' The final word took particular effort, Pa saving up breath so it could come out in one go, rather than splitting it into two syllables.

'Of course.' Dad stood up, then tugged a tissue from the box on the tray-table. He held it out, apparently unsure whether Pa needed help in using it. I watched as Pa closed his shaking fingertips around the tissue. With his other hand, he pulled the oxygen mask away from his throat, then he held the wadded-up tissue next to the hole in his trachea. He closed his eyes. The tendons in his neck stood out as he gave a couple of convulsive splutters. Then his neck relaxed. He opened his eyes, and with some difficulty, replaced the mask over his throat.

He squinted at the contents of the tissue, then held it out for my dad to take. He said something neither of us could hear.

'What's that, Dad?'

Pa steeled himself, drew in as much air as he could manage, then tried again.

'Look… at… that.' He held the used tissue out so me and Dad could examine it. It was soggy with a large yellow-black grot of phlegm and bile, like a rotten egg sat inside a white crocus. 'It's… hard… to… speak.' He paused, let my Dad take the tissue. 'Because… this…' He patted the ventilator mask. 'presses… on… my… throat. I… can't… make…' He took another, sucking breath, like a swimmer coming up for air. 'the… bubble. And… I'm… too… weak… to… cough… up… all… the… phlegm.'

Pa turned to address me. 'What…' He inhaled. 'Are… you… up to?'

I kept my eyes mostly on my twiddling thumbs, glancing up at Pa only occasionally. Suddenly the detail of my life felt shabby and small.

'Oh, you know. Poetry and things.'

Dad put a hand on my elbow. 'You've got a gig next week, haven't you? In London?'

I nodded.

'Is that the one they're recording?' Dad said.

'Yup.'

'So it's quite a, uh… it's quite a good opportunity, then. Did you hear that, Dad? They're recording it. That's good, isn't it?'

'Very… interesting.' Pa closed his eyes.

Off to my left, the man with the newsreader hair was still calling out, his monologue cycling from mournful, through baffled, to pseudo-drunken, and finally into anguished sobbing.

'Mary? Oh God, Mary Daniels, if you can hear me please

come to me! Please tell me! Please, if Mary Daniels can hear this, please come. I can't see you. I don't know where I am! Oh God! God God God! Please! Mary Daniels! Where are you?' And he'd break down into sorrowful howls.

Meanwhile, Dad soldiered on gamely.

'Tim's doing Glastonbury this year. When is that, Tim?'

'Uh... I don't know.'

'Mary Daniels! Please! I need you to find me, please God, Mary Daniels!'

'End of June, maybe?'

I tugged at my fringe. 'Umm. I'm not sure. Maybe.'

'Help me! I'm in Hell! Please God, Mary Daniels!'

'Maybe then. And you'll be doing poetry.'

'That's right.'

'Well, that's good.'

Dad looked over at Pa. Pa appeared to have fallen asleep. The newsreader man had tailed off into quiet whimpers. On the far side of the ward, a man in thick-rimmed spectacles lurched forward and began retching noisily over the side of his bed.

Dad turned to me. 'I'm going to see if I can find a nurse. I think Pa's tube needs emptying.' He pointed to the water pooling in the bottom of Pa's air pipe.

'Okay,' I said, and watched Dad stand and walk off. He disappeared round a corner and a few seconds later an old lady shuffled into view, wearing a powder-blue towel dressing gown and a pair of pink fluffy slippers. She had a distant smile on her face and only made it a couple of yards on to the ward before a nurse intercepted her.

'Are you all right?' said the nurse, a girl with a brown ponytail who looked about twenty.

The old lady nodded enthusiastically. 'Oh yes. The young people were going to put on a play.'

'Okay.' The nurse put one hand on her shoulder, another on her elbow, and began gently steering her back the way she came. 'Shall we get you back to bed?'

'I thought they were over here.'

'Do you know where your bed is?'

'Ooh. You've got me all confused now.'

Dad returned with a nurse. 'Dad?' He waited until Pa opened his eyes. 'Dad? We're just going to clear your tube.'

Pa waited obediently while the nurse unplugged the tube, drained all the water out, then put it back in. Once she had left my Dad persisted with the small talk, and I listened, feeling clumsy.

'Ben is in Paris,' he said, meaning my brother.

'Oh,' said Pa.

'Do you remember speaking French in France?'

'What's... that?'

'Dad?'

'Can't... hear... you.'

Dad leant forward. 'In France, Dad. Do you remember using your French? To speak to people?'

Pa frowned. 'Yes. But that's... all... water... under... the... bridge... now.'

I felt myself growing irritated with Dad. Everything he said seemed almost insultingly banal. At the same time, I was doing my level best not to help him. I kept trying to think of things to say, but they all sounded stupid or crass. I wanted to tell Pa how much I loved him, and how scared I was, but I was afraid I'd start crying – not just little tears, but full, unseemly bawling like the guy across the ward. The hospital was thick with misery, yet as exposed and impersonal as a service station café. In the end, my attempt at stoicism must have looked like sulky indifference.

Dad opened the bag he'd brought with him, and got out the carton of vitamin drink. 'Mum asked me to give you this, Dad.' He put the carton on Pa's tray-table.

Pa picked it up. 'What... is... it?'

'It's got vitamins for you. Mum says you're not eating enough.' Dad grinned. 'Fussing. You know what she's like. Do you think you can manage some?'

Pa nodded. 'Okay.' Slowly, he began turning the carton over and over in his hands.

'There's a straw, Dad.'

Pa put the carton down on the tray-table. With some effort, he managed to rip off the plastic straw sachet attached to the side. As he fumbled to grip it, I noticed that his fingers were badly swollen. After watching him struggle for a minute or so, Dad said: 'Do you want me to help you open it?'

Again, Pa nodded. Dad took the straw, slid it out of its clear plastic sleeve, found the sharp end, then poked it through the silver foil in the top of the carton. He straightened up the drinking end, then lifted it to Pa's lips. He waited while Pa took a few shallow sips.

'Is that enough for now, Dad?'

'Yes... thank... you.'

For a while, we didn't say much. Every so often, Dad would try to restart the conversation.

'So yes, Ben's in Paris.'

'Yes.'

'I read an article in the *Guardian* about a woman who was in France during World War Two. I, uh... I can't remember her name.'

'Antoinette?'

'What was that?'

'Ann... twah... nette?'

'No.'

The man on the bed opposite was screaming again.

A family of four walked past us, out of the ward. They all looked very sad. The eldest son was wearing a football shirt and the guy I assumed was the dad was wiping tears from his eyes. I was annoyed rather than sympathetic. I felt like they were gatecrashing our moment.

Another long gap in conversation, then my dad spoke.

'Would you like a shave, Dad?'

Pa performed a slow, deep blink, then he stared at Dad as if noticing him for the first time. 'What's... that?'

'Would you like a shave?' Dad rubbed a palm over his own beard. 'Fancy a shave?'

'Yes.'

'Okay.' Dad got up from his chair and walked round to the bedside cabinet. 'Let's find your washbag, then.'

For the next few minutes, I watched Dad shave Pa with an electric razor. Every so often, he would use his fingertips to gently tilt Pa's head, saying something like: 'Just move your head back for me, Dad.' It reminded me of how, when I was little, I would sometimes stand and watch Pa in the bathroom while he shaved. I was too young even for bumfluff, but he would put his electric razor against my top lip so I could feel the tickly sensation of the blades buzzing behind the foil guard.

Once Dad had finished, he put the razor back inside the washbag then sat back down. Pa seemed to be distracted by something. Eventually, he spoke, but neither of us could hear what he said. He swallowed, tried again.

'Toi… let,' he said.

'You need to go to the toilet?' said Dad, lowering his voice a bit.

Pa nodded.

'Okay.' Dad got back up out of his chair.

I wasn't sure what was going to happen, until Dad stooped and retrieved a kind of large plastic carafe from under Pa's bed. Pa had a little three-button control panel in his lap that could raise and lower his bed. Dad took it from him and hooked it over the back of the bed. Then Dad reached over and pulled back Pa's blanket.

I didn't know whether to stare down at my hands, or turn away, or whether I ought to pretend that nothing was happening. I didn't want Pa to think I was embarrassed, as if I thought his relying on others was somehow shameful. Dad had to help Pa move his legs. His feet were terribly swollen – they looked like a pair of inflated latex gloves. Dad handed Pa the plastic container. It took Pa a little while to tuck it into place. The curtain gave him a little bit of privacy but it didn't go all the way round. I thought about breaking the awkwardness with a joke, but I couldn't think of anything funny. I had never seen Pa naked before.

'Mary Daniels! Please, can you hear me, Mary Daniels? I need you. I… I'm all alone! Mary Daniels?' The newsreader man in the opposite bed began ramping up towards another sobbing fit.

Eventually, Pa was done. Dad took the plastic container from him, then tucked Pa's blanket back over him.

'I'll just go and find somewhere to put this,' said Dad.

He left me and Pa on our own. I didn't know what to say, so I just sat there. After a few moments, I saw Pa trying to muster the energy to speak.

'So… how's… things?' He spoke with exaggerated mouth movements, as if he were chewing invisible words out of the air.

'They're okay,' I said. I couldn't bring myself to make eye contact. 'Yeah.' I nodded, as if deciding, after consideration, that my first statement was true. 'You know… I'm doing this and that, bits and pieces, little things. But it's all, you know… it's all baby steps, and I'm working in areas that I quite like, and… yeah.'

'Any…' began Pa, but I couldn't hear the end of his question.

'I'm sorry?'

'Any… teaching… work?'

'No.' I shook my head and fidgeted. 'No, I… except I still edit people's manuscripts. But no… I don't do any teaching. Not yet.'

There was a pause. Pa frowned up at the ceiling, then he said: 'You… were… always…' and I couldn't quite hear how he finished the sentence, except it sounded like the word 'emotionless' was in there.

I felt my chest clench. Was he calling me cold? I wasn't sure what he'd said but I was afraid to ask again in case it had been a criticism. I knew I hadn't been talking much but I didn't mean it to come across as if I didn't care. I really cared, of *course* I cared, but we were basically in public and Pa had never been one for big demonstrative displays of affection anyway. I almost asked Pa to repeat what he'd said, but when I looked over his eyes were closed and he seemed to have dozed off.

Dad came back and sat down next to me. He put a hand on my shoulder.

'You all right?' he said.

I nodded, biting my bottom lip.

He looked over at Pa, and we waited for a bit. After a while, Dad started to shuffle uncomfortably.

'Dad?' he said. 'Dad?' Pa opened his eyes. 'We might think about making a move.'

From the moment we'd arrived, I'd been desperate to leave. Yet, as soon as Dad said it was time to go, I started filling up with regrets. Why had I wasted all my time here? Why couldn't I bring myself to say anything? What was I so scared of?

Suddenly, Pa thrust his bare arm out of the bed, and caught hold of my palm. His fingers were clammy, but his grip was surprisingly strong.

'Tell me... what... you're... doing. It... doesn't... matter... how... small... or... silly. Just... tell... me... some... thing.'

I felt cornered. It was as if he knew.

Because I *did* have something to tell him. Something that I hadn't told anyone. Something that, what with the events of the past week, seemed precisely like he said – small and silly. I hadn't wanted to make the visit about me. Mentioning it seemed crass.

But now he was asking.

I started welling up. I couldn't go on being so bloody English.

'Um...' I wiped my eyes with the back of my shirtsleeve. Dad took hold of my other hand. 'Well, I got a phone call this morning.' I inhaled, tried to ignore the catch in my throat. 'I... I've been offered a book deal. I sign in two days.'

Yes, the very book you hold in your hands, dear reader, blah blah blah.

Pa sat up in bed. All at once he was alert, wide-eyed. 'What? Really?'

I nodded.

Pa's face broke into a smile – and when you've got no teeth, you really can smile with your *whole* face.

'Who... else... knows?'

'No one,' I said. 'I didn't want to say anything until I'd signed, but... well...'

Dad caught Pa's gaze and shook his head. 'Don't look at me. This is the first I've heard.'

'What's... it... about?'

'Umm... It's about me.' By now, I was crying openly. I

glanced at my dad, and saw that he was crying too. I couldn't remember ever seeing him cry. 'And, uh... I suppose it's about me being tough on myself. And ambition. And maybe wondering if ambition is, you know... bad.'

Pa shook his head resolutely. 'No. Keep... your... ambition. Just... don't... let it... rule... you.'

And in that moment, I knew he was right. Here was the answer I'd spent so long searching for. The stupidly obvious, common-sense answer.

Keep your ambition. Just don't let it rule you.

Holding my father's hand on one side, and his father's hand on the other, I dipped my head and let myself cry.

After a while, I felt Pa's hand slip loose. When I looked up, he had moved his oxygen mask, and he was hacking into a tissue. Again, he held the wadded tissue out for inspection. This time, there was a much larger, treacle-coloured clot of phlegm. Pa looked pleased.

'Can breathe... a bit... better... now,' he said. He looked over at my dad. 'Could... you... get me... a bag... for... the... rubbish?'

'Okay, Dad.' My dad patted me on the back, then got up and left us on our own.

While he was gone, Pa took my hand in both of his. He gestured for me to move closer.

'We had... some... good... times, didn't... we?'

'Yeah.' I was crying again.

Pa smiled. 'Maybe... we've some... still... to come. You... never... know. I... could... get... better.'

'Yeah.' We both knew that Pa had fairly advanced, untreatable prostate cancer. He was not going to get better.

'You... have... a... good... father.'

'I know.'

'A... good... mum... too.'

'I know.'

And though – except perhaps during some notable teenage sulks – I'd always known that I had good parents, right then, I realised that they were *really* good.

I sat there for a while, with Pa holding my hand, neither of us saying anything, just breathing. Out of the corner of my eye, I saw the confused old lady in the pink slippers wander back on to the ward. With an odd sense of purpose, she shuffled straight towards the newsreader man, who was sobbing quietly. I felt my stomach tighten at the thought of their two bewildering worlds colliding.

Moments later, she was at the man's bedside.

'Hello?' She sounded nervous. 'Who are you? Where am I?'

I expected the man to scream out, but all at once he became subdued. He reached out and took the old lady's hand.

'Are you all right?' he said, very softly, and a little sadly. 'Please – don't be frightened.' It was the first time I'd seem him looking anything close to calm. The two of them stayed like that for several minutes, hand in hand, the man upright in his bed, the old lady standing alongside him, neither of them saying anything, neither of them looking at one another.

Eventually, a nurse came by and guided the old lady back to her bed. When the nurse came back, the man was weeping quietly. She patted his springy grey hair.

'What's the matter?' she said. 'Come on now, there's no need to get yourself all upset. Would you like some squash?' The man nodded, and she gave him a cup with a straw. The squash seemed to soothe him; at last he fell into a state somewhere close to peace.

Dad returned with a small plastic bag marked 'Used Dressings'. After some faffing and confusion, he managed to tape it to the side of Pa's tray-table, and stuff the soggy tissue inside.

'Well,' said Pa, 'this... is... the best... news... since... I took... my... exams.'

I felt a grin spread across my face. 'You realise what that means, Dad?'

'What?' said my dad.

'It rates higher than your birth, the births of all the grandchildren, and the end of the Second World War.'

Dad smiled. He looked at his watch.

'Well... I think we'd better be getting going, Dad.' My dad stood up to go.

Pa took my hand again, brought it up to his mouth, and kissed it. He motioned for me to come nearer. The swelling in his hands made them look pudgy, so what with his lack of teeth and hair and his nakedness, he looked a little like a baby. I leant in close, until his breathing became loud, and the milky smell filled my nostrils. Pa looked me in the eyes, and squeezed my hand tighter.

'You... have... achieved... everything... I ever... wanted... for... myself,' he said.

I nodded, then moved away. Pa released my hand. Dad and I left.

Those were the last words my grandfather ever said to me.

Which might all seem a bit much to swallow. Trust me, I wouldn't have scripted things to play out like that[10]. But it all happened that way, I promise.

Indeed, the incident passed into minor family legend. Pa died less than a week later, and several people commented how 'amazing' it was that he had stayed alive just long enough to hear my news. The adjectives 'incredible', 'wonderful' and 'beautiful' were also bandied about with enthusiasm, the implication being that the whole episode was the handiwork of some interventionist deity or nebulous higher power.

I found their reverence embarrassing, and, more importantly, I felt it missed the point. Coincidences happen all the time, and while I was sure it had been a nice bit of news for Pa to receive, in the grand scheme of things, it didn't really matter. I'd seen amazing, incredible, wonderful, beautiful things on that visit, but they had sod all to do with me.

Seeing my dad help his father to shave, to eat, to go to the toilet – watching his tenderness as he did those things, and realising that they weren't even the exception. My parents lived their whole lives showing humility, patience and kindness. *That* was the amazing, incredible, wonderful and beautiful thing to

---

10 Since you ask, my original plan was to end the book with my suplexing a T-Rex into the Acropolis. And then the Greeks would be all: 'Oh Tim, you saved Athens but it kind of sucks that you destroyed one of our most pre-eminent cultural monuments.' And I'd be like: 'Destroyed… or *improved?*' And they'd look and see the smashed Parthenon *now with added dinosaur carcass*, and realise I was right.

me. The love, in amongst all that suffering and shit – sod it, as far as I was concerned, it really was a miracle.

As we left, I knew my new ambition was impossibly high – that I'd chosen a hero who I could never hope to live up to. But, you know, if I end up being half the man my dad is, I think I'll have done all right.

If you find the whole business nauseatingly schmaltzy, all I can offer by way of compensation is that, while three generations of Clares sat hand in hand around that hospital bed, grandfather, father and son in wordless communion, I, with my head down, was thinking: *This is going to make such an awesome ending for my book.*

It was dark by the time we got outside. Dad and I walked through the hospital car park to the car. We didn't get in straight away, but stood for a while. Then I went over and gave him a big hug.

'I love you, Dad.'

'I love you too.'

We drove in silence for a while. The night was cool.

'That thing you said,' Dad began, 'about the book – was it true?'

'What do you mean?' I said, then realised exactly what he meant. 'What? Excuse me? Are you asking if I lied to Pa? Do you honestly think I'd do that?'

Dad laughed. 'Well, I don't know. You haven't said anything about it.'

'I told you, I didn't want to say anything until I was sure.'

'Can I tell Mum?'

'Wait a couple of days.'

Dad shook his head. He was grinning.

'That's amazing. Truly amazing. Congratulations. I'm so proud of you.'

'Thanks, Dad.'

I looked out the window, up at the night sky. The moon was a huge slice of apple. I realised I was ravenously hungry.

'So... what's it about?' he said. 'Is it non-fiction?'

My heart sank. I'd known this conversation was coming sooner or later.

'Dad... remember that time when I was really upset and we went for a drive at four in the morning?'

'Yes.'

'Well, uh... funny story...'

# Acknowledgements

Firstly, thanks to Paul Reizin, who goaded me into writing down my frustrations. Without his intervention, this book would have never got started.

Obviously, I owe Mum and Dad a massive debt of gratitude. Over the years the two of you have been a constant and uplifting source of money. Thank you.

Thank you also to the rest of my long-suffering family: Nan, Omi, Ben Clare, and of course Pa, who I miss a great deal.

I'm extremely grateful to all the people who appear in the book, or who gave their time to give advice, feedback and support. Thanks to Luke Wright, Chris Hicks, Joel Stickley, Ross Sutherland, John Osborne, Gordon Smith, Ian 'Yanny' McKenzie, Tom Sutton, Steve Aylett, Helen Corner, Mark Le Fanu, Hollis Brown, Amanda Ross, Chris Jukes, Will Borthwick and Sarah Titmuss. Particular thanks to Joe Dunthorne, whose patience, enthusiasm and friendship have been invaluable.

Thanks to Ken Barlow at Ebury Press for taking a punt on me, and for editing the living Christmas out of my purple prose and sloppy penmanship.

Finally, this book exists because of the hard work, tolerance, enthusiasm, shrewd editorial sensibilities and steadfast friendship of Maggie Evans. She poured many, many hours into counteracting defects of craft and character in the text itself, while in the real world she acted as an upbeat, tenacious advocate of my interests. I remain baffled and humbled by her unflagging faith in me as a writer. Maggie, I did my best. Words, as always, are inadequate. Thank you.